NET
PRIVACY

NET PRIVACY

A GUIDE TO DEVELOPING AND IMPLEMENTING AN IRONCLAD EBUSINESS PRIVACY PLAN

MICHAEL ERBSCHLOE

JOHN VACCA

McGraw-Hill

New York   Chicago   San Francisco   Lisbon   London
Madrid   Mexico City   Milan   New Delhi   San Juan   Seoul
Singapore   Sydney   Toronto

Library of Congress Cataloging-in-Publication Data

Erbschloe, Michael.
    Net privacy : a guide to developing & implementing an ironclad eBusiness
privacy plan / by Michael Erbschloe and John Vacca.
        p.   cm.
    ISBN 0-07-137005-6
    1. Internet—Security measures.   2. Privacy, Right of.   3. Electronic com-
merce.   I. Vacca, John R.   II. Title.

HD30.38.E73   2001
658.4'78—dc21   2001018037

McGraw-Hill

A Division of The McGraw-Hill Companies

1 2 3 4 5 6 7 8 9 0   AGM/AGM   0 9 8 7 6 5 4 3 2 1

ISBN 0-07-137005-6

This book was set in Berling by Matrix Publishing Services.

Printed and bound by Quebecor World/Martinsburg.

McGraw-Hill books are available at special quantity discounts to use as premiums
and sales promotions, or for use in corporate training programs. For more information, please write to the Director of Special Sales, Professional Publishing, McGraw-
Hill, Two Penn Plaza, New York, NY 10121-2298. Or contact your local bookstore.

This book is printed on acid-free paper.

To Ronald Spangler for his inspiration, support, and friendship
over the last 40 years and for changing my life forever
by introducing me to the world of sci-fi.

—*John R. Vacca*

To my mother for her growing
tolerance of her children.

—*Michael Erbschloe*

CONTENTS

FOREWORD

"The rules for conducting business today have changed." That sentence isn't news anymore, but it seems to be the magic phrase in every advertisement that touts the "ebusiness" revolution. Your own company has probably had a Web site for quite awhile, and everyone in your office probably conducts some sort of business through email or the Web. So what's new about this statement?

Before the corporate marketers tacked on "e" to everything under the sun, marketing efforts were akin to breaking out the rifle and pith helmet to go on the hunt for customers. It required a tremendous effort to cultivate a prospect list, dispatch literature, track responses, and measure a campaign's effectiveness. But now thanks to the almighty search engine, the tide has turned and customers are now hunting for you.

When customers find you, they will likely know more about your company than many of the people *in* your company do, and they've already scouted out your competitors. If they decide to do business with you, they will likely provide you with something even more valuable than their initial order: name, address, phone, email address, credit card number, and so on. Maybe they've provided the other jewels of the personal information crown like their favorite color, which type of carbonated beverage they prefer, or their pet snake's birth date. So how have the rules for business changed? Your customers now know the value of this crown, and they won't give it to just anyone.

As a Web manager, part of my job is to ensure that visitors to my site are comfortable with the security measures in place. I also need to fortify the reputation of my organization by offering assurances that these visitors' personal information will not be misused. Even more importantly, the organization needs to religiously adhere to its own policies and educate its employees in the proper methods of securely handling personal information.

Most Web surfers are familiar with the lock that appears at the bottom of their browsers when performing a transaction. The lock shows that data sent to a Web site are being hidden from eavesdroppers. But what happens to those data once they have reached their destination? Misuse of a customer's personal information can be just as damaging to an organization's livelihood as an outside security breach. Security holes can be repaired quickly, but trust takes time to earn.

Regular reports of malicious hackers breaking into commerce Web sites have raised sensitivity to the risks involved in the adoption of ecommerce. Today's netizens are not only more aware of security issues, but they will want to establish a level of trust with whomever their information is shared. As the ease of identity theft and other information crimes increases, protecting our sensitive personal information becomes more vital. We need to know who has access to our information and how these data are being used.

Information security companies such as RSA have developed extremely effective ways of scrambling transmissions, encrypting and securely storing sensitive data, and adding safeguards to ensure that only those who are supposed to have access can view these data. But even the most bulletproof security measures can be rendered useless without solid policies behind them and proper implementations of those policies in place.

Whether you're on the server side or the browser side of the Web, you're off to a great start in expanding your knowledge of personal trust relationships with the online world . . . you're reading this book. *Net Privacy: A Guide to Developing and Implementing an Ironclad Ebusiness Privacy Plan* will greatly assist your organization in developing a privacy and security strategy. It provides a view of privacy issues from all sides and includes real-world situations involving privacy mistakes. It outlines legal issues and government regulations that effect policy decisions and provides checklists for implementing security procedures for most any organizational data-sharing situation.

If you're someone just concerned about online privacy, this book will provide a better understanding of how private information is handled and how those data can be abused. It will give insight on what questions to ask when starting a trust relationship with any organization.

Jason Thompson
Webmaster
RSA Security, Inc.

webmaster@rsasecurity.com
http://www.rsasecurity.com/

PREFACE

Governments and businesses face three major challenges in dealing with the privacy of personal and corporate information—philosophical, legal, and procedural. The philosophical debate about what type of information is and should be private has raged on since the beginning of the industrial revolution and shows no signs of ending anytime soon. Since the growth of Internet communications and ecommerce, the legal definition and laws for the protection of privacy have become a tangled mess of international politics, corporate interests, rhetorical advocacy, and economic posturing. These processes will also continue and are likely to become increasingly messy over the next two decades. This book was written to address the procedural side of privacy protection and to provide organizations with a framework and process to develop, maintain, and implement appropriate policies and procedures to protect privacy.

Philosophical debates, especially when they are focused on something as sensitive as the privacy of individuals and the liberty that inherently emerges from the protection of that privacy, are stimulating and thought provoking. The process of enacting laws to protect privacy and the need for international cooperation in the millennium of the global Internet communications, economics, and ecommerce are challenges that are straining provincial mentalities and protectionist tendencies. This is the social and political environment in which organizations must struggle to develop policies and procedures to protect privacy while simultaneously attempting to maximize the use of enterprise information assets. The problems caused by the turmoil in the political and legislative environments are compounded by rapidly evolving Internet technologies. Add to this mix a lack of human experience in coping with rapid change and dealing with the cross-culturalization of philosophies and laws and you have a perfect recipe for chaos.

This book provides managers with step-by-step guidance for developing enterprise privacy policies and procedures. These structured processes and steps can keep a privacy task force from getting lost in rhetoric and overwhelmed by the chaos being created by macro political and economics forces. The basic foundation of the privacy management process is *governance*. As privacy policies are being formulated, governance allows the voicing of all of the perspectives necessary for organizations to successfully accomplish their missions and goals to be heard. A governance approach is necessary because enterprise privacy policies must be balanced to simultaneously meet legal requirements while maximizing the value of information assets. A motivated privacy task force and rational leadership are key to successful privacy management. Also the entire enterprise must be involved in the development and implementation of privacy policies and procedures. In addition to providing a governance framework, this book explains the practical procedural steps of establishing a privacy task force, evaluating privacy needs, formulating privacy policies, devising specific procedures to protect privacy, implementing and testing procedures, and monitoring and modifying privacy protection in the future.

All organizations will face privacy management issues, and, as laws evolve, all organizations could face civil or even criminal litigation for failing to properly protect privacy. Those organizations that have worked to develop privacy policies and procedures must remain vigilant to avoid negative consequences as laws, business relationships, and social conditions change. Those organizations that have not yet established privacy policies and procedures need to start doing so immediately.

Michael Erbschloe and John Vacca

INTRODUCTION

The philosophical focus of this book's privacy management perspective is geared toward the improvement of the business bottom line for private companies and improvement of costs control and resource optimization for nonprofit and government organizations. The book contends that all types of organizations need to develop privacy policies that maximize the benefit of reusing information in as many ways as possible, while minimizing the risks associated with potential privacy violations. Although this balance is essential in an information-intensive world, clearly, organizations will not easily achieve the balance between privacy and the optimization of resources.

The Internet has contributed to the awareness of privacy issues in four ways. First, the Internet has resulted in a huge increase in the number of people using computers to seek information and make purchases. Second, several privacy-related incidents have resulted in considerable and less than favorable press coverage for enterprises that have suffered from privacy problems. Notably, in late 1999 and early 2000, Web technology that tracks how people use the Internet came under fire. Third, many organizations had their first experiences in dealing with large-scale privacy issues. They range from small, new Web-based companies to large enterprises that started using the Internet for marketing, sales, or information dissemination. Fourth, the global cross-border nature of the Internet presented totally new challenges to governments and enterprises. The combination of these trends set the stage for potential privacy conflicts.

In many ways, current and future privacy issues can be viewed as a clash of cultures. The global nature of technology usage, and thus cross-border information exchanges, whether voluntary or not, result from technology architectures or stem from out-and-out deception, putting governments and international organizations into adversarial positions. The desire of new Web-based companies to build viable enterprises by capitalizing on personal data—whether by using this information to develop marketing and sales approaches or by collecting data for the purpose of selling it—throws the entrepreneur into conflict with governments, consumer groups, and private individuals.

IMPLEMENTING AN ENTERPRISEWIDE PRIVACY PLAN IN A CHAOTIC WORLD

The chaos surrounding privacy issues will undoubtedly continue. For that reason, having a comprehensive corporate privacy plan is of the utmost importance. This book shows business managers how to develop and implement an enterprisewide privacy plan. This is important because organizations are becoming more dependent on information systems to manage critical financial data as well as customer records and product data. It is also important because of increasing regulatory and social pressures about the protection of individual privacy and proprietary corporate information.

This book's position on privacy is very straightforward. Enterprises need to avoid potentially costly lawsuits and embarrassing public relations incidents that may result from revealing information that is protected by law, that management has determined could be detrimental to the enterprise if known by competitors or the public, or that customers feel should be kept private.

Privacy management needs to be comprehensive and enterprisewide. Thus to develop a solid privacy plan all departments and functions within the enterprise need to be involved. This includes, but is not limited to, the information technology department, legal counsel, customer relations, public relations, product development, manufacturing, and the accounting or financial management department. In order to successfully implement a privacy plan all departments need to understand the plan, as well as the corporate policies and procedures regarding the protection of privacy. In addition, the implementation and effectiveness of the privacy plan needs to be evaluated on an ongoing basis.

The goal of this book is to provide business managers and executives with a process to manage privacy in their enterprise by giving them basic building blocks that will help them understand the process of developing, implementing, and monitoring privacy plans, policies, and procedures.

BUILDING AND UNDERSTANDING PRIVACY

Chapter 1 begins with an overview of threats to privacy and potential corporate liabilities. These threats include internal and external threats as well as trends in government regulations and public sentiment that need to be addressed in an effective privacy plan. This chapter is *not* a history lesson, but rather, provides a framework to categorize and inventory threats that must be dealt with in managing privacy.

Chapter 2 examines the customer environment. This includes both consumers and business-to-business customers, as well as the dynamics of these relationships that need to be addressed in a strong privacy plan. Chapter 2 reviews some recent privacy problems and shows why and how the customer will influence regulatory trends.

Chapter 3 examines the regulatory environment in greater depth. It covers the role of local, state, and national governments, as well as activities of international organizations and how these activities may affect an enterprise.

PRIVACY MANAGEMENT PHASE ONE: ORGANIZING AND RESEARCH

Chapter 4 moves from the building blocks of understanding to the process of organizing your enterprise to manage privacy. It explains the processes needed to organize the necessary elements to protect privacy in an enterprise. It covers awareness building, staffing and training issues, how to work across internal departments and functions, and how to work external entities such as law enforcement agencies and consulting firms.

PRIVACY MANAGEMENT PHASE TWO: CONDUCTING A PRIVACY-NEEDS AUDIT

Once an organization launches its privacy initiative, it must determine what information in its enterprise needs to be protected. Chapter 5 provides a step-by-step process to identify an enterprise's weaknesses and vulnerabilities, including those vulnerabilities that may arise from relationships with business partners, suppliers, or service providers.

PRIVACY MANAGEMENT PHASE THREE: DEVELOPING POLICIES AND PLANS

The development of the privacy plan involves examining privacy needs and matching those needs with appropriate methods or technology. Chapter 6 reviews the arsenal of technology that an organization may be able to use in protecting privacy. These tools include hardware, software, and networking products that can be useful in protecting privacy.

Once an enterprise has reviewed the tools that may effectively address its privacy issues, it can move into the actual creation of a privacy plan. Chapter 7 overviews the elements of a privacy plan, how to achieve enterprisewide buy-in for the plan, and how to select appropriate technology to implement that plan.

PRIVACY MANAGEMENT PHASE FOUR: IMPLEMENTING THE PLAN

Chapter 8 provides an overview of the implementation process. It covers assigning responsibilities, training staff, setting criteria for new information application development, and addressing potential weaknesses in existing applications. It also recommends ways to measure how well a privacy plan has been implemented.

To ease the process of implementing the privacy plan, Chapters 9 through 15 contain a series of checklists to evaluate how to assure various enterprise technologies are configured to maximize privacy protection. Technologies include enterprisewide information systems, data centers, enterprise storage systems, business unit systems, and corporate communications systems such as Intranets, Extranets, the Internet, and email. These chapters also provide checklists for desktop systems, mobile systems such as laptops, remote access provided to telecommuters, corporate Web sites, ecommerce applications, and Internet supply chain systems.

ACKNoWLEDGMENTS

The efforts of many people have contributed to the successful completion of this book. I owe each a debt of gratitude and want to take this opportunity to offer them my sincere thanks.

A very special thank you goes to my editor, Michelle Reed, whose continued interest and support played a large role in making this book possible. Thanks go as well to editorial assistant Gillian Grady, who provided staunch support and encouragement when it was most needed. Special thanks are due to my technical editor, Dennis Pleticha, who ensured the technical accuracy of the book and whose expertise in cabling and telecommunications system technology was indispensable. I also thank my editing supervisor, Paul Sobel; copy editors, Diana Huber and Edith Baker of Write With, Inc.; and Matrix Publishing Services, whose fine editorial work has been invaluable. Thanks go as well to the marketing team, whose efforts on this book have been greatly appreciated. Finally, I would like to thank all the other people at McGraw-Hill whose many talents and skills are essential to a finished book.

Thanks are due to my wife, Bee Vacca, for her love, her help, and her understanding of my long work hours.

I wish to thank the organizations and individuals who granted me permission to use the research material and information necessary for the completion of this book.

Finally, very special thanks go to my coauthor, Michael Erbschloe, whose initial interest and support was a large factor in making this book possible. His guidance and encouragement went over and above the business of being a coauthor.

John Vacca

In addition to all of those people that John has mentioned, I would like to express special thanks to my research assistants, Catie Huneke and Deby Ellerbrook. I would also like to thank all of my comrades at Computer Economics for their constant encouragement and criticisms.

Michael Erbschloe

NET
PRIVACY

1

THE THREAT To PRIVACY AND CoRPoRATE VULNERABILITY

Maintaining the privacy of enterprise information is a meticulous process and requires coordination across all departments and functions within an organization. Everyone on the privacy management team must understand the basic issues and concepts of privacy management as well as enterprise policies and procedures. An understanding of the basic issues and concepts helps managers make operational decisions about privacy during the day-to-day course of events. It also enables them to more fully participate in formulating policies and procedures.

This chapter examines the basic privacy issues and concepts that the entire privacy management team needs to understand. As an organization starts working on a privacy plan, a basic set of definitions should be included along with policies and operating procedures. This definition set will enable new managers to more quickly develop an understanding of privacy management. It will also leave fewer items open to misinterpretation by all employees responsible for managing privacy.

This overview of basic issues is based on the questions that have been most frequently asked about the topic of privacy. These topics were selected as a result of several meetings and focus groups where managing privacy in an organization was discussed. The following points provide a basic understanding of key privacy topics, many of which are expanded upon in subsequent chapters.

DEFINING PRIVACY IS A CHALLENGE

Unfortunately the definition of privacy is not straightforward. Many cultural, societal, political, legal, and national viewpoints exist as to what privacy is and what constitutes a violation of privacy. Thus establishing an operational definition of privacy in an enterprise is important. A strong definition of privacy will help prevent inadequate interpretations of policies and procedures. It will also help prevent poor decisions regarding the privacy of information when specific procedures do not exist for specific incidents or information elements.

At the most basic level, the privacy of information is tied to the ownership of information. Ownership of information is clear in many cases. If an enterprise, for example, creates information about its products, business strategies, or operations, that information belongs to the enterprise. The information is the property of the enterprise. Managers in the enterprise then get to determine who has the right to know that information and when and where it can be disseminated.

Disseminating the information, however, is not the same as giving away ownership and the rights inherent in that ownership. Here the definition of privacy becomes more complicated. In common practice, an organization may provide another organization with proprietary information in order to facilitate a business relationship. During this process the two organizations establish a basis for the exchange of information and expectations, and they agree upon the requirements as to how that information can be used.

Individuals also have ownership of information about themselves. If, for example, you as an individual apply for a loan, you provide information about yourself to a bank or finance company. You give this information within the context of expectations as to how it can be used. Considerable controversy has recently emerged regarding individuals providing personal information in order to gain access to Web sites or services. When consumers provide the requested information, have they given up the right to expect that such information is no longer theirs and is no longer private? The ultimate outcome will be highly dependent on the *privacy contract* between the information provider and the information user. A privacy contract is usually put forth in the privacy policy or statement on the Web site.

PRIVACY IS IMPORTANT FOR MANY REASONS

When organizations exchange information to help facilitate business processes, the importance of privacy has been fairly well established and has become customary. An organization wants its information kept confidential to prevent damage that may occur if the information is obtained by competitors or other parties that could use the information to negatively affect the competitive position or the well-being of the information-providing company. The information provider has a public image to protect, and the misuse of confidential information could result in bad publicity. In the case of publicly held companies, improper dissemination of proprietary information could negatively influence stock value.

Individuals who provide information to businesses or government organizations can also be negatively influenced by the misuse of information. Such misuse may impact their jobs, career choices, and lifetime earnings. An individual who is gay or lesbian may choose to keep this information private in order not to have to deal with potential social or financial negative consequences. People who are making investments decisions, who are considering changing jobs, or who have decided to get divorced may suffer damages from the release of information related to their lives or their plans.

The common thread between the privacy of proprietary corporate information and of personal data provided by individuals is that the improper dissemination and use of such information can cause damage. In some cases improper use of private information can damage finances, while in other cases it can damage reputations.

UNDERSTAND THE PRIVACY CONTRACT

Since we have no universal definitions as to what constitutes the ownership of information and the privacy of information, the privacy contract is essential to establish an agreement between the information provider and the information recipient as to the use of the information exchanged. The example of a business-to-business exchange of information to facilitate business processes is done under specific conditions with agreed upon procedures and rights to use the information. Likewise the exchange of information between a consumer and a business needs to be governed by a similar contract that establishes rights and expectations.

When information is exchanged, the parties who are giving and receiving information must have a contract as to the scope of use of that information. Both parties should not be expected to share a common view for the rights to use the information. Where local or national law governs the use of information, the contract should, of course, be in compliance with such laws. Where no specific laws exist, the exchange of information should be governed by a binding contract that both parties can understand.

The concept of the privacy contract is exemplified in the privacy statement on a Web site. To be in compliance with the Safe Harbor principles of the European Union, an organization must inform individuals as to why information about them is collected. The privacy statement must also state how to contact the organization with inquiries or complaints and must indicate the types of third parties to whom the information will be disclosed. This notice must be provided to individuals in clear language at the point when individuals are first asked to provide personal information or as soon thereafter as is practicable. In all circumstances the organization must inform individuals before it uses information for any purpose other than that for which it was originally collected or before it discloses information to a third party.

Companies Need to Be Concerned About Privacy

Issues of social responsibility are certainly important, but the most important privacy issues with which an organization needs to be concerned are the potential for litigation and the possible damage to its reputation for ignoring or blundering on a privacy issue. This does not mean that individual people are unimportant in the myriad of privacy concerns. In fact just the opposite is true. Because people are so important, a company may face litigation or reputation-damaging public relations disasters if it doesn't adequately address privacy issues.

The social nature of privacy and the rising concerns among citizen groups and governments will likely keep privacy issues at the forefront of social concerns. The focus on privacy issues will be fueled in part by a desire to deal with the many Internet issues that have emerged. State attorney generals, the U.S. Justice Department, the Federal Trade Commission, and the Securities and Exchange Commission are expected to step up their efforts to enforce existing laws in Internet communications and business as well as eventually push for additional laws and regulations.

The U.S. Congress, state legislatures, and governments in countries around the world are also expected to become more aggressive in the regulation of the Internet, and those privacy issues will be a part of those efforts. Internet regulation will not be easy for governments to cope with and thus many false starts, high levels of rhetoric, and the pursuit of test cases to show regulatory prowess or to reinforce the popularity of political entities or candidates are anticipated. This is another element of the chaos that will continue to embroil the Internet and the privacy of information.

A legal requirement already exists for managing the privacy of information obtained from children: the Children's Online Privacy Protection

Act of 1998 (COPPA). This law requires that specific steps be followed when data are collected by any person or organization that operates a Web site, chat room, message service, email newsletter, or any other Internet-based or online service directed to children or that knowingly collects information from children under 13 years old. In many cases, a site must obtain parental consent before collecting, using, or disclosing personal information about a child. Consent is not required under some circumstances.

Therefore, an organization should develop a strategy to keep it out of the line of fire when investigations of privacy violations become wider spread or as governments attempt to make new laws and regulations. As with past social issues, such as environmental protection and equality in human resources, practices being labeled as "bad" are not going to be good for a company. The best possible strategy is one of risk avoidance.

MANY ORGANIZATIONS HAVE EXPERIENCED PRIVACY PROBLEMS

Several relatively high-profile privacy problems have surfaced during the last few years. An overview of these problems is provided in Chapter 2. Enterprise problems with alleged privacy violations have resulted in lawsuits as well as considerable amounts of really bad press coverage. The chapter does not judge the merits of any particular case but attempts to gauge, or at least illustrate, the impact on corporate reputation. The managers with whom we had confidential conversations about the privacy problems they encountered all had different perspectives toward the incidents in which they were involved. The one consensus, however, was they all would rather not have had the experience. All of the managers interviewed noted that legal costs can potentially be very high, even if courts rule in your favor or even if the incident eventually fades away. In addition, the process of dealing with the public relations aspect is emotionally draining, physically tiring, and has a negative impact on productivity. Overall, these managers recommended that the best approach is to avoid privacy-related incidents.

EVERY COMPANY IS VULNERABLE ON PRIVACY ISSUES

Every company is always at risk of having trade secrets compromised, intellectual property stolen, and business plans revealed in an untimely manner. Industrial espionage and spying remain at a high level and are practiced on an international scale. An organization's privacy planning process needs to take these threats into consideration. However, theft of propriety information is only part of an organization's vulnerability in the privacy wars. How an organization uses the information it collects about its customers or even its suppliers can increase its vulnerability.

One of an organization's greatest points of internal vulnerability is a lack of knowledge about the types of data that it has and how those data are being used. Far too many organizations do not know all the data they collect and how they are being used. Those companies without privacy plans in place are the most vulnerable. Although the companies with a track record in collecting and using a wide variety of data may be better versed in privacy issues, they still may create privacy problems by not understanding exactly what happens with those data.

mANAGERS NEED To DETERmINE HoW VULNERABLE THEIR oRGANIZATIoN IS

One of the key steps in developing a privacy plan is to conduct a privacy vulnerability audit. This process is examined in Chapters 4 and 5. A privacy vulnerability audit is a complex and meticulous process. It involves all departments in an enterprise and examines how data and information are protected, how the data are used inside the enterprise, and how they are shared with business partners. The privacy vulnerability audit is a very important step in determining how to develop a privacy plan and in deciding the type and scope of privacy-related policies and procedures that need to be established to avoid privacy problems.

THREATS EXIST WITHIN THE oRGANIZATIoN

Two types of privacy management threats occur within an organization. First is deliberate misuse or theft of information. This can range from incidents where employees deliberately remove proprietary information, including trade secrets, customer lists, or financial data, and provide that information to unauthorized parties. The second type of internal threat stems from ignorance or carelessness in how proprietary data and information are used. This can result in information being unnecessarily compromised, putting an organization at risk or, having a negative impact on its ability to function or compete. In addition, improper disclosure can result in civil litigation by the parties who believe their privacy rights have been violated.

A lesser internal threat has to do with how professionals interact with each other at conferences, workshops, scientific or engineering meetings, and now even over the Internet in communities and chat rooms. Professionals like to network, share ideas, and learn from each other. They like to help each other solve problems and accomplish research or advance their profession in some way. While this sharing of information may be good for society as a whole or for the professionals involved in the networking activity, it may not be the best thing for an organization. The privacy plan must define appropriate behavior in these circumstances.

THREATS EXIST OUTSIDE THE ORGANIZATION

Certainly privacy threats occur from outside an organization. Competitors, market researchers, and even social action groups can benefit from obtaining another organization's proprietary information. In many cases such groups will work with people inside the organization and plot to steal trade secrets or customer lists. In other cases researchers will use extreme means to find out about operations or business plans. Although much of this activity is deemed legitimate and is a customary business in many countries, an enterprise can still experience a negative impact if the wrong type of information is revealed to individuals outside the organization.

Even the most innocent-looking research effort can be detrimental to an organization. Numerous survey organizations, for example, send questionnaires to purchasing or information technology departments or conduct telephone surveys about issues or buying plans. The privacy plan needs to address such surveys and set a policy about how these situations should be handled.

SOCIAL TRENDS WILL AFFECT PRIVACY REQUIREMENTS

Social trends will definitely influence the need to assure that data and information in any organization are protected. Such an impact will occur in two ways. First, tighter regulation of privacy in the United States is to be expected. In addition, Web sites that are accessible in other countries will likely come under pressure to meet local privacy requirements and laws. In this case, enforcing such laws will be difficult, but the existence of the laws will increase social and governmental pressure on a global basis. This conclusion is based on a continued increase in international cooperation to deal with Internet issues such as virus attacks and hacking. Once cooperation moves faster on issues like security, privacy issues will logically follow shortly thereafter. While this impact is not imminent, it will occur around 2005.

The more immediate concern is what will happen within a country as the Internet grows and more people use the Internet for communications, community activities, and commerce. Social trends tend to put pressure on the political process. In the United States social pressure can translate into lobbying efforts that politicians find impossible to resist. The Internet and information technology in general will no doubt come under greater scrutiny by the U.S. Congress. This scrutiny, in turn, will result in more rhetoric and probably more legislation. Although Congress may not be particularly effective at such efforts, it is good at putting pressure on the business community, which means that having a privacy plan in place and a good privacy track record will be a corporate advantage over the long-term.

DATA SECURITY PROGRAMS ARE NoT ENoUGH To ASSURE PRIVACY

The necessity for good data security is absolute and is a fiduciary responsibility of corporate management. However, even though data security and privacy are related, the concept and practice of data security are generally

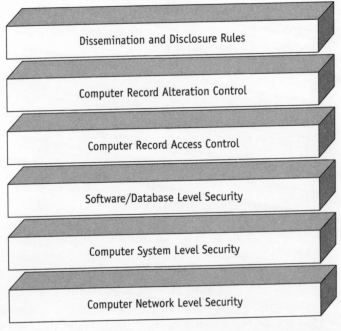

Figure 1-1. Achieving Information Privacy System Level Requirements

geared toward *restricting access* to data. Restricting access to data does not automatically assure that privacy is not being abused or violated. If organizational policies and practices regarding the use or sale of sensitive private information are not appropriate for a specific environment, privacy problems will still surface despite a secure information and technology infrastructure. For privacy plans to be effective security measures are necessary at all system levels to assure that privacy of information stored in or processed by computers is properly protected. This means that application developers need to address security and privacy protection for the system levels shown in Figure 1–1.

LAW ENFoRCEMENT AGENCIES WILL Do LITTLE To PRoTECT PRIVACY

In theory, law enforcement agencies in most major countries will get involved when unauthorized parties access information systems or misappropriate trade secrets. However, most law enforcement agencies are rather underequipped to deal with cyber crimes. Thus, the reality of getting help from law enforcement agencies is far different than the theory. Law enforcement officials may write a report and may be of help when physical property is stolen, but be wary of counting on them to be of much assistance in information theft or the intentional violation of information privacy.

Our experience working with several law enforcement agencies over the last decade has taught us several things. First, law enforcement personnel can generally be expected to be responsive and courteous. Second, law enforcement agencies would like to do more about cyber crimes and information theft, but they also recognize that they are understaffed and undertrained for such work. Third, the overall ability of law enforcement agencies to deal with information or computer crimes has improved considerably over the last decade, but that has been mostly at the national level or in large cities that have enough money to support adding specialized staff or training existing staff. Finally, the abilities of law enforcement personnel are expected to improve considerably over the next decade because of the prevalence of information or cyber crimes.

PRIVACY oF CoRPoRATE INFoRMATIoN MAY NoT BE INSURED

Companies need to check their insurance policies for coverage, but probably their insurance policies cannot or will not cover the potential extent of damage that major privacy violations could produce. Unless an organization has demonstrated due diligence in protecting its data and information and has clear policies for privacy management in place, its insurance company representative may just laugh and tell stories back at the office about how dumb the organization was to think that it had coverage. Companies should conduct an insurance audit to determine if they have coverage as well as the extent of any possible coverage. This audit includes a legal review of the policies and also involves conferences with the insurance companies.

PRoFESSIoNAL ASSoCIATIoNS CAN PRoVIDE SoITIE HELP WITH PRIVACY EFFoRTS

Certainly professional associations may provide some information about privacy. Occasionally, annual conferences have sessions dealing with privacy management. The professional associations may be a good starting place for various managers to learn how other organizations have addressed specific private issues. However, each organization must forge out its own privacy plan and make strategic, policy, and procedural decisions as to how to deal with privacy issues. The framework established in this book will guide companies through the process of researching, developing, and implementing their privacy plans.

PRIVACY LAWS ARE NoT THE SAITIE IN EVERY CoUNTRY

Privacy laws differ considerably from country to country. If an organization is doing business in multiple countries, its privacy plan must address requirements to comply with the privacy laws of all of the countries in which it conducts business or has operations. The management team in each country or those managers in the corporate headquarters responsible for business operations in each country need to address specific requirements. In addition, an organization's privacy plan, policies, and procedures must address varying privacy requirements by country. Also, if a company plans on expanding its operations or sales efforts into new countries, it should evaluate privacy requirements and modify its privacy policies and procedures before it expands into a new country.

ASSURING PRIVACY oF INFoRmATIoN IS A CoMPLICATED PRoCESS

Every company needs an enterprisewide privacy plan from which to formulate policies and procedures. This plan should be produced in written form so department managers and individuals responsible for managing information or data can refer to the document for guidance when making decisions. Organizations should also have a standing privacy task force or committee that systematically reviews the plan and updates it as new business efforts are launched or new technology is implemented. Critically, managers should inform their clients, customers, and business partners about the company's privacy policies and procedures to assure that they understand the organization's position and how very seriously it takes properly managing privacy. The process of building an enterprisewide privacy management program is broken down into four major phases as shown in Figure 1–2. Phase One is organizing and research; Phase Two is actually conducting the privacy-needs audit; Phase Three is developing policies and plans; and the final phase (Phase Four) is implementing policies and plans.

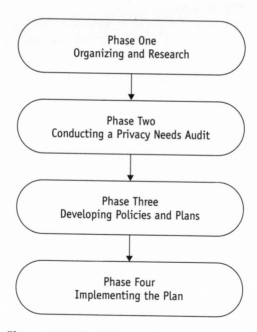

Figure 1–2. The Privacy Management Process

THE PRIVACY MANAGEMENT PROCESS ALL DEPARTMENTS SHOULD BE INVOLVED IN MANAGING PRIVACY

Yes, all departments should be involved in creating and implementing privacy plans, policies, and procedures; however, not all departments will have the same level of involvement. Each department needs to be involved to assure that all possible weaknesses in managing privacy are identified and that proper policies and procedures are created. In addition, each department should be involved because it can help create a greater awareness of the need for privacy procedures and also help to promote enterprisewide buy-in to the privacy plan.

ALL EMPLOYEES SHOULD BE TRAINED oN PRIVACY PROCEDURES

Yes, all employees should be trained on privacy policies and procedures, but not all employees will need the same level of training. All employees should be aware of what is and is not sensitive information or data and why it may be considered sensitive. Those employees with greater public contact need to be very well trained so they understand how to deal with public inquiries, what type of information they can release, and what data are restricted. Employees who are involved in record keeping, information processing, or database management also need to have an exceptional understanding of the privacy issues and requirements of the information they work with on a day-to-day basis.

ARE oRGANIZATIoNS WITH WEB SITES MoRE VULNERABLE To PRIVACY PROBLEMS?

This question has no cut and dry answer. The answer really depends on how an organization uses its Web site. If it does not post sensitive material and does not collect, compile, or process customer data on its Web server, then it is not more vulnerable for having a Web site. If the Web site is used to collect, compile, or process customer data, then the company has an added point of vulnerability. The increased vulnerability in this situation arises from the potential of a hacker breaking into the Web site and stealing data such as names, addresses, account information, or credit card numbers. In addition, if the Web site is integrated with back-end applications or connected to other systems in the enterprise, then hackers and information thieves have a greater possibility of accessing sensitive information that otherwise may be kept private. Therefore, organizations with Web sites should pay special attention to these types of vulnerabilities when conducting privacy audits and developing privacy plans.

ORGANIZATIONS WITH CUSTOMER OR CLIENT DATA ARE MORE VULNERABLE

Organizations with customer or client data are more at risk: Customer or client data are not only confidential, they are also the types of information that thieves and hackers seek out. This is especially true when financial records or credit card numbers are at risk. Also, organizations with customer or client data have the burden of added social pressure because of the sensitive nature of personal information. Pressure to protect personal data will increase over the next several years as privacy legislation is passed in countries around the world. This means that organizations that collect or use personal data on customers or business partners will need to take extraordinary steps to assure privacy and, of course, to avoid potentially costly litigation or embarrassing public relations incidents.

DETERMINE WHO SHOULD BE IN CHARGE OF PRIVACY

An important first step in any organization is to establish a privacy task force or committee made up of representatives from all departments in the enterprise. The privacy task force can determine if a full-time staff person will be required to oversee the implementation of the privacy plan. Although appointing a privacy director or czar is becoming rather vogue, such a position may not be required in all organizations. Chapter 4 provides a step-by-step process for organizing the privacy plan development efforts.

DEVELOPING A PRIVACY PLAN TAKES CONSIDERABLE TIME

The amount of time it takes to develop a privacy plan will obviously vary depending on the nature of an organization and the type of data and information that need protection. Generally speaking, the first draft of a good privacy plan, with appropriate input from all departments, should take from three to six months to develop. Once developed, a privacy plan takes three to six months to implement. Note, however, that managing privacy is an ongoing effort. After the plan is implemented, outcomes must be measured and policies and procedures must be updated as business and legislative conditions change. In other words, the work on privacy management is an ongoing process and should not be considered finished once the privacy plan is implemented.

TECHNoLoGY CAN HELP PRoTECT PRIVACY

Several technologies can help protect privacy, but none will assure that privacy efforts are being managed effectively. Technologies are useful in protecting data processing and storage facilities as well as data transmitted over networks and the Internet. Do not be self-deceptive and think that technology is all that is needed to protect privacy. Technology helps, but privacy protection is a human effort that requires coordinated efforts across all departments in the enterprise. Chapter 6 provides an overview of many technologies that are useful in helping to protect privacy. Chapters 10 through 16 provide checklists to evaluate privacy protection in enterprise systems, desktop and mobile computers, and Web sites and supply chain systems.

ENSURE ALL EmPLoYEES UNDERSTAND THE ImPoRTANCE oF PRIVACY

All employees must understand the importance of the organization's privacy protection efforts. The human resources (HR) department can play an essential role in the process of training all employees. HR can establish briefings for new employees upon hire and set up and manage ongoing training for existing personnel. HR departments are also experienced in information campaigns and can help create instructional content for corporate newsletters, Intranets, or Web sites. Involve the HR department early in the privacy planning process.

2

THE NATURE OF PRIVACY PROBLEMS

Numerous privacy issues have arisen over the last several years in both the private sector and the public sector. Many more incidents have made news headlines since the mid-1990s and the growth of Internet users. The general trends are toward a greater concern for privacy and increased media and public response over privacy violations. This chapter examines many of the recent incidents that have contributed to the great concern toward privacy. These examples of privacy-related incidents and responses to these incidents help to illustrate the potential problems an enterprise could encounter. Our purpose is to illustrate the nature of recent privacy problems. The content of this chapter does not judge the validity of the privacy concerns or the behavior or response of the organizations involved in the privacy incidents.

CONSUMER-RELATED PRIVACY ISSUES

If it can happen on the World Wide Web, it will happen on the World Wide Web. At least that is what the security specialists, Internet consultants, and public relations people that helped put together this overview of Internet-related privacy scandals felt. Talking to public relations people in Internet companies is always interesting in that they have such great stories to tell. The consensus among those people who put out public relations fires around Internet companies is that they need to be ready for anything.

DoubleClick, Inc.

As the most highly publicized company accused of endangering consumer privacy, DoubleClick, Inc., has had a tumultuous history. The culmination of privacy-rights group outcries, lawsuits, and Federal Trade Commission (FTC) investigations has resulted in a good deal of backtracking and policy realignment for this Web advertising network organization. A synopsis of the battle between privacy advocates and DoubleClick follows:

- By January 2000, major newspapers were publicizing the fact that DoubleClick, through the use of cookie technology, was beginning to connect Internet users' names to their Web-surfing patterns.
- Privacy advocates had long been warning consumers that the anonymous cookie technology used to track individual Internet use would soon be connected with the individual's names and real-life identities. In January, DoubleClick acknowledged that several of the Web sites in its advertising network were indeed putting the real names they required in Web site registration together with those individuals' surfing trails.
- To maximize the benefits of putting together user names and online surfing patterns, DoubleClick purchased Abacus, a huge database of consumer's off-line catalog-buying habits. DoubleClick's Abacus Online Alliance would then serve online advertisements to Internet users based on both their off-line and online activities.
- Following these events, a New Jersey senator proposed a law that would forbid Web sites from gathering personally identifiable information without permission.
- At the same time the New Jersey legislation was introduced, the privacy-rights group Center for Democracy and Technology launched a campaign to encourage users to opt out of DoubleClick's tracking methods.
- Meanwhile, a woman in California sued DoubleClick for unlawfully obtaining and selling her private information without her permission or knowledge.
- To defuse the large amount of criticism DoubleClick faced by this time, the company's president Kevin Ryan said the company would use 50 million Web banner ads to inform consumers on how to opt out of the Abacus Online Alliance database. However, privacy advocates pointed out that DoubleClick still did not ask permission for consumer information.
- The Electronic Privacy Information Center lodged a compliant with the FTC. The complaint alleged that DoubleClick was unlawfully tracking the online activities of Internet users and that this information was being used to develop a national marketing database. The FTC began their investigation of DoubleClick at the end of February 2000.

- In addition to the FTC investigation, DoubleClick faced a separate inquiry from the New York State Attorney General, and the Michigan State Attorney General said her state would sue DoubleClick unless it changed its practices.
- In the midst of these allegations and investigations, DoubleClick began revamping its privacy policy to allow Internet users to opt out of being tracked. The company hired PricewaterhouseCoopers to ensure that it was adhering to this new policy. By February 24, the company had lost almost a fifth of its market value since the beginning of the FTC investigation.
- By March 2, DoubleClick announced that it dropped its plans to track Internet users by name as they surf the Web. The company formally acknowledged that it had made a mistake in planning to link names with user activity and that it would not do so again until privacy standards were set.
- Following this announcement, the Michigan Attorney General applauded DoubleClick but said the state would continue to monitor the company's activities.
- Six days after its formal apology, DoubleClick announced that it had hired two former government officials to create a new privacy policy for the company. Former New York State Attorney General Robert Abrams was hired to head the company's new privacy advisory board. New York City's former consumer-affairs commissioner Jules Polonetsky was appointed as the company's new chief privacy officer.
- By May 17, DoubleClick created a seven-member board designed to review the company's services for potential privacy threats. The members include consumer advocates and experts in security and Internet privacy.

RealNetworks.com

- Like DoubleClick, online music software company RealNetworks has run into a series of privacy problems that have forced the company to rethink its strategies. Yet, despite its troubles, this company continues to think of new ways to gather information on its users, only to face new complaints when consumer groups discover RealNetworks' practices.
- In the months prior to November 1999, consumers and privacy groups complained to RealNetworks about its online information-gathering practices. The company produced a popular software program for listening to music on computers. When users downloaded the software

and played music on it, the program secretly transmitted to the company's headquarters details about which music CDs each customer listened to, how many songs they copied, and the serial numbers that could be used for identification purposes.

- Following the consumer complaints, RealNetworks apologized publicly for their practices and distributed a small patch that would block the tracking technology. In this apology, RealNetworks assured consumers that it had never stored the information it had been gathering.

- RealNetworks also changed its privacy policy on its Web site to state that the tracking it had previously done using the software was only intended to understand its users in order to provide more personalized services.

- After RealNetworks changed its privacy policy and made its formal apology to consumers, several privacy lawsuits were filed against the company. One suit filed in federal court in Chicago asked for unspecific damages and was seeking class-action status. Another suit sought $500 million in damages and was filed by a California man.

- In response to these lawsuits, RealNetworks filed a suit of its own to stop the consumers' action against the company. The suit claims that any disputes between the company and its users should be settled through arbitration as stated in the licensing agreement that all customers agree to before downloading RealNetworks software. This lawsuit was filed in early January 2000.

- By May 2000, RealNetworks was again raising more privacy concerns in the news. This time the company had released a new simplified downloading process called RealDownload 4. Although the program makes downloads easier, it also sends details of all downloads of any programs from the site back to the RealNetworks headquarters. That information is then used by RealNetworks to display customized advertising based on consumer behavior. Accumulated information is used for statistical analysis. Consumer groups complained that this new download option creates a privacy problem even though it allows users to opt out of the data-gathering process. Opponents say that to opt out, users must read through a license agreement and that this option is made too cumbersome for most users.

America Online

America Online (AOL) succeeded in keeping a rather clean slate in terms of privacy issues until early 1999 when the company mistakenly released individual information that caused a sailor to face expulsion from the Navy. Nearly a year after that episode, AOL was again in the news for seemingly underhanded practices that made it difficult for users to opt out of a program that could jeopardize their privacy.

- In a mistake that AOL attributed to human error under unusual circumstances, the company released to the Navy the identity of AOL profile page author Senior Chief Petty Officer Timothy McVeigh who described himself as gay on his AOL page.
- AOL's privacy policy forbids company representatives from giving out the names of profile page authors. In addition, a 1986 federal electronic privacy law prevents disclosure of information to the government without a warrant or court order. Despite the policy and law, an AOL representative provided the profile information to an investigator from the Navy who failed to identify himself as a government official and who did not reveal the true purposes of his call.
- Based on the information gathered from AOL, the Navy wanted to honorably discharge McVeigh. That action was put on hold until the AOL case was decided.
- In December 1999, AOL upset many more of its users by telling those who had previously opted out of receiving customized ads that they must fill out new forms if they wanted to keep their no-ad status. AOL messages told users that they would automatically begin receiving ads again, unless they completed what users called a cumbersome process.
- Consumer privacy groups said the new policy made it a yearly chore to be left alone, but AOL has tried to play down the inconvenience.

Geocities

As the first online privacy violator to come before the FTC in January 1999, Geocities was accused of using and distributing personal identifying information about its users without their consent or knowledge.

- In exchange for providing free Web pages, Geocities gathered the names, street addresses, e-mail addresses, personal interests, education levels, occupations, incomes, and marital statuses of all users.
- Geocities assured users that an individual's personal information would not be shared with other parties without user permission, but that Geocities advertisers would receive some aggregate data. However,

individual information was given to third parties that targeted members through advertisements and solicitations to which they did not consent.

- Children who used Geocities were especially vulnerable to the company's misleading practices. Through the "GeoKidz Club," Geocities allowed third parties to arrange contests for children and gather personal information from them. This information was gathered without parental consent, and the third parties were not disclosed. It appeared to users that only Geocities had control over the GeoKidz Club.

- In their settlement of the case against them, Geocities agreed to post a new privacy statement that explains what user information it gathers and distributes. It also agreed to obtain parental permission when gathering information on children under 13 years old. In addition, Geocities must provide a prominent link to the FTC's Web site, where visitors can find information about privacy.

Federal Deposit Insurance Corporation

In August 1999, 23,000 people complained to the Federal Deposit Insurance Corporation (FDIC) about a federal proposal designed to help banks identify suspicious financial activity in accounts that the banks handled. Consumers believed the "know your customer" proposal would jeopardize their banking privacy.

- Under the "know your customer" proposal, banks would be required to develop profiles of customers' regular banking behavior, monitor transactions for suspicious activity, and report any unusual activity to a federal database.

- Prior to this proposal, the Bank Security Act of 1970 required banks to report cash transactions of over $10,000 and to report suspicious activity to a federal database. The 1970 act did not require a formal monitoring system of individuals' accounts, and most banks did not have one in place.

- The new proposal was criticized as too vague, and privacy advocates feared that individuals could easily be reported to the government for laundering money if they received an inheritance or other infusion of money.

- Privacy groups have also been concerned about regular bank account monitoring, because, under the Fair Credit Reporting Act, banks can share information about a customer as long as the customer gets one chance to tell the bank not to disclose the information. Currently, banks typically only share information gathered from credit reports and loan applications, but with the monitoring required by the "know your customer" proposal, banks would have significantly more information to share with each other about their customers.

The Young Investor Web Site

In May 1999, the FTC found the Web site Young Investor guilty of collecting personal information from its underage visitors without their parents' consent.

- Promising prizes and a newsletter, the Web site enticed children to complete a survey in which they provided name, address, age, and email address, and answered questions about their own and their family's finances.
- None of the respondents received the promised prizes or newsletters before the FTC investigation.
- In addition, although the survey told respondents that all of their answers would be anonymous, the FTC alleged that Young Investor used the information for purposes other than sending newsletters and prizes to respondents.
- The owners of Young Investor, Liberty Financial, assert that the information gathered from children without parental consent was never used by the organization or shared with any other party. The company has agreed to post a privacy notice on its sites for children and to obtain verifiable parental consent before collecting personal, identifying information from children under 13 years old.

ABC ONLINE

In September 1999, ABC news with Sam Donaldson held its first Internet news broadcast and allowed online visitors to electronically chat with the show's anchor. When viewers logged on to the show's chat room, some of their personal information was displayed to all other users and passive visitors.

- All viewers participating in the ABC news chat with Donaldson not only had their user names and comments posted on the Web site, but they also had their unique Internet Protocol addresses disclosed.

- The provided IP addresses allowed users and visitors to trace other users' real-world identities.
- In one situation during the event, a chatter who criticized the FCC and Donaldson's guest, FCC Chairman William Kennard, was discovered to be an employee at the Justice Department. This situation caused some concern within that department and prompted officials to remind Justice Department employees that, according to the department's Internet policy, employees must make it clear that their personal activities online are not official business of the department.
- Following the broadcaster's initial Internet newscast and the associated privacy problems, ABC decided to stop publishing chat room users' IP addresses. Before the event, ABC had stated within its privacy policy that some chat room boards would display IP addresses of anyone posting a comment, and that users should review the site's various chat rooms before using them to ensure their comfort level with the information disclosed in each room.

ReverseAuction.com

Using personal user information gathered from the eBay Web site, competitor ReverseAuction.com sent spam email to many eBay users in an attempt to persuade the recipients to use the ReverseAuction.com site instead of eBay. The FTC charged ReverseAuction.com with violating the eBay privacy policy in January 2000.

- To obtain user email addresses from its competitor, ReverseAuction.com registered as a user on the eBay site. Registered users on eBay have access to other users email addresses, but eBay discourages users from collecting or misusing these addresses in its privacy statement. ReverseAuction.com violated this policy when it spammed the eBay user email accounts.
- In the spam emails, ReverseAuction.com told recipients that their eBay registration was about to expire and encouraged them to start a new registered account at ReverseAuction.com.
- Because ReverseAuction.com violated the eBay privacy policy and invaded eBay users' privacy, the FTC took action against the company. In this situation, eBay was not accused of any wrongdoing.
- To settle the FTC charges, ReverseAuction.com agreed to cease its spamming of eBay users. The company also agreed to delete all information gathered from the eBay site when it registered as an eBay user.

Additionally, ReverseAuction.com gave users an opportunity to cancel their ReverseAuction.com accounts.

Privacy Advocacy Site

In a demonstration of the ease of gathering personal information online, Pennsylvania privacy advocate Glen Roberts posted information on his private Web site that was used by others to create hundreds of fake credit card accounts.

- On his Web site, Roberts provided the names and Social Security numbers of high-ranking military officers. He obtained this information from the *Congressional Record*, which published this information whenever the officers were promoted.
- Visitors to Roberts' Web site, Nevison Stevens and Lamar Christian used the information on the site to create credit card accounts in the names of the military officers.
- Stevens and Christian then used the fake credit cards to purchase $161,000 worth of computers and jewelry online.
- In May 2000, a U.S. District Court found both Stevens and Christian guilty of conspiracy to commit bank fraud, and they now face up to four years in prison. Assistant U.S. Attorney Beth Moskow-Schnoll reported that the *Congressional Record* has ceased publishing the Social Security numbers of military officers who receive new promotions. However, the Social Security numbers that were included in the *Congressional Record* prior to this year remain there.

Business Related Privacy Issues

During the last few years many concerns have been raised about the privacy of corporate information, industrial spying, and international commercial espionage. Most of these issues are very valid, and private companies will face increasingly difficult privacy and security challenges in the future. These challenges range from something as complex as having an entire operation monitored, including voice, data, and physical activity, to something as simple as employees accidentally revealing trade secrets over the Internet. Major security incidents or the unauthorized access and distribution of corporate information is at least embarrassing and in extreme cases can negatively affect stock prices, erode investor confidence, and scare away prospective customers. The following examples illustrate some of the new technology-based threats to corporate privacy that businesses should be concerned about today.

Satellites

Industrial espionage is becoming increasingly easier with the recent successful launches of commercial satellites. In the past, only government entities owned and operated observation satellites, but the release of commercial satellites has made high-level surveillance accessible to private companies for the first time. This opportunity has brought substantial benefits to the private sector but has also opened significant privacy concerns.

- The capabilities of these satellites can allow organizations to significantly improve performance in agriculture, environmental monitoring, map making, energy exploration, and other diverse areas. However, companies can also use satellites to track and monitor the activities of their competitors.
- Images taken from commercial satellites are now capable of displaying features as small as 1 meter. This would allow observers to easily distinguish a car from a pickup truck.
- Currently, over 500 satellites orbit the earth, and the United States owns 220. In the next 10 years, another 1,000 launches are expected. While the majority of existing satellites are government controlled, most of the satellites planned for launch over the next decade will be commercial.
- High-resolution satellite data are digital and can be transmitted to many destinations quickly and easily. For a company trying to maintain its privacy, the rapid distribution of confidential images is a significant threat.
- Legislation cannot realistically protect businesses from capturing and distributing satellite images. Current U.S. policy requires commercial satellites to be licensed by the National Oceanic and Atmospheric Administration. This entity does not attempt to control image distribution, but it does limit the resolution of satellite images to one meter. However, increasingly high-resolution satellites are available on the international market and are not subject to U.S. regulation.

Amazon.com

Starting in August 1999, businesses began to face a new threat to corporate privacy. At this time Amazon.com initiated its Purchase Circle programs in which the purchasing patterns of groups of consumers working at major U.S. corporations were released to the general public on the Amazon.com site. Many companies felt that such information could provide competitors with clues about corporate strategies and plans.

- The Amazon.com Purchase Circles were designed to let Amazon.com visitors find out what others were buying without disclosing individual information. In the Purchase Circle program, the purchasing pattern of at least several hundred individuals from the same corporation is made public.
- To find the buying trends of individuals from certain companies Amazon.com tracks the ZIP codes and domain names of all users on its site. Whenever a user purchases an Amazon.com item from their work computer, the purchase is tracked to the employer's domain name.
- The major corporations covered in the Purchase Circles were concerned that the purchasing patterns of their employees would reveal private corporate information or corporate mentality. For example, when Hewlett-Packard split and a new CEO stepped up, the top seller was a book on dealing with changes in the workplace.
- Despite complaints from corporations, Purchase Circles continue to be popular special features on Amazon.com. In addition to corporations, users can find purchasing patterns for groups of people by ZIP code, government agency, nonprofit or professional organization, educational institution, and more.

Yahoo! Chat

In early 1999, defense contractor Raytheon filed a lawsuit against 21 people who allegedly disclosed the company's financial secrets in a Yahoo chat room. The company eventually dropped the suit, but not before its privacy and the privacy of the chat room users was put at risk.

- The suit filed by Raytheon claimed that postings by a group of chat room users, some of whom were Raytheon employees, cost the company $25,000 and hurt its business reputation. The organization said that they had to file the suit to protect their financial information.
- The content of the questionable chat included discussion of the company's stock price and complaints about the chief executive.
- The chat room users believed that their activities were anonymous because they used aliases such as "Rayman-mass" and "Raytheon Veteran."

- Raytheon, however, was able to obtain the names of the chat room users by filing discovery motions against Yahoo! and other Internet providers.
- Although this action brought criticism from consumer privacy and free speech groups, it gave Raytheon the information it needed to handle the situation internally and the suit was dropped. Four of the employees named in the suit left Raytheon.

Government Privacy Issues

Many government organizations have been under fire from advocacy groups and the media for not protecting the privacy of personal data. It has been commonplace that defense and national security related organizations are accused of poor security, a lack of concern for individual privacy, and inappropriate monitoring of individual activities. Most of these incidents, however, do not touch the consumer directly and eventually fade away into history. With the help of several associates, three major incidents that touch the consumer in a direct manner are provided next. They involved the U.S. Internal Revenue Service (IRS), the Social Security Administration, and the use of prisoners to process consumer information.

IRS

In October 1999, privacy groups became concerned about an IRS proposal to release taxpayers' records to third parties in electronic form. The electronic delivery method would dramatically speed up the process of sharing taxpayer information, and consumers feared that this would endanger privacy.

- In the older off-line model of taxpayer information delivery, third parties such as credit bureaus and mortgage brokers could request information from the IRS. The information exchange would usually take about two weeks, and total requests per year did not exceed 6 million.
- In the new electronic format, requests should be processed within 24 hours. Due to the added ease and speed, the IRS estimates that the number of information exchanges will jump to 50 million per year.
- Privacy advocates are not only concerned about the increased number of information exchanges involved in the new program, but they are also worried about the security of the online system. If unauthorized parties can access the electronic delivery method, individual taxpayers' information could easily be used and distributed.

- The IRS claims that the new system actually increases taxpayer privacy. In the old information exchange program, entire tax returns were sent to third parties. With the electronic delivery method, only the necessary 26 line items will be sent.

State Prisons

In December 1999, a reporter discovered that local, state, or federal governments have contracted at least 20 state prisons to allow inmates to access records with personal identifying and financial information of average citizens. Providing convicted criminals with this information has resulted in increases in a wide variety of identity crimes.

- In an article for the Scripps Howard News Service, reporter Richard Powelson found that government agencies have used contracts with prisons in which inmates handle incoming calls to government offices.
- To handle the calls or perform other contracted tasks, the inmates have access to citizens' names, addresses, telephone numbers, birth dates, Social Security numbers, and in some cases credit card numbers.
- According to the U.S. General Accounting Office, government agency contracts with state prisons have given over 1,000 inmates access to personal information about U.S. citizens.
- Investigators have found that credit card fraud, theft of official birth certificates, harassing phone calls, and unsolicited letters to citizens have been a result of these contracts.

Social Security

In bringing the Social Security system online, the Social Security Administration (SSA) faced significant privacy challenges. After an initial launch of an online system in March 1998, the SSA shut down the site due to security troubles. By the beginning of 1999, the SSA relaunched a much more secure site and had taken several precautions to limit access to personal information.

- The original SSA online program was designed to allow citizens to access information on their Social Security benefits through the Internet. Users were able to view the Personal Earnings and Benefit Statement, which showed a person's earnings history and estimated retirements, disability, and death benefits.

- The information available in the original system could be obtained by providing only a name, Social Security number, mother's maiden name, and state and date of birth. Officials determined that this level of security would not adequately prevent unauthorized access to benefits information.
- The revamped site limits access and the information available online. Users are now able to get online estimates of their retirement benefits, but the earnings and tax histories that are the basis of those estimates are only available through regular mail. Users will also have access to work credits and will be able to see if their benefits are insured.
- To access the more limited information, users must have an individual email account that is verifiable, such as through an employer or online subscriber service. Through this verified email account, the user must send a specific email request to "unlock" their benefits estimates. After sending the email, users receive an activation code to open the record. When they are finished looking at the information, users are able to then lock the record.

REACTING TO CONSUMER REACTION TO PRIVACY INCIDENTS

From discussions with several public relations managers and business developers, the viewpoints toward consumer reaction to privacy issues vary considerably. On one extreme, public relations workers were adamant that they would just as soon not have to deal with privacy-related incidents or scandals. Business developers, on the other hand, seem less concerned about consumer reaction and feel that consumers have short memories and all incidents will fade away. The big thing that both public relations managers and business developers agreed on was that the reaction of consumers towards privacy violation incidents was not as much of a concern as the potential impact on the legislative process.

Indeed, the response of individuals must be dealt with, but how isolated incidents potentially influence public opinion or at least the political view of public opinion is a major concern. As many as 3,000 pending privacy bills are pending in various legislative bodies around the United States. This legislation often goes nowhere because, for the most part, it is merely political fodder. The main problem with fodder is that it sometimes grows into actual legislation, and when it does, it is usually bad legislation. This is best exemplified by the Communications Decency Act (CDA), which was the first attempt of the U.S. Congress to regulate the Internet. The

CDA was ruled unconstitutional by U.S. Federal courts because the law was poorly written and could not hold up to constitutional tests.

No doubt an organization needs to put on the best possible public relations face if it is confronted with a privacy issue by individuals or by advocacy groups. An organization must not alienate individual clients or customers, who may get mad enough to complain to the FTC or to an advocacy group, which could create even bigger problems. Dealing with an advocacy group also requires considerable public relations tact. However, an organization may not need to immediately cave in to any or all advocacy group demands. If an organization is unfortunate enough to become an example case for an advocacy group, life can become pretty miserable.

Overall organizations should try not to overreact to consumer reaction or advocacy group attacks. In addition, the FTC and probably other government organizations will attempt to do some muscle flexing over privacy issues during the next several years. Privacy is expected to remain a political hot button during election campaigns. Public relations groups, or departments, need to be prepared to respond to such attacks and, of course, to be prepared to deal with the media in a damage control mode. As illustrated in the examples in this chapter, many organizations take a defensive posture when confronted with privacy issues too quickly. How a company reacts to such privacy incidents may have a far greater effect on the outcome than the incident itself.

3

THE REGULATORY AND
LEGISLATIVE ENVIRONMENT

As the concern for privacy increases, governments around the world are working on legislation or have formed cross-border task forces to deal with privacy issues. This chapter examines international privacy activities as well as the privacy efforts in selected industrial countries. The outcome of international privacy efforts will take several years to unfold, and even longer to be implemented on a global basis. The national laws regarding privacy will continue to evolve around the world. This chapter provides a basic understanding of major privacy-related activities and attitudes in countries in which many organizations may do business. It also examines the source of Internet users, the countries involved in business-to-consumer Internet sales and business-to-business Internet and supply chain transactions, and some of the privacy challenges that result from the global nature of Internet business systems.

Historically, the Organization for Economic Cooperation and Development (OECD) has been the leading international organization addressing privacy issues, especially issues related to cross-border flow of data and the development of national laws governing privacy. The origins of OECD privacy-related activities can be traced back to 1960, and some observers believe the work actually began before that date. The European Union's Directive on Data Protection and many national laws have been cast following the guidelines developed over the years by the OECD. The guidelines, which are continuously updated, are published on the OECD Web site www.oecd.org in a document entitled *Guidelines on the Protection of Privacy and Transborder Flows of Personal Data.*

THE EUROPEAN UNION'S PRIVACY INITIATIVES

The European Union's (EU's) privacy legislation called the Directive on Data Protection became effective on October 25, 1998. The directive requires that transfers of personal data take place only to non-EU countries that provide acceptable levels of privacy protection. This resulted in a long series of negotiations between the United States and the EU and the development of *safe harbor* standards. As it now stands, compliance with safe harbor requirements is voluntary, and organizations may qualify for the safe harbor in different ways. Organizations that do decide to voluntarily adhere to safe harbor principles can obtain and retain the benefits of the safe harbor and publicly declare that they have done so. The principles of safe harbor are as follows.

An organization must inform individuals as to why information about them is collected, how to contact the organization with inquiries or complaints, the types of third parties to which the information will be disclosed, and the options and means the organization provides individuals to limit its use and disclosure of information. Notice must be provided to individuals in clear language at the point when individuals are first asked to provide personal information or as soon thereafter as is practicable. In all circumstances the organization must inform individuals before it uses information for any purpose other than that for which it was originally collected or before it discloses information to a third party.

An organization must provide individuals with an opportunity to choose if and how personal information that they provide is used or disclosed to third parties if such use is not compatible with the original purpose for which the information was collected. Individuals must be provided with clear, readily available, and affordable mechanisms to exercise this *opt out* option. For sensitive information such as medical and health information, racial or ethnic origin, political opinions, religious or philosophical beliefs, trade union membership, or information concerning the sex life of the individual, the individual must be given the opportunity to specifically affirm (opt in) that the information can be used.

An organization is allowed to disclose personal information to third parties in manners that are consistent with the original principles of notice and choice. When passing on information of which an individual has approved the use, an organization must first determine that the receiving party subscribes to the safe harbor principles. As an alternative to meeting general safe harbor requirements, the receiving party must enter into a written agreement with the organization providing the information, in order to assure that the receiver will provide at least the same level of privacy protection as is required by relevant safe harbor principles.

Organizations that create, maintain, use, or disseminate personal information must take reasonable measures to assure that it is reliable for the intended use. In addition organizations must take reasonable precautions to protect its information from loss, misuse, unauthorized access, disclosure, alteration, and destruction.

An organization may only process personal information for the purposes for which the information was originally collected. In doing so an organization is responsible for assuring that data are accurate, complete, and current.

Individuals who provide information must have reasonable access to personal information about them that an organization holds and must be able to correct or amend that information where it is inaccurate.

In addition to the steps that an organization must take internally, nations and states face the need for providing privacy protection mechanisms to assure compliance with the safe harbor principles. Recourse must be available for individuals affected by noncompliance with the principles, and an organization that violates safe harbor principles must face consequences. Such mechanisms must include readily available and affordable independent recourse for an individual's complaints and a method by which disputes can be investigated and resolved as well as damages awarded where the applicable law or private sector initiatives provide. Procedures must be in place to verify that the assertions businesses make about their privacy practices are true and that those privacy practices have been implemented as they were stated at the time the information was originally collected. Sanctions against organizations who violate the principles must be rigorous enough to ensure compliance.

Notably the Online Privacy Alliance guidelines for privacy on the Internet are consistent with the EU safe harbor requirements. Also, many laws being passed at the national level in countries around the world are fairly consistent with EU requirements.

PRIVACY LAWS AND REGULATIONS IN THE UNITED STATES

Privacy laws and regulations in the United States are a mixed bag of vague constitutional protections, laws governing information protection in different industries (such as health care, banking, and finance), and socially oriented laws that affect both the disclosure of information and the infringement of personal freedoms. Laws at the state and local levels are emerging in an attempt to govern privacy or to specify what type of activities constitutes an infringement. These laws range from antistalking ordinances to the prohibition of Web cams in public places. Overall privacy laws in the United States are a fragmented mess that no single government entity has attempted to make sense of or is empowered to control or guide. Meanwhile the debate among federal, state, and local powers regarding privacy rages on with no end in site.

After discussing privacy laws with several seasoned observers, an overview was pulled together of privacy laws and regulations in the United Sates. These observers pointed out that privacy in the United States is often discussed at a theoretical and constitutional level with ongoing attempts to interpret the vagueness of and the basis of laws that were enacted over 200 years ago. These laws were created to keep the government in check. They were created before the computer, before the telephone, and before mass merchandising. Currently over 400 laws in the United States address privacy issues in some manner for medical records, telecommunications, financial services, and insurance. Several expert sources speculated about how many privacy-related laws were being considered at different levels of government. The estimates ranged from over 1,000 to over 3,000 legislative bills in process.

Several fundamental concepts provide the basis of understanding privacy in the United Sates. First, an individual's privacy shall not undergo unreasonable intrusion. Second, making private facts public, including income tax data, sexual relations, and medical treatment records, is not appropriate. Third, privacy rights relate more to government actions. This concept is demonstrated by the protection of privacy of an individual charged with a crime. Law enforcement agencies are prohibited from such things as the intercepting of conversations in a house or hotel room, opening envelopes sent via first class mail, and tapping telephone conversations unless a specific court order allows the investigators to perform such intrusions.

However vague, there are numerous laws, rules, and regulations at various levels of government that protect personal information in specific situations. These include medical records, bank statements, academic records, the court records of minors, the protection of telephone conversations, and many more. Also laws protect trade secrets of private corporations and the records and technical information related to national defense and security. The strength of these laws are debated by several experts, most of whom agree that individuals as well as organizations of all types need to be concerned about privacy, partially because of the contradictions and conflicting laws among federal, state, and local governments.

THE ROLE OF THE U.S. FEDERAL TRADE COMMISSION AND COPPA

The most active U.S. government department on the privacy front is the Federal Trade Commission (FTC). The FTC has a basic responsibility of monitoring and assuring compliance with laws of trade and consumer protection in the United States. The FTC has been active in working on privacy legislation and provides numerous reports and guidelines covering privacy. More information can be obtained at the FTC Web site, www.ftc.gov. One of the primary roles of the FTC in privacy is the administration of the Children's Online Privacy Protection Act of 1998 (COPPA). In the United States and for the purposes of COPPA, a child is defined as anyone under the age of 13 years.

COPPA requires that any person or organization that operates a Web site, chat room, message service, email newsletter, or any other Internet-based or online service directed to children or that knowingly collects information from children under 13 years old must post a notice of their information collection practices. This notice must include how the site will use the information collected, whether personal information is forwarded to advertisers or other third parties, and how to contact the site to inquire about the use of data. In many cases, a site must obtain parental consent before collecting, using, or disclosing personal information about a child. Consent is not required under some circumstances, including:

- Collecting an email address to respond to a one-time request from the child
- Ensuring the safety of the child or the site
- Sending a newsletter or other information on a regular basis as long as the site notifies a parent and gives the parent a chance to say no to the arrangement

Web site operators must notify parents and get consent again if they plan to change the type of information they collect, change how the information is used, or offer the information to new and different third parties. In addition, Web sites must give parents the option to revoke their consent, and the sites must delete information collected from their children at

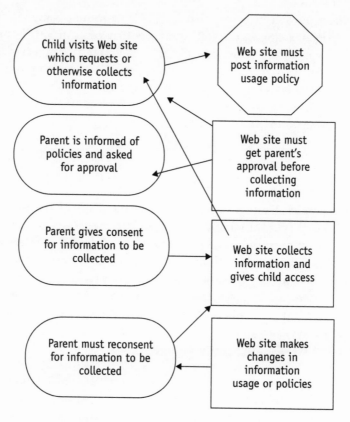

Figure 3-1. Meeting COPPA Requirements

the parents' request. Parental consent must be verifiable, which means any reasonable method must be used to ensure that a parent of a child receives notice of the operator's personal information collection, use, and disclosure practices, and authorizes the collection, use, and disclosure before information is collected from that child. The COPPA requirements are outlined in Figure 3-1.

PRIORITIZING EFFORTS TO COMPLY WITH NATIONAL PRIVACY LAWS

Being aware of privacy laws around the world is certainly important but very difficult given that over 200 countries have Internet users. Each organization should track the source of its customers or Web site users and make every effort possible to assure that known laws are not being violated. In addition, organizations with Web site users that come from EU member countries or countries with laws similar to EU member countries need to prepare to meet strict EU requirements. Another way to plan privacy management efforts is to examine the laws of countries that expect growth in Internet business-to-consumer activity and those that expect growth in Internet business-to-business systems such as supply chains and demand chains.

EU-INFLUENCED COUNTRIES

Privacy planners should also recognize that members of the EU all have similar privacy laws. In addition, those countries that are negotiating for EU membership and those countries that have expressed an interest in EU membership will comply with broad EU guidelines on privacy and implement any specific laws necessary to gain membership. EU members and countries interested in membership are shown in Figure 3–2. All of the countries in Figure 3–2 will be enforcing consistent privacy laws, and Web site users in countries as small as Estonia will eventually have the same privacy protection and expectation as those in larger countries like France or Germany.

It is important to understand that many countries outside Europe have privacy laws similar to those of EU member states. Although Canada does not constitutionally protect privacy, laws and regulations that do cover individual privacy in Canada are consistent with the requirements of the EU.

Members of the European Union	Austria, Belgium, Denmark, Finland, France, Germany, Greece, Ireland, Italy, Luxembourg, the Netherlands, Portugal, Spain, Sweden, and the United Kingdom
Countries Negotiating for Membership in the European Union	Czech Republic, Estonia, Hungary, Poland, Slovenia
Countries Interested in Membership in the European Union	Bulgaria, Latvia, Lithuania, Romania, Slovakia, Switzerland, Turkey

Figure 3–2. EU Members and Countries Interested in Membership

Canadian law is somewhat ambiguous in that it contends that an organization may collect, use, or disclose personal information only for purposes that a reasonable person would consider are appropriate in the circumstances. This ambiguity places a considerable, although theoretical, burden on the courts in Canada because they must interpret the concept of *reasonable*. In Japan the 1946 Constitution covers the basic privacy of home, personal correspondence, and personal data, and the 1988 Act for the Protection of Computer Processed Personal Data is consistent with EU requirements.

The Australian Privacy Act of 1988 established a set of eleven information privacy principles based on the OECD guidelines. The 1988 act applies mostly to federal government agencies. A similar act was passed in 1989 to regulate privacy of consumer credit information that applies to all private and public sector organizations. Australia also has laws against the unauthorized access of computer systems, mail, and telecommunications. In 1998, Australia passed a data protection law that restricts access to government computers and establishes penalties for unauthorized access.

In Argentina, a data protection law was passed in 1996 upon request of the Central Bank. The president vetoed the law and efforts to revive are pending. The law applies to privacy of data files, registers, banks, and other electronic or manual technical means of data treatment. Consistent with EU regulations, the Argentina law provides provisions for consent, notification, security, uses, scope, confidentiality, and international transfer of personal data. Additional protection of sensitive data is addressed under the Code of Penal Procedure, which requires judicial intervention to allow interception of telephone communications or other means of communication for the purposes of building a legal case against an individual suspected of criminal behavior.

COUNTRIES WHERE INTERNET USERS WILL COME FROM

Depending on the type of Web site an organization operates, being aware of where users originate may be important. Organizations with the general purpose of informational Web sites could easily have users around the world. If information about users is collected or compiled, Web sites that provide services to or receive traffic from those countries with the largest populations of Internet users may face significant challenges. The largest number of Internet users resides in the United States, which will continue to lead the world in the number of Internet users through 2003. The next highest ranking country in the number of expected Internet users for the next several years is Japan, followed by China, Germany, and Great Britain. The number of Internet users in countries with more than one million users is shown in Figure 3–3.

Of the 55 countries expected to have more than one million Internet users by 2003, 18 are either EU members or countries interested in EU membership (Austria, Belgium, Czech Republic, Denmark, Finland, France, Germany, Great Britain, Greece, Hungary, Italy, Netherlands, Poland, Romania, Spain, Sweden, Switzerland, and Turkey). In addition, Argentina, Australia, and Canada, who have privacy laws similar to those of EU countries, are also on the list of the top 55 countries that will have more than one million Internet users.

Country	Projected Internet Users In the Country by 2003 (millions)	Importance Ranking by Number of Users
United States	165	1
Japan	55	2
China, Germany, Great Britain	30	3
Canada, South Korea	20	4
Australia, Brazil, France, India	15	5
Indonesia, Italy, Russia	11	6
Taiwan	9	7
Netherlands, Spain	8	8
Mexico, Poland, Sweden	5	9
Belgium, Hong Kong, Thailand, Turkey	4	10
Austria, Denmark, Finland, Norway, Switzerland	3	11
Argentina, Greece, New Zealand, Malaysia, Singapore, South Africa	2	12
Afghanistan, Chile, Colombia, Czech Republic, Egypt, Hungary, Ireland, Israel, Pakistan, Peru, Philippines, Portugal, Romania, Saudi Arabia, Slovakia, Slovenia, U.A.E., Ukraine, Uzbekistan, Venezuela	1	13

Figure 3–3. Ranking of Countries by the Number of Internet Users

Brazil, among the top 55 countries from which Internet users will come, also has well-developed privacy laws. The 1988 Constitution of Brazil states that the private life, honor, and image of an individual are inviolable. The constitution provides individuals the right to compensation for property or moral damages if the secrecy of their correspondence, telegraphic, telephone, or data communication is violated except in the course of a legal investigation of criminal activity. In addition, the 1990 Code of Consumer Protection and Defense grants individuals the right of access to information that an organization compiles on them and the right to have any incorrect data corrected.

In Hong Kong, also in the top 55 countries from which Internet users will come, privacy rights have traditionally been viewed as weak by many human rights observers. The 1995 Personal Data Ordinance, for example, does not address the varying levels of sensitivity of personal information. The Telecommunications Ordinance provides broad powers of interception of private telecommunications, including email, based on the protection of public interest. Overall, many of the privacy protections that advocates around the world consider important are very vague in Hong Kong law and thus lack procedural safeguards necessary to protect individual privacy.

In India, the government has been slow to address privacy issues. Investigators there can easily get government permission to use wiretaps, and people have a severe lack of judicial recourse in controlling, or limiting, government monitoring of private telecommunications and email. Much of the ambiguity regarding privacy or the lack of strong regulations in India is probably tied to years of political turmoil and unrest.

COUNTRIES WHERE BUSINESS-TO-CONSUMER ECOMMERCE WILL OCCUR

Companies engaged in Internet business-to-consumer sales should evaluate from which countries they will generate sales activity and prepare to meet the privacy requirements of those countries. As shown in Figure 3–4, 22 countries are expected to have over one billion dollars in annual Internet business-to-consumer sales in 2003. Each of these 22 countries is on the list of the top 55 countries from which Internet users will originate as shown in Figure 3–3. The process of providing business-to-consumer sales requires collecting far more information than does providing general information such as news, community services, or content that can be found in a typical search engine.

Country	Projected Business-to-Consumer Internet Sales in 2003 (U.S. $ Billions)
U.S.	160
Japan	70
Germany	27
Great Britain	22
Canada	14
France	14
Australia	10
South Korea	7
Italy	7
Netherlands	7
Sweden	5
Switzerland	5
Norway	4
Denmark	4
Spain	3
Hong Kong	3
Belgium	3
Finland	3
Austria	3
Brazil	2
Singapore	2
New Zealand	1

Figure 3–4. Ranking of Countries by the Projected Business-to-Consumer Internet Sales

COUNTRIES WHERE BUSINESS-TO-BUSINESS ECOMMERCE WILL OCCUR

Companies engaged in Internet business-to-business transactions face the challenge of protecting the privacy of the parties for whom they are acting as well as potentially the end consumer of a product or commodity. Internet business-to-business organizations should evaluate the countries in which their suppliers or service providers are located to determine the extent of privacy that the law provides for their transactions. Under safe harbor principles, Internet business-to-business companies are responsible for assuring that the privacy of data used to accomplish a transaction is not compromised somewhere in the supply chain or order fulfillment process.

As shown in Figure 3–5, over 50 countries are expected to participate in over 10 billion dollars in annual Internet business-to-business transactions in 2003. Most of these countries supply raw material or play a role in the production process of finished consumer goods. What should cause concern for privacy managers in dealing with the business-to-business transactions in some of these countries is a lack of privacy laws and in some cases a fairly high level of lawlessness. The fundamental principle of supply chain systems is to integrate the ordering and fulfillment process from

Country	Projected Internet Business-to-Business Transaction in 2003 (U.S. $ Billions)
U.S.	3,060
Japan	1,680
Germany	680
China	550
Canada	500
France	410
Great Britain, Italy	350
Brazil	240
India	200
Mexico	170
Australia, Spain	150
Netherlands, Russia, South Korea, Thailand	115
Argentina, Hong Kong, Switzerland	80
Austria, Belgium, Turkey, Taiwan	60
Denmark, Poland, Sweden	50
Finland, Greece, Indonesia, Norway, Saudi Arabia, Singapore	40
Colombia, Ireland, Israel, Malaysia, Philippines, Portugal	30
Egypt, New Zealand, South Africa, U.A.E.	20
Algeria, Ecuador, Jordan, Kuwait, Lebanon, Morocco, Oman, Tunisia, Uruguay, Venezuela	10

Figure 3–5. Ranking of Countries by the Projected Business-to-Business Internet Transactions

end to end. If that principle is implemented to its fullest extent, some ends of the supply chain are going to be located in countries that, because of different views towards business, may pose a threat to privacy and perhaps even to system security. In addition, many of these countries are not among the EU-influenced countries that have relatively strict privacy laws and business practices.

PUTTING PRIVACY LAWS INTO PERSPECTIVE

The material presented in this chapter intends to provide only an overview of the types of privacy laws and regulations that organizations face when conducting business internationally. The complexity of privacy laws that every organization must deal with will be compounded by the nature of the organization itself. If the organization uses the Internet and collects or uses data from individuals, it faces a situation of increasing complexity. If an organization deals with personal information such as medical records or financial records, the complexity of its privacy problems also increases.

Although this chapter received considerable input from several first-hand observers, they did not feel like they had the final solution to privacy laws or regulation. Also, these observers had several contradictory perspectives as to the quality of privacy law. One thing that was agreed on was every organization, no matter how large or small, public or private, needs the ongoing support of legal counsel. As laws evolve and social pressure to protect privacy increases, companies will likely be faced with a constantly changing legal landscape.

4

ORGANIZING TO
PROTECT PRIVACY

The first step in developing a privacy plan is to create an organization structure in which to conduct work: a *privacy task force*. The privacy task force is composed of representatives from all departments in an enterprise. Leadership of the task force must be determined and an agenda for action needs to be set. The privacy task force will require several months to compile the data needed to determine what information must be protected and to formulate policies and procedures to assure privacy is maintained. The process of building an enterprisewide privacy management program is broken down into four major phases:

- Phase One: Organizing and research
- Phase Two: Conducting a privacy-needs audit
- Phase Three: Developing policies and plans
- Phase Four: Implementing the plan

Each phase has been broken down into steps. This chapter provides a step-by-step guide to Phase One, which involves organizing and conducting basic research to develop and implement a privacy management program. This chapter divides the organizing and research phase into 10 major steps as shown in Figure 4–1.

The 10 steps of Phase One involve organizing the privacy task force and conducting basic research to move forward on developing the privacy policies. In addition to listing the steps in Phase One of the privacy plan, this chapter also comments on the obstacles that a business can encounter at each step in the process. These candid comments are based on experience working on organizational change by implementing the task force

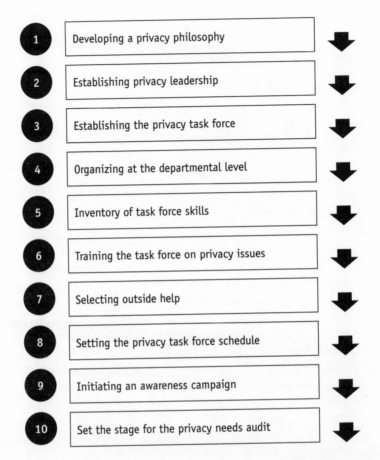

Figure 4-1. Organizing and Research: Phase 1 of Privacy Planning

approach to accomplish major enterprise initiatives. Understanding how the process can be stalled is as important for the privacy task force members as understanding the task force processes themselves. Since the long process of implementing an enterprise privacy plan must be moved along steadily, the task force should know and anticipate the possible stumbling blocks before they deter the process.

STEP 1: DEVELoPING A PRIVACY PHILoSoPHY

The concept and process of privacy can be viewed from a number of perspectives ranging from political to economic. The philosophical focus of this privacy management perspective is geared toward the improvement of the business bottom line for private companies and toward costs control and resource optimization for nonprofit and government organizations. This book contends that all types of organizations need to develop privacy policies that maximize the benefit of reusing information in as many ways as possible, while minimizing the risks associated with potential privacy violations.

The economics of resource optimization are relatively easy to get a handle on, but the definition of risks varies widely depending on the type of organization. Privacy factors that vary across organizations include the existence and detail of privacy policies and the degree of central control over the use of corporate information. Opposing perspectives on privacy ranging from low risk to high risk are illustrated in Figure 4–2. In a low-risk environment, a privacy policy is in place, information dissemination is tightly controlled, policies are set by data type, and all disclosures of information to outside organizations require approval. In a high-risk environment, only nominal policies are in place, information is loosely controlled, usually only global nonspecific policies on privacy of information exist, and business units and departments are allowed to make their own decisions on the use of information.

The major challenge in developing a privacy philosophy is working

Figure 4–2. Risks Perspectives on Information Privacy

through the process of consensus building among departments and managers in your enterprise. Some departments will be far more willing to take the higher risk perspective, while others may advocate moving toward a low-risk perspective. Typically, marketing and sales departments are more willing to take higher risks in dealing with privacy. This is the nature of sales and marketing departments, which are measured by their abilities to target customers, generate revenue, and expand market share. In addition, the management teams in sales and marketing typically have compensation plans that are tied to performance, which means that they will feel threatened by any action that limits their abilities to target customers and achieve performance goals.

On the other end of the continuum are the public relations departments and at times corporate counsel who are responsible for cleaning up any disasters that befall the organization. These parties will clearly push for a low-risk perspective for the organization. In addition, stockholders may tend toward a low-risk privacy philosophy because they know privacy scandals can negatively affect stock prices as well as earnings. However, contradictory positions may occur among stockholders because they want to improve revenue and sales and are willing to take higher risks to accomplish these goals. Yet those same stockholders will be embittered when higher risks result in negative consequences such as privacy-related problems.

To move to the next step in the privacy plan process, the organization must have a consensus and initiate a philosophy that attempts to take all of the diverse attitudes from various departments into consideration. At this point then, a leader should be appointed who can take the corporate philosophy and mold it into a practical privacy action plan.

STEP 2: ESTABLISHING PRIVACY LEADERSHIP

The highest levels of management—chief executive officers (CEOs), chief operating officers, chief financial officers, and chief information officers—need to support privacy planning and privacy managing efforts across the enterprise. The support of the highest level of management helps to illustrate the importance and the seriousness of all privacy efforts. The general agreement of high-level managers should be developed in the privacy philosophy development stage. Yet, although their consensus is key, chief officers will not likely be effective in the day-to-day management of privacy or in leading the development of a privacy plan.

A midlevel manager should be assigned the coordinating role in developing a privacy plan. The person assigned this task will need to put considerable time into the process and often be required to give it their full attention. The manager of the privacy task force needs to be detailed oriented without getting lost in the forest. This leader also needs to be able to manage a diplomatic relationship with all of the departments in the enterprise as well as work well with external resources.

The major challenge in establishing effective leadership for the privacy task force is finding people in the organization who have both the internal political clout and the motivation to be involved in the long and time-consuming task of developing privacy policies and plans. Although the ideal leader is driven to accomplish the company's privacy goals, some of the people who will be most willing to step up to the responsibility may be motivated by personal philosophies that lean toward greater privacy protection; such people will cause a significant problem for an organization. A privacy task force leader who is perceived as having already decided about privacy may very well alienate managers who are seeking a more balanced perspective. The leader should be a representative of all corporate privacy concerns and who can balance the various department perspectives. The leader's goal must be to decrease risk but not completely close off the use of information resources in the name of privacy.

Once the person who can handle this leadership position has been identified, it is important to create a cross-department task force that can help build and implement the directives of the task force leader.

STEP 3: ESTABLISHING THE PRIVACY TASK FORCE

The privacy task force is the next essential element in organizing a company's privacy planning efforts. Every department in the enterprise needs to be represented. Each department should have two representatives, a primary and an alternate. Appointing two representatives from each department ensures a better chance of maintaining continuity of involvement as well as decreasing the difficulty in scheduling meetings. In addition, department representatives need to be from the top managers in the department, and they need to have a complete understanding of operations and the authority to make decisions and implement plans.

The big challenge in pulling together a privacy task force is getting the time and attention of managers throughout the organization. Everyone is busy and all managers already have a long list of goals they would like to achieve—many of which may affect their own personal incomes. CEO clout must be behind the task force. The best possible role of the CEO is to make sure that the privacy task force gets the resources, participation, and cooperation necessary for the privacy policy development efforts to succeed. The CEO should probably not lead the privacy task force because CEOs usually have a busy schedule. The initial response may be favorable if other managers see that the CEO is leading the task force. However, probable sporadic attendance of the CEO at meetings and the CEO being too busy to keep up with the step-by-step processes of the task force could result in other managers diminishing the importance of the process.

The CEO must be in a symbolic and supportive role that conveys the importance of the privacy task force to managers across the organization. If managers know that an overseeing CEO will recognize their efforts within the task force, they will be much more likely to push for progress at both the corporate and departmental levels. To encourage adherence to the privacy plan within departments, the privacy task force members will be expected to coordinate activities with the appointed privacy team within their own departments.

STEP4: oRGANIZING AT THE DEPARTMENT LEVEL

Each department should have its own departmental privacy team. The departmental team should work with their privacy task force representatives to conduct specific departmental research to help establish the corporate privacy plan, to help evaluate the plan as it is drafted by the task force, and to implement the plan at the departmental level once it is developed. The size and membership of the departmental team will vary depending on the diversity of data used by the department. Departmental level privacy teams should be made up of a mix of supervisory personnel and technical experts in the areas in which the department has enterprise responsibilities.

The major obstacle in pulling together well-rounded departmental privacy teams is similar to what one encounters in establishing the enterprise privacy task force—time and interest. Supervisors and technical experts are busy and are focused on departmental performance goals that may very well affect their own personal compensation. In addition, they may feel threatened by the entire privacy protection movement. The departmental managers must assure that they have assembled a well-rounded team, and they must motivate the team to participate fully in the privacy-needs audit as well as the policy and procedure development phases. One way to overcome such resistance and objections is to establish a bonus program for departmental team members. Bonuses for involvement in such special projects can range from $1,000 up to five percent of the team member's annual base salary.

STEP 5: CREATING AN INVENTORY OF TASK FORCE SKILLS

The next step is to determine the skill set of the task force members. An inventory of their background and training is helpful, as is determining who has specific experience in managing privacy-related policies, procedures, and issues. This information should be made available to everyone on the task force. The task force should also determine if they feel any skill sets are missing from the group, and, if so, how to fill the gap. Filling the gap may require contracting with an outside consultant or seeking outside legal advice.

In addition, all task force members need to conduct an initial assessment of their own departments to determine if any staff member already has experience dealing with privacy issues. Those employees working on the departmental privacy teams who have had related experience need to be cataloged as a potential resource to help other departments assess their privacy needs and implement the enterprise privacy plan.

The major obstacle to inventorying the skills of the task force is time. The privacy task force needs a staff person who can conduct the inventory and follow up with personnel who have not completed their skill assessments by deadlines. Then, once the skills have been assessed, they need to be catalogued, which is also a time requirement. Some resistance may be encountered in the skills inventory process. Some individuals on the departmental teams are not on the team by choice and, as a result, may be less cooperative. The key person to help overcome such resistance is clearly the department's task force representative.

Once the skill sets of the enterprise task force team and the individual department teams are understood, the task force can begin training members to make up for whatever skill deficiencies were identified in the skill assessment process.

STEP 6: TRAINING THE TASK FORCE ON PRIVACY ISSUES

The task force must understand what they are attempting to do as well as the issues and basic concepts of privacy. All task force members should be familiar with this book as well as other sources of information or analysis that may be used to develop and implement a privacy plan. If necessary, bring in outside speakers to get the task force members up to speed as fast as possible.

Each task force member should have responsibility for researching privacy issues that affect their disciplines or departments. This responsibility includes reviewing professional papers and case studies of what other organizations may have done or are considering regarding privacy protection and also researching government regulations that an individual department needs to adhere to in its business processes. The departmental privacy teams should do this research. Each departmental representative should report back to the task force on results of this research.

The major obstacle to training the task force members is getting them all together in one place at one time and getting them to focus on the topic. The most formal training sessions should be conducted at a location away from organization facilities. Hotel and meeting-center facilities are readily available and are not expensive. Of course, while training, as well as attending any meetings, the basic contemporary rules of attendance etiquette should be observed, including turning off cell phones and beepers and having business casual dress code.

All members of the task force will benefit from these training sessions, which will make the organization more effective in reaching its privacy goals. However, simply training the staff will not likely address all of the skills required for the privacy plan. For the skills that are not covered internally, companies should recruit outside assistance.

STEP 7: SELECTING oUTSIDE HELP

Most organizations need outside help at some stage of their privacy policy and plan development process. The type of outside support that is needed should be evident once the skill set of the privacy task force has been inventoried and members have undergone some initial training. Most organizations do not have in-house legal staff, so they need to employ outside legal counsel. In other cases the need for trained policy and procedure manual writers is evident. Companies need to identify the skills that they will need to contract for and recruit appropriate individuals early in the privacy planning process. Acquiring these skills early will help a business maintain its momentum as the planning process proceeds.

The major obstacles to finding outside assistance for developing privacy policies and plans are determining just what expertise is needed and then locating individuals with the appropriate experience. As privacy concerns grow and new legislation continues to be passed at the national and state levels, more privacy consultants will appear on the market. Companies should be cautioned, however, upon relying too heavily on outside experts to develop privacy policies and plans. This book provides an easy-to-understand process and encourages an organization to work through the process with internal personnel as much as possible. This approach will improve everyone's understanding of privacy issues as well as have a positive influence on the enterprise cultural perspective toward privacy. It will directly encourage the privacy task force to make progress and accomplish the goals they see on their privacy plan schedule.

STEP 8: SETTING THE PRIVACY TASK FORCE SCHEDULE

Companies are encouraged to establish a privacy task force agenda and set a schedule for accomplishing goals immediately after the task force is formed. All task force members can use this book as a guide in developing and meeting such a schedule. The first step in the scheduling process is to set a regular meeting schedule. Weekly meetings are recommended for the first several weeks. Within these initial meetings, the task force should establish a communications process, and, if a company so chooses, form subcommittees, identify responsibilities, and assign interdepartmental tasks. The departmental privacy teams should meet as often as necessary to keep their tasks on schedule and to support the enterprisewide privacy task force.

The major problem in setting a schedule for the task force work is not knowing how complex the privacy policy development and planning process will become. Companies should plan for one year from the time the task force is established until they have implemented their plan. This time will of course vary, depending on many factors, including the size and geographic distribution of the organization, the amount and types of data the enterprise has or uses, and how many people can dedicate time to the process. In addition, enterprises with highly centralized and organized information management departments may find that they can move through the privacy planning process at a faster pace. This chapter has examined several other factors that influence the time required to develop privacy policies and plans. Figure 4–3 shows factors that can decrease and those that can increase the time required to accomplish the privacy-planning mission.

Factors That Decrease Time Requirements		Factors That Increase Time Requirements
Well-organized information management (IS/IT) departments		Resistance from departments in working on the planning or research process
Thoroughly developed data dictionaries for databases		Multiple business units in several countries working in different languages
Well-trained and organized task force that agree on agendas and philosophies		Highly independent subsidiaries that resist corporate control
High levels of cooperation from all departments		Turn over on the privacy task force

Figure 4–3. Factors That Influence Time Required for Privacy Plan Development

STEP 9: INITIATING AN AWARENESS CAMPAIGN

To successfully implement a privacy plan, creating an enterprise task force and departmental teams is not enough—every organization will need the support of all the employees in an organization. Therefore, the organization should start building awareness of its privacy efforts early in the process. In-house media campaigns are helpful in achieving this goal, as is enterprisewide training. Media campaigns can include articles in employee newsletters, postings on enterprise Intranets, and posters on bulletin boards. Public relations people are really good at this type of work. In addition, an organization should start planning for training of new hires and existing staff on the privacy policy and on privacy topics in general. Because getting such campaigns rolling can take a long time, awareness building should start during the early stages of the policy development and planning process.

The major obstacles to implementing an effective privacy awareness campaign are adequate funding and experienced communications staff to work on the campaign. The funding required to accomplish an awareness campaign will of course depend on the size of an organization and the geographical characteristics of the organization. The goal of the awareness campaign is to reach all of the employees in an enterprise. Already existing communications processes such as newsletters, annual or quarterly meetings, and Intranets will make the awareness campaign less expensive to launch because the communications infrastructure is already in place. If these communications mechanisms do not exist, special efforts will be needed to facilitate the communications process.

In addition, many smaller enterprises do not have in-house communications staff and will need to contract with outside organizations to manage the awareness campaign. Regardless of whether an organization uses in-house or external staff, the communications staff working on the campaign should have experience in awareness-building efforts. If an organization is using in-house staff inexperienced with awareness campaigns, it should send the communications staff to training on awareness building. If the organization is using outside agencies, it should select an agency with demonstrated experience in awareness building.

STEP 10: SETTING THE STAGE FOR THE PRIVACY-NEEDS AUDIT

A key step in the privacy planning process is the privacy-needs audit. This entire process is covered in the next chapter. Preparing for the audit and reducing the costs of the audit can be achieved by notifying employees as to the type of information that must be collected during the audit process. Using the awareness campaign to promote the audit process has a double benefit. As employees are made more aware of privacy needs and issues, they can also be drafted as willing participants into the audit process.

Fundamentally the audit process helps identify data or information that needs to be protected, and it highlights other areas of weakness in terms of privacy management. Input gained from across the enterprise can unveil areas of vulnerability that may not be discovered during the audit process, and such input could help guide parts of the audit process itself. In general, the awareness campaign is a good starting point for launching the privacy-needs audit.

Launching the privacy-needs audit should be relatively straightforward if steps one through nine of the organizing and research phase have gone well. If a well-functioning privacy task force has not been established and if departmental privacy teams are not in place, then an organization has not set the stage for launching the privacy-needs audit. The biggest obstacle to setting the stage is fostering cooperation among all departments. Before an organization actually launches the audit, it should closely examine the progress it has made in preparing for the audit. The task force should be very realistic about how different departments have cooperated or not cooperated. If any doubts exist, the task force should take two or three weeks to evaluate the level of readiness before starting the audit process.

ASSESSING PROGRESS AND PREPARING TO MOVE AHEAD

As an organization establishes a privacy task force and works through phase one of developing the enterprise privacy plan, upper-level managers, department managers, and privacy task force members will all be confronted with massive amounts of new material and a long list of challenges. Taking a moment to absorb new information and contemplate the challenges ahead may make these challenges easier to face. The challenge of developing an enterprisewide privacy plan can seem endless and overwhelming during the early stages of the process. Enterprise managers should evaluate progress as the process moves from one phase to the next. The following goals should be accomplished during Phase One:

- A leader should be identified who can embody the privacy philosophy of the organization and who is provided resources to accomplish the development of the privacy plan.
- The privacy task force should be in place and functioning.
- Departments should identify and staff their privacy teams.
- The skill base of the task force and department teams should be assessed.
- Training to round out the skills of the staff working on the privacy plan should be conducted.
- If outside help is necessary, a consultant should be identified and selected.
- A schedule for the work of the task force should be developed.
- An internal awareness campaign should be kicked off.
- The task force and department teams should be ready to conduct a privacy-needs audit.

If all of these things have been accomplished, the privacy task force and department teams should be ready to move into phase two, which is conducting a privacy-needs audit. Phase two can require considerable time and effort, and upper-level managers may not be hearing a lot from the task force during that phase. The privacy-needs audit is far less ceremonial than phase one and requires thoroughness and a great attention to detail.

5

CoNDUCTING A
PRIVACY-NEEDS AUDIT

Conducting a privacy-needs audit is phase two in the privacy policy development and planning process. Once there is a privacy task force and other necessary groups in place to tackle the privacy plan, the organization must begin to understand the many types of data and information it collects and uses. The privacy-needs audit helps the organization identify those data, determine where or whom it comes from, establish how and where it is used, and identify if and where it is disseminated. In addition, the audit process will identify laws, government regulations, and internal requirements that could possibly govern the collection, use, and dissemination of the data. Conducting the needs audit is a time-consuming task that will require the cooperation of all departments or business units in an organization.

This chapter provides a step-by-step approach to conducting a privacy-needs audit. It has divided the privacy-needs audit phase into 10 major steps that follow the first 10 steps of the organizing and researching process discussed in Chapter 4. The steps are illustrated in Figure 5–1.

In addition to describing the 10 steps for conducting a privacy-needs audit, this chapter covers the type of obstacles that an organization can encounter at each step. As in other chapters, these candid comments about obstacles are based on several decades of experience in working on organizational change using the task force approach to accomplish major enterprise initiatives.

STEP 1: ESTABLISHING A DATA
INVENTORY SYSTEM

To begin the privacy-needs audit, the organization needs to create a data inventory record system to help track and organize the information col-

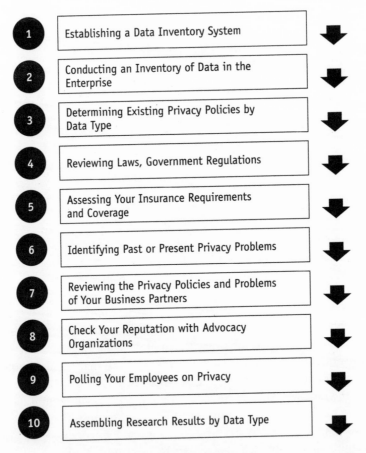

Figure 5-1. Conducting a Privacy-Needs Audit: Phase 2 of Privacy Planning

lected during the audit. A database is helpful in managing the information collected. The organization should collect as much information as possible on each piece of data in its enterprise and record it in its data inventory database. The minimal information collected about each piece of data will probably vary, depending on the organization. The following list provides a starting point for the information that an organization needs to collect:

- Description of the data
- Which department is responsible for the data

- Source of the data
- Which computer (or computers) the data reside on, if applicable
- Where paper copies of the data are filed, if applicable
- Where the data are used in-house
- How the data are used in-house
- Where the data are disseminated
- How the data are disseminated
- Any existing policies on using the data
- Laws covering the use of the data
- Previous incidents regarding privacy of the data
- The position of advocacy groups toward the use of the data
- Privacy task force notes on the data

The major obstacle when establishing a data inventory system is that the volume of work required can be very high in large enterprises. Therefore staff resources are needed to conduct the audit by department, to compile the information, and to keep the inventory updated over time. Another obstacle, which is closely tied to resource requirements, is resistance to thoroughness because of the cost and time involved. This data inventory step should be as thorough as possible. If the company does not take a comprehensive look at its data, it is not taking a comprehensive look at its vulnerability.

The objective of the privacy-needs audit and the entire privacy-planning process is to reduce the organization's vulnerability when it comes to privacy. No organization should have a false sense of security about how vulnerable it is to privacy problems. Many organizations read the latest story in the newspaper about privacy issues that pertain to certain types of data, then take a brief look at their own in-house treatment of that particular type of data, and prematurely conclude that they are not vulnerable. Building a complete and thorough data inventory system to begin the privacy-needs audit will help reduce tendencies to take short cuts as the company develops and implements the privacy plan.

STEP 2: CONDUCTING AN INVENTORY OF DATA IN THE ENTERPRISE

Once a comprehensive data inventory system is in place, the organization should begin to populate the database with detailed information on the data that it controls. Each department must determine what data or information it collects, creates, or uses. Working with the department teams, the task force should catalog all of the data, their source, and their current use. This time-consuming process must be thoroughly executed. The central information technology department can be very helpful in this process. Well-organized data management operations usually have data dictionaries that describe all of the data fields in enterprise databases. In most cases, these data dictionaries are an excellent starting place to learn about the large quantities of data your organization collects, processes, or uses. The central information technology department, sometimes called the MIS department, can be assigned to assist with the data inventory process.

Companies should not, however, assume that the central information technology department is aware of all the data used by departments or business units. All too often databases and information systems have sprouted up around an organization. These databases can be standalone systems that departments have created, or they can be derivatives of centralized databases that have been extracted for specific data mining or data analysis tasks.

A formal cataloging approach should be used in inventorying data and information. To move further into the planning assessment and planning process, the company needs a uniform and thorough description of all data and information. Setting up a database that is accessible by the entire privacy task force is a good way to facilitate the cataloging process. Expect the inventory process to take a considerable amount of time; it can take weeks and sometimes months to do a data inventory, depending on the size of the organization.

To find the data and information used in the enterprise, the privacy task force and the department teams need to look everywhere. For example, data may be found in the following locations:

- Customer data files
- Supplier data files
- Channel partner records
- Accounts payable files
- Accounts receivable files
- Web site registration records
- Employee records
- Research and development files
- Subscription records for corporate newsletters

The major obstacle when actually conducting a data inventory is getting the cooperation of all departments or business units. Cooperation comes on two levels. The first is how nice people are about the detailed task of a data audit and how timely they respond. The second is how well they really cooperate and how much effort they really put into the process. Companies need to be very realistic in this phase and understand that departments and business units feel as if they have ownership of data, and in many cases, their performance ratings or compensation, especially for managers or sales people, may depend on exploiting a variety of data sources.

All the obstacles basically come down to what is referred to as *cultural barriers to change*. This defensiveness or fortress-building response has always been encountered in organizations that are faced with new threats, shifts in marketplaces, or social pressure. For example, heavy resistance to environmental protection requirements lasted for decades and still exists in some parts of the country and in many places around the world. Resistance to equal opportunity such as gender and racial equality in the workplace is something that has yet to be completely overcome. Progress has been made on both the environmental and equal opportunity fronts, but it has taken over 30 years.

Simply stated, companies should be warned against an observed tendency on the part of departments and business units to not fully cooperate with enterprisewide initiatives. Do not establish an environment of distrust and paranoia when dealing with departments or business units. Just take an approach of thoroughness during the data inventory step. A company's best weapon in the quest for thoroughness may not be lengthy forms for each supervisor to complete, but a softer awareness-building approach in which key supervisors or technical experts are polled about how data are being used.

To help achieve thoroughness and overcome potential resistance to the data inventory process, count on taking a three-prong approach. First, as pointed out in phase one, the organization and research phase, start an awareness campaign about the importance of privacy efforts and provide employees with a mechanism for giving feedback about potential vulnerabilities. Second, start the formal inventory process as outlined in this chapter. Third, create and distribute a survey to key personnel as a separate data collection effort to get their inputs on privacy vulnerability. The company can then triangulate the three sources of information and cross-check them as it builds the data inventory.

STEP 3: DETERMINING EXISTING PRIVACY POLICIES BY DATA TYPE

Once the data and information have been located in the enterprise, the organization needs to determine if it has any preexisting privacy policies and procedures related to each type of data. The data inventory database should include fields to track existing privacy policies. As the task force identifies data and their location, it can also inquire about any existing privacy policies related to the different data sets. These policies need to be recorded and evaluated. In the absence of a written policy or procedure, the privacy task force needs to determine what de facto or unwritten policies, if any, govern use of the data in question. For an existing policy, the task force needs to determine if it is adequate or appropriate for current activities. One of the roles of the task force is to examine any and all existing policies and procedures regarding the privacy of data. All written copies of existing policies should be collected for analysis by the task force at a later date.

The major obstacle during this step is the volume of documentation that may have to be pulled together. Existing privacy or data management policies may be difficult to sift through and actually determine what if any privacy management aspects they actually covered. In addition, some policies may not be labeled as policies that have governed past or present behavior toward privacy of data. Going through this process helps prevent new privacy policies and procedures from contradicting existing ones. The new privacy policy should not be seen as an overlay to existing policies or procedures. This means that all of the existing policies related to data privacy need to be reviewed to make sure they do not conflict with new policies. Contradictions in various types of policies will be eliminated in the policy development and implementation phase.

STEP 4: REVIEWING LAWS, GOVERNMENT REGULATIONS

Following an examination of internal policies that may govern data use and collection, the next step in the audit process is to determine if any external laws or government regulations apply to each of the types of data that have been identified. This complex process will require assistance from legal counsel. Appropriate representatives from departments should be responsible for various data types and should be involved in the legal review process along with counsel. Bringing these parties together and reviewing the information can be a rather lengthy process and may require international assistance if the enterprise operates across international borders. The organization needs to conduct the legal requirements phase for each country in which it conducts business.

The major obstacles in accomplishing a thorough review of laws and regulations related to information privacy requirements are time and expertise. Medical organizations have already been confronted with a variety of privacy requirements, and financial services companies have long been dealing with privacy issues. Most organizations, however, are just beginning to deal with privacy issues and probably have very few staff familiar with privacy requirements. If in-house legal counsel is not available, contracting with an outside specialist in the field of privacy law is the best course of action.

Although outside legal counsel can be a very expensive aspect of privacy policy development, taking the do-it-yourself approach is not advised. For interpreting laws and regulations covering data privacy, and especially when the organization needs to comply with laws in several countries, the organization needs legal counsel that is expert in privacy law. Laws and regulations are seldom self-contained, but rather relate to other laws and regulations. Therefore a lack of familiarity with the structure of such laws can result in improper interpretations and incorrect actions. During this regulation review step, small organizations with limited budgets, especially start-up companies, are at risk. If such organizations do not have the budgets to deal properly with this legal review step, they are ill equipped to handle the entire privacy plan development process.

STEP 5: ASSESSING YOUR INSURANCE REQUIREMENTS AND COVERAGE

Along with laws and government regulations, an organization's insurance company's guidelines can determine how data are used and collected. The company should consult with its insurance company on any coverage that may relate to privacy planning, management, or protection. Most insurance companies provide coverage of corporate assets and many provide some sort of business disruption coverage. Both types of coverage could potentially relate to the violation of corporate privacy or the violation of the privacy of others by the enterprise's actions. A straightforward inquiry with the insurance carrier is best. Seeking the insurance carrier's input on the privacy planning approach could also be helpful.

The major obstacle in assessing an organization's insurance coverage is finding the expertise to do an adequate assessment. Larger organizations often have a risk management department to evaluate risks and insurance coverage. Smaller organizations tend not to have such expertise in-house, which means that they will need an outside consultant to help with this step. Basically, coverage from insurance companies regarding privacy violations is not expected. If it is a matter of data theft, they may provide some coverage. On the other hand, if inappropriate risk taking or an employee blunder causes a privacy violation, then the insurance company is not likely to provide coverage. During this step the enterprise must determine what if any coverage its insurance policies provide.

STEP 6: IDENTIFYING PAST OR PRESENT PRIVACY PROBLEMS

Once an organization has a good understanding of all the internal and external factors that control and govern data collection and use, it should analyze any privacy problems that the organization is facing or has faced in the past. Unfortunately, many organizations do not start dealing with privacy issues until they have a privacy-related incident. If privacy management problems have occurred, the task force must have a full understanding of those problems. Such problems can include customer complaints, litigation, and government inquires. In addition to understanding the problems, the task force must also be informed on how the organization responded to those issues.

The company is urged to take a comprehensive look at existing or past issues. This process may include a review of customer complaint forms or records in all business units and departments. If it has a Web site, the company should review any email or inquiries regarding privacy. All too often these inquiries get buried in an email box somewhere on a server and are never reviewed. If visitors to the Web site have made inquiries, these inquiries could provide insight into the perspective of the organization's Web customers or users.

The major obstacle in identifying past data privacy issues is what is referred to as *institutional memory*. In some cases people who have been involved in privacy incidents may have left the company. In other cases memory tends to be selective, and the task force may have difficulty assembling an objective perspective on past privacy incidents. As major incidents of the past are identified, the task force should contact the people who are no longer with the organization and attempt to get their perspectives on specific incidents. If employees involved in an incident are still with the company, the task force should talk to as many people as possible to make sure a well-rounded perspective of the incident develops. All of these efforts will help the task force develop a full understanding of what the organization faces and has faced in terms of privacy problems created within the enterprise.

STEP 7: REVIEWING THE PRIVACY POLICIES AND PROBLEMS OF YOUR BUSINESS PARTNERS

Along with internal privacy problems, the task force needs to understand the privacy issues in which the organization's external business partners are involved. The task force should examine privacy policies, problems, or issues that the business partners have experienced. An organization could be vulnerable because of poor privacy management practices of suppliers, channel partners, or other companies with which it has some business arrangement. These organizations should be informed that a privacy plan is being developed. This part of the privacy planning process can be very problematic; however, the enterprise must recognize that even the best privacy policies and procedures cannot protect it from encountering problems if a business partner obtains data that it misuses in a way that exposes that data to unauthorized parties.

The major obstacle is getting business partners to cooperate. If a company has long-standing relationships with the business partners, it will probably not be too difficult to foster cooperation. The most difficult scenario occurs when large numbers of channel partners are affiliates. This scenario especially applies to newer Web-based companies that use affiliate programs or to the large technology companies that have relationships with resellers, VARs (value added resellers), OEMs (original equipment manufacturers), or consultants. In these cases, collecting information on each affiliate may be impossible. The best course of action in these situations is to focus on the largest partners first. In addition, once the privacy policies are formulated, the organization can require all partners to adhere to its policies as a condition of having the business relationship.

Along with assessing the privacy policies and problems of business partners, the company should establish a process that follows news stories in which the partners are mentioned. Even if self-reporting of privacy problems is required, a business partner that gets bogged down in a privacy scandal may not place a high priority on calling to discuss the problem. Thus, a monitoring process is advisable. Any privacy-related information found through such monitoring, as well as all self-reported information from business partners, should be catalogued and analyzed by the task force.

STEP 8: CHECKING YOUR REPUTATION WITH ADVOCACY ORGANIZATIONS

In addition to understanding the organization's internal and external history of privacy problems, the task force should know how the organization is known among privacy advocacy entities. Some organizations have become targets of various advocacy organizations, so the task force should make sure that problems are not looming from these advocacy groups. Corporate counsel, public relations departments, and outside agencies that handle public relations are a good source of information about which, if any, advocacy groups may be watching the organization's activities. Companies should contact advocacy organizations in a very straightforward manner and inquire if its members or constituents have raised any issues about it. To help improve the relationship between an organization and these groups, inform them of the development of a new privacy plan.

Several people have criticized this recommendation by saying that it is just looking for trouble. In a way this is true. The purpose of all of the research is to help develop a privacy plan that identifies existing or potential trouble spots. The task force needs to dig and find things out. Not identifying the potential and existing problems results in a privacy plan with several holes. Leaving these vulnerabilities unprotected will mean that all of the organization's efforts will not be maximized simply because it was not thorough in the research stages.

The major obstacle to accomplishing this step is that it can consume a considerable amount of time. Many organizations have sprouted up to track privacy performance of all types of organizations and, contacting them all will be a significant task. In addition, as previously mentioned, many enterprises may be reluctant to even pursue this step. These organizations, or departments, will tend not to give the process adequate time or resources and, thus will defeat the purpose of identifying trouble spots.

STEP 9: POLLING YOUR EMPLOYEES ON PRIVACY

As part of the first phase of privacy planning, the organization should widely publicize its privacy policy development efforts throughout the organization to help raise awareness and build an understanding of the importance of privacy. As previously noted, the awareness campaign is a good way to enlist the help of all employees in identifying data being used and potential privacy problems with those data. In the privacy-needs audit phase, the task force should build on the momentum of the awareness-building process and formally survey key employees regarding the whereabouts of data and any privacy problems that they may be aware of or believe may be possible in the future. Conducting formal surveys and tracking responses from key supervisors, especially those in remote or branch offices that for some reason may not be full participants in the privacy-needs audit process, will help to manage this process.

The major obstacle to accomplishing this step is getting employees to respond to a survey. Detailed tracking of questionnaires will determine who has answered the survey and who has not, and thus facilitate the follow-up process. Do not work toward 100% participation in the survey or even 100% responses. The important thing to accomplish is to have fairly good representation by department or by type of expertise that is being polled. As previously mentioned, the purpose of this step is to obtain information that can help verify other aspects of the privacy-needs audit.

STEP 10: ASSEMBLING RESEARCH RESULTS BY DATA TYPE

The purpose of the entire privacy-needs audit and building the enterprisewide data inventory is to enable the privacy task force to determine the necessary scope of the privacy policy and to set procedures for assuring privacy. In order to make sense of the vast amounts of information compiled during the audit process, an organization should create a report listing the type of data being used. This report will ease the process of examining data and ranking each type of data according to their level of sensitivity and the importance of maintaining their privacy. Sorting audit results in this way also facilitates the process of dividing work among the task force members so that they can work in teams to evaluate related types of data and to start drafting privacy policies and procedures.

Once the information about the data is properly sorted and evaluated by the task force members, the task force will need to prioritize its efforts and determine the work that needs to be done by designated departments. This prioritization will allow an organization to move the privacy plan into draft stages of the privacy policy. As the inventory of data is completed, start immediately on developing policy for the data that is the most vulnerable and could cause the most damage if revealed to the wrong parties. This of course will all be based on the assessment of the privacy task force. Those data items that are ranked as a 10 on a scale of 1 to 10, for example, need to be attended to quickly. These rankings will help set the stage for moving into the next phase of privacy management, which is the development of privacy policies.

The major obstacle to this step is the time required to sort and assemble large quantities of data into a usable form. Larger enterprises will have more data elements to review. The privacy task force should plan on several weeks to accomplish this step. The best way to accelerate this step is to assign knowledgeable staff to the task. Depending on the availability of their time, task force members from various departments and their alternates could be responsible for the bulk of the process. If an enterprise is large enough to warrant a full time privacy office, then staff in that office should be responsible for this step.

ASSESSING PROGRESS AND PREPARING TO MOVE AHEAD

As the privacy-needs audit, phase two of developing a privacy plan, comes to a close, the privacy task force and department teams will have gone through another major absorption of information. Even when the results of the privacy-needs audit are compiled and boiled down into a workable inventory, large volumes of information will still need to be examined and understood. The staff conducting the privacy-needs audit may well be exhausted and maybe even bored. To help keep the morale of the staff high, this would be a good time for a break.

The measure of success in phase two is an inventory of data and an understanding of the laws and regulations that affect the privacy of those data. The inventory must be in a form that can referenced in the future to assure that privacy is maintained after privacy policies are solidified and procedures developed. Before moving into phase three, the actual development of a privacy plan, a subcommittee of the privacy task force should work with the information technology department and outside consultants if necessary to conduct an evaluation of the types of technology that could help the organization manage privacy needs. The subcommittee should conduct the security evaluation and report findings back to the privacy task force.

6

EVALUATING
TECHNOLOGY NEEDS FOR
PRIVACY PROTECTION

The privacy task force needs to evaluate the enterprise capabilities required to implement and manage technologies that are necessary to assure the privacy of corporate information. This evaluation requires a detailed analysis of technologies, security staffing, security funding, and security plans. Because this aspect of managing information privacy is highly technical, a subcommittee of the privacy task force should work with the information technology department and outside consultants, if needed, to conduct the evaluation. The subcommittee should conduct the security evaluation and report findings back to the privacy task force. Meanwhile the entire privacy task force and department privacy teams need to become familiar with the basic security and privacy functions that technology can achieve. The following should be performed by the technology subcommittee of the privacy task force:

- Advise the task force on technology
- Prepare briefings on specific technology issues
- Educate the task force on the potential and limitations of technology
- Benchmark information technology security capabilities
- Review technology issues arising from the privacy-needs audit
- Review existing information security plans and procedures
- Test information technology security
- Assist in testing for weaknesses in privacy management procedures

GETTING A GRIP ON FIVE IMPORTANT TECHNOLOGY FUNCTIONS

Several types of technology can help maintain the privacy of corporate information. Although the privacy task force will not necessarily be responsible for selecting privacy technology, it will likely set policies and procedures that help establish the requirements determining the selections of various privacy protection technologies. Task force members should be aware of what technology can and cannot do to maintain corporate privacy. The key role of technology is to control access and allow only authorized individuals to view, manipulate, or use information.

Chapters 9 through 16 provide detailed checklists that should be used to audit the vulnerability of enterprise information on various types of computers and in data communications applications. Those checklists should be used during the implementation phase of privacy protection.

This chapter provides an overview of different types of technology and how they may be helpful in privacy protection efforts. As technology evolves, the ability of privacy managers to use technology to enforce privacy rules is improving. Technology that can be used to help maintain privacy of corporate information can be classified into five basic categories:

- Technology to protect computer-based information
- Technology to protect data communications
- Technology to protect voice communications
- Technology to protect physical copies of information
- Technology to meet safe harbor requirements

TECHNOLOGY TO PROTECT COMPUTER-BASED INFORMATION

Computer systems are highly vulnerable to hacking attacks, break-ins, and virus attacks designed to either cripple the systems or steal information. Computer criminals have stolen large quantities of credit card numbers, customer names and addresses, and confidential financial information. Once the security of a computer system is breached, the privacy of data can be readily compromised.

Each type of computer system has its own strengths and weaknesses, but all are vulnerable to break-ins or data theft, and this makes them potential points of failure in corporate efforts to protect privacy. Because an enterprise cannot be expected to operate without computers and because computers are so vulnerable, the privacy plan needs to address not only the security of data, but also the rules and procedures governing the use of computer-based data. A privacy plan needs to address the protection of information in several types of computer technology, including the following examples:

- Large enterprise systems most often found in centralized data centers
- Desktop computer systems found throughout an enterprise
- Laptop systems used by employees to access data from remote locations
- Web-based systems, including supply chain and extranet applications and Web sites

The privacy of computer-based information can be protected through two primary methods. The first method, which is a fundamental requirement to assure that information privacy is maintained, is to control access to computer-based information. Access is controlled through a variety of means, including rights assigned to individuals and groups of computer users in an organization, password protection of information assets, and a user-authentication system used to verify that users are who they claim to be when they are using computer systems.

The second method to assuring privacy of computer-based information is to control what individuals and groups of users can do with the information to which they have access. Usage is controlled through several means, including restricting who can modify, delete, add, move, or manipulate computer-based information.

Access control and user rights are most often managed through readily available and commonly used network management software programs produced by Novell, Microsoft, IBM, Computer Associates, and other similar companies. In general, these companies make reliable products, and a fairly good supply of labor is available to work with network management and access control products. The biggest challenge to effective access management is assuring that the software products are properly installed, configured, and managed. Proper training on the software products must be provided to information technology (IT) staff or other people in the organization who may have some degree of administrative or supervisory responsibility for the network management and access control.

Professional staff installing and managing the software products should be trained and certified as to their skill levels. The technology subcommittee of the privacy task force should review the skills and certifications of all staff responsible for network management and access control software products and make recommendations for additional training if necessary.

Another area of weakness in the use of network management and access control software products is that too many users in the organization are allowed access to possibly sensitive data and information. During the 1980s, when online transaction processing was becoming widespread, access control was maintained primarily by host-based computing systems like mainframes and minicomputers. The central IT department was responsible for developing, implementing, and maintaining these systems. Access to these massive online transaction-processing systems was usually accomplished through the use of computer terminals. The technology of the 1980s was more capable of controlling access because most end users could not easily copy, manipulate, or otherwise improperly handle data and information.

In the 1990s, the growth in the use of desktop computers (personal computers) in client-server computing environments became more popular and is now almost universal. One of the major selling points vendors relied on when marketing the new client-server and desktop solutions was that it provided greater access and usability of corporate data. The new marketing philosophy was that the more employees could do with data and information, the more productive they could be and the more successful the organization would be in meeting goals and expanding market share. These assertions may be true to some degree, but with greater information access and usability come greater security threats. In addition, new IT staff with different skill sets and different mentalities came into the picture during this time. The typical Web developer was far less trained in structured development techniques, documentation requirements, and IT architecture building than the host-based computing staff of centralized IT departments. The PC revolution and the growth of desktop computing brought a clash of cultures between the host-based mentality and the whiz-bang PC jocks. Depending on which of these groups became dominant in an organization, companies now have varying degrees of privacy challenges with which to deal.

Predicting the state of information security in client-server environments is not easy. Generally speaking, if a strong centralized IT department controls desktop standards and has a properly funded and staffed security effort, many of the gapping holes in access and security that were created during the PC revolution have likely been plugged. On the other hand, if many less experienced IT staff are working in departments and business units installing desktop units and working frantically building out computer networks, the enterprise is likely at greater security risk and privacy protection efforts are going to be weak. The security subcommittee of the privacy task force needs to assess the overall conditions in the organization and make a judgment call as to how much time and effort needs to be expended in evaluating the weaknesses in the organization's overall computing environment. This situation may be impossible to quantify, but a general portrayal of the security conditions can be obtained by doing a high-level assessment of overall conditions, benchmarking centralized security staffing and funding, and using the feedback from the employee poll conducted during the privacy-needs audit. If these efforts set off alarms, the security subcommittee should conduct a more in-depth audit of security procedures and also review who has access to organization data.

TECHNOLOGY TO PROTECT DATA COMMUNICATIONS

The increased vulnerability of information stored on computer systems is only one of the weaknesses in technology that organizations now face. The vulnerability and potential compromise of information that is electronically transmitted from one corporate site to another, information transmitted from an organization to a client or customer, and information that is transmitted to and from suppliers or service organizations has also increased. The use of the Internet to move information between organizations and their constituents is very dangerous and increases the potential of compromising privacy. The use of virtual private networks (VPNs) to move data is a safer approach, but it still not completely secure.

In addition to examining technology to protect computer-based information, the technology subcommittee also needs to determine potential vulnerabilities by evaluating the data networks and transmission methods that the organization is using. Just as user access and information rights changed significantly in the past two decades, data transmission has undergone considerable transition during the last 20 years. During the 1980s, most data transmissions were accomplished by using private networks, leased lines, or dedicated point-to-point circuits. These methods provided a relatively high degree of security because they were definable, identifiable, and easier to protect than the Internet. As the growth of the Internet increased in the 1990s, more organizations, as well as individuals, started to move data and information between organizations and other people using the Internet. This was done largely without organizations or individuals understanding the process of data transmission or how the Internet differed from private networks. The transmission of sensitive and private information over the Internet in raw text form, in attached word documents, or spreadsheets has become commonplace because few people realize how dangerous it can be.

Unfortunately, most organizations do not have strong policies about how to use the Internet, and most employees are not trained on the vulnerabilities of using the Internet for data transmission. The technology subcommittee of the privacy task force faces two major challenges in evaluating the vulnerability of data transmission. The first challenge is determining who is transmitting what types of data, documents, or information. The second challenge is to determine how to change habits and implement new rules or procedures. The poll conducted during the privacy-needs audit will probably yield some useful information. Interviewing a random sample of employees from different parts of the organization can also provide some insight into data transmission habits. The departmental privacy teams can also be a good source of information about data transmission habits within their respective departments.

Once a profile of the data transmission habits of the organization is created, the technology subcommittee should advise the privacy task force on steps to take to improve the security and maintain the privacy of transmitted data and information. The most common response to identified weaknesses is to implement an organizationwide-training program. This is a good first step. However, depending on the sensitivity of data and how widespread sloppy habits may be, the company may need to install filters and monitors on its email system to scan for key terms or to examine in some way all email being sent from the organization. Although using filters and monitors may be the best thing to do in order to protect privacy, implementation needs to be handled correctly and carefully to avoid problems within the organization in order to avoid or ease internal political ramifications.

Overall, employee education is a very good approach to help change bad habits. Most employees do not clearly understand how computers work or even how to use much of the functionality on their desktops. This lack of skill runs across the organization as well as up and down the ranks. Most employees probably do not understand that their email can be read, stolen, retransmitted, or sent to the wrong addressee. The technology subcommittee needs to address the skill levels of employees and formulate an education approach.

In addressing data transmission issues, the technology subcommittee should also recommend viable methods to protect the data being transmitted. Encryption is the most popular approach and is relatively easy to implement and manage. Most organizations, however, have not recognized the value of encryption and have not been willing to spend the money to protect data being transmitted. Most organizations, large and small, that handle sensitive data will likely move to an encrypted data transmission model. The technology subcommittee needs to evaluate the need for encryption and set an agenda for implementing encryption technology.

TECHNOLOGY TO PROTECT VOICE COMMUNICATIONS

While more people are becoming aware of the security issues surrounding data communications and computer-based information, the security of voice communications is most often taken for granted. People have become so accustomed to using the telephone that they do not think about the need for security or how privacy can be compromised using the telephone. Numerous dangers lurk in the realm of voice communications. Illegal wiretapping, monitoring the use of wireless 900 MHz phone systems, or using scanners to listen in on cell phone calls is very easy to accomplish. A trip to the local electronics store or a visit to a few Web sites can equip even amateurs with all the technology they need to easily drop in on voice communications.

The technology subcommittee will not have an easy task addressing the use of voice communications. Incoming calls from customers, clients, and suppliers are virtually impossible to control because the organization cannot readily set requirements for incoming calls. In addition, the organization can attempt to control cell phone communication privacy by simply introducing basic education programs for employees on the use of cell phones, but changing the cell phone habits of field staff may take far more than education. Securing voice communications between organization locations can be more easily accomplished because the organization controls both ends of the call and voice encryption technology is fairly easy to implement. On top of all of the technical difficulties involved in voice communications security, the biggest challenge is convincing management that voice communications is even worthy of protection. In addition, many companies are now starting to deliver Web content and services to users of wireless Internet devices and are thereby creating an entirely new set of technology challenges. The technology subcommittee must be prepared to educate managers and employees so that the organization views voice communications as equal to data communications and to computer-based information in terms of potential security problems.

TECHNOLOGY TO PROTECT PHYSICAL COPIES OF INFORMATION

The security of physical property has traditionally been left to alarm systems and perhaps a few after-hours security guards. Although the technology subcommittee does not need to worry too much about physical protection, it does need to address physical security as it relates to privacy. A smaller evaluation team composed of one member of the technology sub-committee and representatives from the security and facilities management departments are more appropriate to address the protection of physical copies. The physical-properties team should focus primarily on reviewing these areas:

- Building and facility security procedures and technology
- Securing long-term storage of physical copies
- Disposing of physical copies
- Disposing of used and obsolete computer equipment
- Disposing of used magnetic media such as disks and tapes

Just as many organizations are unaware of the potential problems cre-ated by telephone communications, many organizations are complacent about the security of physical property and protecting the privacy of infor-mation contained in printed records and files. This complacency is very dangerous for many reasons. First, without rigorous security protection, someone could easily gain access to physical premises and just as easily walk away with printed reports and files from almost any office complex. Second, because of high volumes of paper within the organization, the fact that documents are missing may not be realized immediately; therefore, the discovery of a security breach may take weeks or even months. Third, old records and files, as well as those that are not accessed frequently, are often put in some form of ancillary or offsite storage that may not be well protected or that may have no security at all. This potential combination of circumstances may make customer records and other material for which privacy must be maintained very vulnerable to compromise. Thus, the physical-properties team should evaluate the storage and potential physi-cal access of all records, files, and printed material.

As with the management of physical-document storage, the disposal of physical records at most organizations is currently very haphazard and is a major point of privacy vulnerability. The physical-properties team needs to pay special attention to the disposal process of the documents to assure that it does not become a huge privacy leak. Most organizations fill trash containers full of old records and then assume that those records will be safely hauled off to the trash dump where no one would have an interest in the contents. This is a grievous error. Corporate spies and competitive intelligence analysts know very well that one of the best ways to find out anything about anyone or any company is to go through their trash. The physical-properties team needs to evaluate record disposal at all organization sites and establish procedures for the proper disposal of paper records.

The disposal of used and obsolete computer equipment is also another major weakness in efforts to protect privacy. Old computer equipment is often not operable when it is disposed of and it is often cleared out of corporate premises in bulk. What often remain intact on old computer equipment are the hard disk drives. Problems arising from the bulk disposition of obsolete equipment are compounded because usually a company does not have an adequate budget for cleaning disk drives. The physical-properties team needs to establish enterprisewide procedures for proper disposal of computers to assure that they do not have any records, files, memos, or email left on them when they leave the corporate property.

In addition to data and records being left on computer disk drives, data may be accessible from the millions of floppy disks and computer tapes disposed of each year. The disposal of magnetic media is equally as hazardous as the disposal of old computer equipment. The only way to assure that data and information that are or were on magnetic media are not accessible is to physically destroy the disk or tape. Thus the physical-properties team also needs to evaluate existing procedures and processes for disposal of magnetic media and set enterprisewide standards for disposal.

TECHNOLOGY TO MEET
SAFE HARBOR REQUIREMENTS

While technology solutions can help protect computer-based information, data communications, voice communications, and physical copies of information, no single technology enables an organization to meet safe harbor requirements. An organization can lose safe harbor compliance status when privacy is compromised due to any one vulnerability in the protection of computer-based information, data communications, voice communications, and the disposal of records, old computers, or magnetic media. Thus one of the first steps in assuring the continuation of safe harbor compliance is for the technology subcommittee and the physical-properties team to conduct enterprisewide audits and set standards for information protection.

Safe harbor requirements also require that individuals about whom data are collected have the right to have errors corrected. The technology subcommittee needs to start addressing how to meet this requirement. Currently, several approaches can be used to give individuals access to the data that an organization has compiled about them:

- Providing access and correction procedures through a Web site
- Furnishing scheduled updates of information by printed means, with records mailed to individuals for review and correction
- Providing telephone support to allow individuals to correct or update data
- Offering a combination of these approaches

Until privacy policies are firmly established and a decision is made to establish safe harbor compliance, the technology subcommittee can only evaluate the previously mentioned alternatives and determine what is required to implement and maintain them. This assessment is best done before an enterprise decides to declare safe harbor status. The technology subcommittee should conduct a cost analysis of each alternative, or combination of alternatives, and report back to the privacy task force. The privacy task force should have the ultimate decision as to the pursuit of safe harbor status. In some cases, implementing the safe harbor requirements may not be cost effective. That decision, however, cannot really be made unless a full cost analysis is performed.

BENCHMARKING INFORMATION TECHNOLOGY SECURITY CAPABILITIES

Controlling access to corporate information is the first basic step in assuring that information privacy is maintained. Control of access to corporate computing systems is absolutely essential. Information technology departments in large organizations are usually well versed in the necessary technology and procedures required for controlling access to computer-based information. The main problem most organizations face in achieving the highest level of access control is proper funding levels for information protection technology and information security staff. Information security efforts in an organization are best if they are centralized and coordinated across the enterprise. During the privacy-planning process, the ratio of information security spending to total information technology spending should be examined.

Computer Economics, Inc. estimates that corporate information security funding is less than one half of what is necessary to achieve proper access control. The benchmarking studies performed by Computer Economics have consistently shown that adequate information security budgets should be between 2.5 percent and 3.5 percent of total information technology spending. The studies have also shown that, to achieve adequate access control, four information security employees are required for every 100 IT professionals employed by an organization. In addition to maintaining adequate spending levels for information security staff and technology, the company should review the effectiveness of security efforts on an ongoing basis and make appropriate changes to technology, staffing ratios, and staff skills to keep up with changing technology, business practices, and legal requirements. The technology subcommittee should compare internal spending with the benchmarks provided by Computer Economics and determine what funding and staff should be added to the existing organization resources.

RELEVANT RESULTS OF THE PRIVACY-NEEDS AUDIT TECHNOLOGY

An important step in the privacy-needs audit is to poll employees of all types to get input on potential privacy problems. The technology subcommittee should review the results of the poll to help identify potential privacy maintenance problems. In addition, the technology subcommittee should follow-up with poll respondents who made comments regarding technology and potential weaknesses. The knowledge and viewpoint of individual respondents can be very helpful in identifying problems and may even be able to contribute to the development of solutions. The process should be easy enough to accomplish if the results of the poll have been organized and comments classified and packaged in a way that is easy for the technology subcommittee to quickly review.

REVIEWING EXISTING SECURITY PLANS AND PROCEDURES

The technology subcommittee also needs to review existing data security plans and procedures for both content and compliance. Many security plans, although well conceived, are not fully implemented. A textbook-perfect security plan does little good if it is not implemented, but sits on a shelf collecting dust, only to be updated with new names and the most recent software versions. Unimplemented plans are a definite sore point with many information security managers who have been attempting for more than a decade to explain that corporate data are vulnerable to compromise. The technology subcommittee should review the security plan's comprehensiveness and interview appropriate staff as to the status of the plan's implementation. The technology subcommittee should render an opinion to the privacy task force and make appropriate recommendations.

TESTING INFORMATION TECHNOLOGY SECURITY AND PROCEDURES

The technology subcommittee should arrange for a variety of tests of information technology security and procedures. If the organization is going to maintain privacy of data and information, it must assure that common weaknesses and mistakes in the management of information security are eliminated and that security procedures are strong and well managed. This testing approach differs from testing for weaknesses in privacy management in that it is geared toward testing specific procedures and processes. This approach, known as *hard testing*, should be considered a nuts-and-bolts-oriented procedure and is designed to find weaknesses that may not necessarily result in the compromise of data privacy. After the hard testing is done, the soft test detailed in the next section needs to be done to help illustrate practical results of weaknesses.

Testing of security weaknesses needs to be done in several major areas:

- Support provided by the information security unit and help desk
- End-user compliance with procedures and end-user security habits
- Actual conditions and capability of the technology in place to protect information

To test the strengths and weaknesses of the information security unit, the technology subcommittee should recruit 10 employees from different departments of the organization. The goals are to determine how well the information security unit handles potential security problems and whether that unit or the help desk provides appropriate answers to end-user questions. Specifically, the subcommittee will want to know if the information security unit or help desk reveals information about security that they should not divulge. The testers should be interviewed to determine their level of computer skills and the types of computer problems that they have encountered. Each of the 10 testers should then follow enterprise procedures to report a computing problem. The problems should range from "easy to solve" to "complex, ambiguous, or difficult to explain." If possible, produce an audiotape of these conversations. If taping is problematic then have one member of the technology subcommittee listen in on the phone calls. The results of each test should be noted, and the technology subcommittee should render an opinion about the level of service and appropriateness of answers and report their conclusions to the privacy task force. In addition to conducting these tests, the technology subcommittee should review the trouble logs of the last 12 months to determine trends from the types of questions that have come into the help desk or the information security staff. This review should also be included in the report to the privacy task force.

Testing end-user compliance with procedures and evaluating end-user security habits also requires a random sample of employees from different departments. The technology subcommittee should interview the employees to determine what they know about enterprise information security procedures and rules. The goal is not to punish the individual participant, but rather to create a profile of the employees' understanding of security issues. The technology subcommittee should make this goal clear to participants before interviews are started and reiterate it at interview closure. The technology subcommittee should note the results of each interview, render an opinion about the level of end-user understanding of security procedures and rules, and submit a report to the privacy task force.

Testing the capability of the technology that has been put in place to protect information most often involves *intrusion testing*, and, for which, most organizations contract a reputable computer security company. This testing can be fairly expensive, with prices ranging from $5,000 to $50,000 depending on the types of systems involved. In addition, or if budgets do not allow for intrusion testing, the technology subcommittee should review the security logs for the last 12 months to determine any trends and to identify potential weaknesses in technology. The technology subcommittee should also interview the information security staff, applications developers, and systems analysts to get their inputs on potential security weaknesses in the organization's information systems architecture or product mix. The results of these tests, reviews, and interviews should be reported back to the privacy task force, which should determine any actions needed to improve security.

TESTING WEAKNESSES IN PRIVACY MANAGEMENT

A member of the technology subcommittee and two other members of the privacy task force should conceive various audit procedures to test how well privacy is being managed in the organization. Tests should be conducted as the privacy plan is being developed and after the plan is implemented. Tests conducted while developing the plan will help to identify weaknesses and areas where training or new procedures are needed. This testing approach differs from testing information security and procedures in that it is not designed to test specific elements or procedures. This approach to testing is not a nut-and-bolts approach, but is designed to illustrate the practical consequences of having weakness in security that could result in compromised privacy.

The best way to conduct these tests is to hire an outside consultant or have a member of the testing team pose as an information seeker, while using a telephone number and email address outside the organization. The test team should identify various points in the organization from which information could be obtained. Posing as an information seeker, the tester should call various people inside the organization and attempt to extract information on specific customers or groups of customers. Assumed identities that work well in convincing people to give out information include newspaper reporter, private investigator working on a divorce case, attorney working on a probate case, and government official. The tester should make the calls over a period of a few weeks and have a phone number available to allow those contacted within the organization to return calls. The tester should keep detailed notes on each of the scenarios that they used to attempt to get information, the people they spoke with in the organization, the number of calls made or emails sent, copies of the emails, and the results of each inquiry. Each test should be summarized and the summaries compiled into a report to give to the privacy task force.

The test team and the privacy task force should decide how to handle the results and whether any disciplinary action will be taken with employees who are duped by the tester's attempts to extract information. Although the decision to take disciplinary action rests with individual organizations, bear in mind that the purpose of these tests is to gain a greater understanding as to how the organization responds to attempts to gain information.

REPORTING RESULTS TO THE PRIVACY TASK FORCE

This chapter recommends several methods to assess an organization's security and privacy management habits and culture. Because the tests vary so much in intent, target, and methods, each effort should be reported separately to the privacy task force. Besides, a separate subcommittee of the privacy task force should be created to evaluate the results of these tests and to make inquiries for clarification or further explanation to the technology subcommittee, the physical-property team, and the security and privacy management testers. The addition of this extra review step will help assure that the reports are fair and thorough with well-balanced conclusions.

7

DEVELOPING THE ENTERPRISE PRIVACY PLAN

Working to develop the enterprise privacy plan is a long and difficult process. To reach the point of being able to develop a plan, organizations have had to go through several phases. In phase one, resources were organized and the privacy task force established. In phase two, considerable effort was put forth to determine what information and data need to be protected and to understand the laws governing privacy protection. In addition, the technology subcommittee conducted an evaluation of technologies and existing security policies and procedures, and the physical property team tested existing systems for weaknesses. With all of this preparation accomplished, the task force is ready to start the third phase of privacy plan development, which is establishing enterprise privacy statements, policies, and procedures. This chapter goes through a step-by-step process to developing privacy policies, writing the privacy plan, and creating procedures to maintain privacy.

As the privacy plan is being developed, the task force should sort issues and data types into two major categories. The first category covers data privacy issues that are required by law, regulation, business practices, custom, or business conditions. If, for example, the organization deals with specific types of data such as health records or financial records of private individuals, it has little choice in how to handle the information; the company must comply with the law or risk facing severe consequences.

The second category covers data privacy issues for which the company has options or the process of protection is open to wide interpretation. Category two could include information collected from individuals who voluntarily signed up for an email newsletter for which no specific guarantees of privacy were provided upon registration.

Thoroughness is important when developing privacy policies and procedures and creating the written privacy plan. This chapter covers the following necessary elements of the privacy plan and the process of making policy decisions:

- Preparing to write and assemble a privacy plan
- Understanding the elements of the privacy plan
- Setting the tone for making decisions on privacy policies
- Organizing the Policy Development and Plan Writing Process
- Organizing the decision-making process and assigning tasks
- Writing draft policies and procedures
- Reviewing draft policies and procedures
- Revising draft policies and procedures
- Approving the final privacy plan document and procedures
- Preparing and publishing the final privacy plan document

PREPARING TO WRITE AND ASSEMBLE A PRIVACY PLAN

The physical creation of the privacy plan is an important part of the development process. People throughout the organization will use the document, which will embody and communicate the privacy philosophy, policies, and procedures. The privacy plan could also be used in legal proceedings to help defend and conversely help attorneys of other parties and government agencies to take action against the organization. The privacy plan should be carefully crafted and reviewed by management, legal counsel, and all members of the privacy task force before it is made public (see Figure 7-1). When preparing the privacy plan, the following guidelines are helpful:

- The written plan must be easy to read and understand by all employees in the organization.
- The language of the plan must be clear and concise in order to avoid misinterpretation.
- The document must be easy to distribute to employees, business partners, and even customers.
- The document must be easy to update and maintain and should be published in either electronic or loose-leaf form.

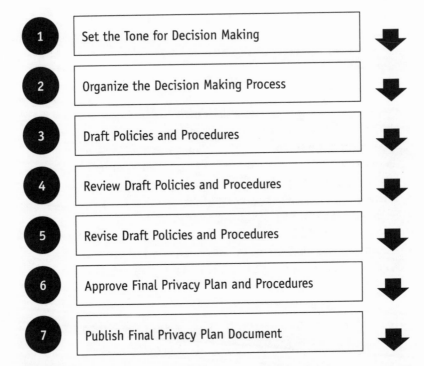

1. Set the Tone for Decision Making

2. Organize the Decision Making Process

3. Draft Policies and Procedures

4. Review Draft Policies and Procedures

5. Revise Draft Policies and Procedures

6. Approve Final Privacy Plan and Procedures

7. Publish Final Privacy Plan Document

Figure 7–1. Developing the Enterprise Privacy Plan: Phase 3 of Privacy Planning

- The document may be placed on an Intranet for inexpensive dissemination, along with other material, such as employee handbooks and safety guidelines, if the organization is large and geographically dispersed.
- The privacy plan should be clearly marked as the property of the organization and should include instructions on how the document should or should not be distributed outside the organization.
- The document should have a professional appearance and be consistent with the enterprise's communication standards.
- The document should be professionally copyedited.

In addition to being treated as an official corporate document, the written privacy plan must be comprehensive and contain all of the elements necessary for employees throughout the organization to use when making decisions that could influence the privacy of enterprise information. The plan needs well-organized contents that should include, but not necessarily be limited to, the following elements:

- A cover page with a title and explanation of what the document contains. The cover page should also identify the organization's primary contact person for dealing with the privacy plan and privacy issues.
- A preface explaining how the document should be used and distributed both within the organization and outside the organization.
- A detailed table of contents to help employees use the plan as a reference tool.
- A clear disclaimer that states that an employee should ask an appropriate manager if anything in the plan is not understood or if a new situation arises that the plan does not specifically address. The disclaimer should clearly indicate that the employee should ask an appropriate manager how to deal with a situation for which appropriate privacy protection action is unclear.
- An introduction covering the basic elements of the privacy plan and the importance of maintaining the privacy of corporate information.
- An explanation and procedure as to how employees should deal with public inquiries regarding the privacy policies of the organization.
- Instructions to employees on what they should do if they feel that privacy of information has been compromised.
- An explanation of how to handle complaints from the public, customers, clients, or suppliers about privacy.
- An explanation, in plain language, of the major laws that affect the organization and what these laws require for maintaining privacy.
- A set of guidelines for how employees should explain the privacy policies of the organization to customers, clients, or suppliers.
- An individual section for each major type of data, information, database, or data element for which privacy must be maintained. (This element will probably result in the creation of several sections.)
- A clear explanation as to the roles each department plays in maintaining enterprise information and protecting the privacy of that information.
- A policy that clearly addresses the organization's expectation of suppliers, business partners, and distributors in protecting the privacy of the enterprise's information that may need to be exchanged during the normal course of business.

- A section that specifies how information should be maintained over long periods of time. This section should address on-site and off site storage.
- A section that specifies procedures for proper disposal of data. This section should cover both printed and electronic documents, including data filed on computers and magnetic media.
- A glossary with definitions of terms and acronyms used in the plan.

SETTING THE TONE FOR MAKING DECISIONS ON PRIVACY POLICIES

The process of making policy decisions can be very political and laden with conflict. When a department feels threatened by changes in policy or loss of control over its business decisions, debate will be heated. In addition, some individuals may feel that their compensation is threatened because they may be restricted in the way they can use information and thus do business. This dynamic necessitates a strong enterprise leader who sets the tone for the decision-making process.

The enterprise leader must be capable of facing the reality that a shift in policy and procedure may have a negative economic impact on parts of the organization and may very well influence the short-term revenue-generating ability of a for-profit corporation. The goal of developing a privacy plan is to strike a balance between the organization's short-term gain and its long-term stability and health. The chief officers of a company, as well as each of the department managers, need to reconcile this conflict within themselves as well as among each other. Managers must accept that governments, advocacy groups, and class action attorneys are wandering the business landscape and are ready to pounce on any organization that they suspect may be violating the privacy of customers or prospects. Representatives of these advocacy groups and government agencies have nothing to lose and everything to gain and are willing to do so at the expense of any business or nonprofit organization.

To avoid the potential costs of a shortsighted privacy plan, the decision-making process on privacy policies must take place in the spirit of cooperation and not an arena of conflict. Individual managers within the enterprise need to remember that they are not fighting with each other, but are unifying to prevent a siege by advocacy groups and government investigators. The spirit of cooperation does not mean that there cannot be dissent among the ranks. Having a balanced perspective during the decision-making process is important, and dissenters should not be rejected, unless of course they demonstrate bad manners. The dissenters are necessary to assure that the organization does indeed achieve a balance. The enterprise does have a social responsibility to abide by the laws of the lands in which they do business, but it also has a responsibility to the stakeholders and employees to assure its long-term stability and profitability.

Healthy debate during the first days of meetings on privacy policies will be helpful in achieving a balance in perspectives. Advocates and dissenters alike should note that the first few days are really just the beginning. Policies must be drafted and reviewed, with more room for continued debate. Hopefully, for the sake of tasks, the debate will become more centered on specifics and procedures than an overall philosophical discussion of the role of government and the evilness of advocacy groups and class action attorneys.

ORGANIZING THE POLICY DEVELOPMENT AND PLAN WRITING PROCESS

At this point, the privacy task force is faced with a series of decisions that could help avoid risks, but at the same time hamper the ability of the enterprise to grow and be profitable. Poor privacy management put in place at this stage could result in litigation and, in some cases, even criminal prosecution. In the first step of phase one, the privacy task force's goal was to establish a philosophy that could run the spectrum of low-risk to high-risk handling of personal information on clients, customers, or prospects. In a low-risk environment, a privacy policy is in place, information dissemination is tightly controlled, policies are set by data type, and all disclosures of information to outside organizations require approval. In a high-risk environment, only nominal policies are in place, information is loosely controlled, information privacy policies are global and nonspecific, and business units and departments are allowed to make their own decisions on the use of information. The privacy task force should revisit and rethink the enterprise position on privacy before continuing the privacy plan development process.

The process of making decisions about privacy policies and procedures needs to be very formal. These decisions are official company actions, and the decision-making process itself could come under as much scrutiny as the policy decision. This process could be very lengthy and take several days, if not weeks, to accomplish. The privacy task force, all subcommittees, departmental teams providing input, legal counsel, and other parties necessary to the process should plan on spending a week going through the process. The agenda that follows is recommended as a step-by-step process to review all material compiled during phases one and two of the development of the privacy plan. During all report reviews, time should be allowed for questions and answers.

Day One—Review of Research and Reports of Subcommittees:

- Call the meeting to order.
- Review the agenda.
- Review reports from legal counsel on legal requirements.
- Review reports from the technology subcommittee.
- Review reports from the physical properties team.
- Review other reports as necessary.
- Conduct general discussion of issues and procedures.
- Adjourn the meeting.

Day Two—Sort the Big Issues From the Small:

- Call the meeting to order.
- Review the agenda.
- Identify what must be done to comply with laws and regulations.
- Discuss necessary policies and procedures to assure compliance with legal requirements.
- Make policy decisions on required issues.
- Assign work on drafting policies on required issues.
- Assign work on creating the required elements of the privacy plan.
- Review secondary issues that relate to information privacy, but may not be required by law.
- Discuss secondary policies and procedures.
- Make policy decisions on secondary issues.
- Assign work on drafting policies for secondary issues.
- Assign work on creating the elements covering secondary issues that must be addressed in the privacy plan.

- Set the date to reconvene and move forward on the review of draft policies.
- Adjourn the meeting.

The outlined agendas for days one and two are straightforward enough, but only in that the agendas are sequential and orderly. The dynamic of discussion and decision making is not so straightforward. As indicated previously, an enterprise leader should help set the tone for the meetings in order to encourage both cooperation and healthy debate. Once the privacy task force has gone through the initial processes of hearing reports, discussing questions and answers, assigning tasks, and making policy decisions, the plan writers will need time to work on the plan. The drafting process, which can take many days and sometimes weeks, is a time when the entire process can get stalled. Members of the privacy task force must make the drafting process their highest priority in their workday or the process will fall even farther behind. If necessary, full-time clerical or word-processing support should be assigned to the privacy task force to assure that the process runs smoothly during the drafting stage.

WRITING DRAFT POLICIES AND PROCEDURES

Writing draft policies and procedures to protect the privacy of enterprise information is a time-consuming process. Writers should bear in mind that they are producing a draft and that the draft will be reviewed and modified during the policy adoption process. The process of *drafting* policies should indeed be a *drafting process*. Final language can and will be decided upon during the next meetings of the privacy task force. The important thing for the draft writers to keep in mind is that they must thoroughly and concisely express their meaning in each section of the policies that they are drafting. All writers should use uniform style sheets and a simple and straightforward layout out for the documents they create. All writers should also adhere to the following guidelines for creating the draft documents:

- Use the same word-processing, spreadsheet, and graphics package when creating the draft.
- Use the same formatting templates for word documents.
- Use only one font in the document.
- Use uniform subheads and paragraph styles.

- Double-space the draft and leave 1.5-inch margins on the top, bottom, and sides to allow reviewers to write comments.
- Clearly mark each document as *company confidential.*
- Use standardized organization names and acronyms when referring to the enterprise or departments.
- Use titles, rather than the names of individuals, when discussing responsibilities within the organization.
- Use an agreed-upon style manual such as the *Chicago Manual of Style.*
- Write in a very straightforward business style.
- Avoid compound lengthy sentences and keep sentences to 28 words or less.
- Keep paragraph formats simple and avoid long paragraphs.
- Keep any diagrams or exhibits simple and easy to understand.
- Be very clear when writing about specific items, such as procedures, in what people should do in certain circumstances.
- Avoid philosophical statements about privacy.
- Do not include the names of specific advocacy groups or organizations outside the enterprise.
- Keep electronic backups of all documents.
- Have another person on the team review the draft for clarity, grammar, and language before submitting it to the task force for review.
- Send drafts to the privacy task force three to four days before the first review meeting.

REVIEWING DRAFT POLICIES AND PROCEDURES

Reviewing draft policies is a multiple-step process. The drafts should be sent to the privacy task force three or four days prior to the prearranged review meeting so that the task force can review the documents before the meeting. Each task force member should have read the drafts before the meeting and should be prepared to discuss each policy and procedure. The privacy task force should reconvene for day three of their development meetings.

During the meeting, a recording secretary should note changes and dissenting comments so the draft can be revised. The process is tedious and repetitive; however, the review must be as thorough as possible, and all departments must feel like they have had input and their comments have been noted. A following detailed agenda for the review process recommended:

Day Three—Discuss the Draft Policies:

- Call the meeting to order.
- Review agenda.
- Discuss the overall review process and major issues.
- Discuss the privacy plan's front matter, including the cover page, preface, table of contents, disclaimer, and introduction.
- Agree to and note changes to the front matter.
- Take a vote on the front matter and record dissenting comments.
- Discuss the privacy plan's introduction.
- Agree to and note changes to introduction.
- Take a vote on the introduction and record dissenting comments.
- Discuss the instructions to employees on what to do if they feel that privacy of information has been compromised and on how to handle complaints from the public, customers, clients, or suppliers about privacy.
- Agree to and note changes to the instructions on data compromises and privacy complaints.
- Take a vote on the instructions regarding data compromises and privacy complaints, and record dissenting comments.
- Discuss the overview of major laws that affect the organization and their requirements for maintaining privacy.
- Agree to and note changes to the overview of major laws.
- Take a vote on the overview of major laws and record dissenting comments.
- Discuss the guidelines for how employees should explain the organization's privacy policies to customers, clients, or suppliers.
- Agree to and note changes to the guidelines for explaining the privacy policies.
- Take a vote on the guidelines for explaining the privacy policies, and record dissenting comments.
- Conduct separate discussions of policies for each major type of data, information, database, or data element for which privacy must be maintained.
- Agree to and note changes to the policies for each major type of data, information, database, or data element for which privacy must be maintained.
- Take a vote on policies for each major type of data, information, database, or data element, and record dissenting comments.

- Discuss the explanations as to each department's roles in maintaining enterprise information and protecting the privacy of that information.
- Agree to and note changes to the explanations of department roles.
- Take a vote on each of the explanations of department roles, and record dissenting comments.
- Discuss the policy that addresses the organization's expectation of suppliers, business partners, and distributors regarding the protection of privacy of enterprise information that may need to be exchanged during the normal course of business.
- Agree to and note changes to the policy that address the organization's expectation of suppliers, business partners, and distributors.
- Take a vote on the statement of the organization's expectation of suppliers, business partners, and record dissenting comments.
- Discuss the section on how information should be maintained over long periods of time.
- Agree to and note changes to the policy that address how information should be maintained over long periods of time.
- Take a vote on the policy that addresses how information should be maintained over long periods of time, and record dissenting comments.
- Discuss procedures that specify proper disposal of data, including printed and electronic data.
- Agree to and note changes to procedures for proper disposal of data.
- Take a vote on the procedures for proper disposal of data, and record dissenting comments.
- Discuss the glossary that defines terms and acronyms used in the plan.
- Agree to and note changes to the glossary.
- Take a vote on the glossary, and record dissenting comments.
- Set a date for the final review of the privacy plan.
- Adjourn the meeting.

REVISING DRAFT POLICIES AND PROCEDURES

Revising the draft policies and procedures is relatively easy to accomplish. The revisers must maintain attention to detail and not take editorial prerogatives when interpreting changes. They should revise the privacy plan, prepare it according to the guidelines set forth for the draft document, and then send the final plan, with the notes from the revision meeting (day three), back to the privacy task force. This final revision should be accompanied by a cover letter that explains the purpose of the final review and outlines the review meeting agenda. Each task force committee member should then examine the document changes and compare them with the agreed-upon changes before the final review meeting. This time-consuming process is important for gaining the support of all departments when the organization reaches the implementation phase.

APPROVING THE FINAL PRIVACY PLAN AND PROCEDURES

Once the revision of the draft policies and procedures is made, approval of the final privacy plan and procedures should be easy. All members of the privacy task force should understand that the time for debate is over and that they are meeting to give their final approval to a written document that embodies the philosophy, policies, and procedures of the corporation's privacy plan. If such a consensus has not been reached, then the final review process could turn into a final debate. The privacy task force should meet for final approval of the document and then set the stage for implementation.

To ensure that all elements of the privacy plan are reviewed and approved, the following specific agenda for the approval meeting is recommended.

Day Four—Approval of the Final Plan:

- Call the meeting to order.
- Review the agenda.
- Discuss the final review process.
- Review the privacy plan's front matter, including the cover page, preface, table of contents, disclaimer, and introduction.
- Agree to and note corrections for errors in changes to the front matter.
- Take and record a vote to approve the front matter.
- Review the privacy plan's introduction.
- Agree to and note corrections for errors in changes to the introduction.
- Take and record a vote to approve the introduction.

- Review the instructions to employees on what to do if they feel that privacy of information has been compromised and on how to handle complaints from the public, customers, clients, or suppliers about privacy.
- Agree to and note corrections for errors in changes to the instructions on data compromises and privacy complaints.
- Take and record a vote to approve the instructions on data compromises and privacy complaints.
- Review the overview of major laws that affect the organization and their requirements for maintaining privacy.
- Agree to and note corrections for errors in changes to the overview of major laws.
- Take and record a vote to approve the overview of major laws.
- Discuss the guidelines for how employees should explain the organization's privacy policies to customers, clients, or suppliers.
- Agree to and note corrections for errors in changes to the guidelines for explaining the privacy policies.
- Take and record a vote to approve the guidelines for explaining the privacy policies.
- Conduct separate discussions of policies for each major type of data, information, database, or data element for which privacy must be maintained.
- Agree to and note corrections for errors in changes to the policies for each major type of data, information, database, or data element for which privacy must be maintained.
- Take and record a vote to approve policies for each major type of data, information, database, or data element.
- Discuss the explanations as to each department's roles in maintaining enterprise information and protecting the privacy of that information maintained.
- Agree to and note corrections for errors in changes to the explanations of department roles.
- Take and record a vote to approve the explanations of department roles.
- Discuss the policy that addresses the organization's expectation of suppliers, business partners, and distributors regarding the protection of privacy of enterprise information that may need to be exchanged during the normal course of business.
- Agree to and note corrections for errors in changes to the policy that address the organization's expectation of suppliers, business partners, and distributors.

- Take and record a vote to approve the statement of the organization's expectation of suppliers, business partners, and distributors.
- Discuss the section that specifies how information should be maintained over long periods of time.
- Agree to and note corrections for errors in changes to the policy that address how information should be maintained over long periods of time.
- Take and record a vote to approve the policy that addresses how information should be maintained over long periods of time.
- Discuss procedures for proper disposal of data, including printed and electronic data.
- Agree to and note corrections for errors in changes to procedures for the proper disposal of data.
- Take and record a vote to approve the procedures for proper disposal of data.
- Discuss the glossary.
- Agree to and note corrections for errors in changes to the glossary.
- Take and record a vote to approve the glossary.
- Set a date for the next privacy task force meeting. This date should give each department ample time to first have an implementation meeting. The purpose of the next privacy task force meeting is to discuss issues and progress.
- Adjourn the meeting.

PREPARING AND PUBLISHING THE FINAL PRIVACY PLAN DOCUMENT

The final privacy plan document should be published in electronic or loose-leaf form. These formats allow easy update and maintenance over time. Since the document must be easy to read and easy to understand, the privacy task force should conduct a simple readability test. A good way to test readability is to select employees from different parts of the organization to read the plan and provide input on the readability of the final privacy plan document. This employee input on readability can be organized and presented at the next meeting of the privacy task force.

As implementation begins, many employees in the organization will need to go through training on the privacy plan. Trainers and employees in training will need access to the copies of the plan. In addition, new employees and especially those in some sort of supervisory role will also need access to the plan during their orientation process. The size of the organization will certainly influence the publishing methods and help determine the quantity of printed and electronic copies needed. To help determine the number of copies needed, the privacy task force should consult with the human resources department regarding employee turnover, headcount at various locations, Intranet availability, and the type of available training facilities.

8

IMPLEMENTING THE ENTERPRISE PRIVACY PLAN

The implementation of a privacy plan takes considerable time and effort and requires more than making copies and distributing them to departments or business units. Goals need to be set for achieving levels of implementation, and the entire process must be evaluated on an ongoing basis. Training needs to be accomplished at all levels of the organization and in all departments and business units. Implementation of a plan is a coordinated and directed effort that requires the cooperation and support of all employees. Implementation also requires communicating with suppliers, customers, clients, and business partners. This chapter outlines the entire implementation process.

DEVELOPING THE IMPLEMENTATION PLAN

The privacy task force has traveled a long and probably difficult road to develop the enterprise's privacy plan. Task force members and departmental teams may feel that their task is over. Although a milestone has been reached, the work is far from finished. The privacy task force needs to meet and decide how the privacy policies, plan, and procedures will be implemented and who will be responsible for specific steps in the implementation process. Without thorough implementation, the privacy protection cannot be achieved. The privacy task force needs to assign responsibilities for several tasks to assure proper implementation, including:

- Setting timelines for implementation
- Recording and reporting implementation progress
- Distributing the privacy plan documents

- Training executives and middle managers
- Training employees who have specific privacy responsibilities
- Training employees across the organization
- Promoting privacy protection awareness within the company
- Providing appropriate notice to business partners, suppliers, and customers
- Developing appropriate and compliant language for contracts, notices, customer agreements, Web sites, brochures, and marketing material
- Implementing new procedures for storage and disposal of records and media containing sensitive material
- Evaluating implementation of the privacy plan

The privacy task force should establish working groups to be responsible for different areas of implementation. These working groups should report back to the task force on a regular basis to discuss goals, budget requirements, and obstacles encountered. The implementation process is going to take time and cost money. Enterprise executives and department managers need to quickly come to grips with this reality and be prepared to provide the staff with the time and financial resources necessary for a thorough implementation of the privacy policies, plans, and procedures.

ASSIGNING RESPONSIBILITIES FOR IMPLEMENTATION

Assigning implementation responsibilities is often easier in a large organization than in a small organization. Large organizations usually have departments that specialize in the areas in which work needs to be done. Smaller organizations may need to use an ad hoc approach in assigning responsibilities for privacy plan implementation. The privacy task force should assign responsibilities in a logical fashion and spread responsibilities across the organization. Departments that will need to be involved in the long-term for specific aspects of privacy management should be in charge of implementing related procedures. The records management department, for example, should be responsible for implementing new procedures for the management, storage, and disposal of corporate records, files, and customer data. The public relations department should be assigned the tasks related to corporate communications, internal awareness campaigns, and materials for customers and business partners. A recommended assignment of responsibilities is shown in Figure 8–1.

Department	Examples of Implementation Tasks
Privacy Task Force	• Oversight and direction. • Monitoring implementation.
Public Relations Department	• Corporate communications. • Internal awareness campaigns. • Preparation of material to send to customers and business partners.
Human Resources Department	• Developing and managing the training process for existing employees. • Creating orientation process for new employees.
Central Information Technology Department	• Setting standards for application development and maintenance to improve information security. • Implementing improved computer security procedures. • Training employees on computer security. • Setting standards and selecting more secure computing and software products.
Security Departments	• Implementing new procedures to protect the privacy of physical records. • Work with other departments in an advising capacity.
Facilities Management Department	• Implementing new procedures for the disposal of obsolete and used computer equipment and magnetic media. • Work with records management to implement new procedures and improve storage facilities.
Records Management	• Implementing new procedures for the management, storage, or records. • Implementing new procedures for the disposal of enterprise records, files, and customer data.
Sales Department	• Work with PR department on implementing awareness campaign for customers. • Work with marketing and legal counsel to revise materials.
Legal Counsel	• Interpret new laws and regulations. • Review customer notices and contract language for accuracy and compliance.
Marketing Department	• Work with sales and legal counsel to revise materials. • Create new material or modify existing marketing material and campaigns to incorporate privacy policies. • Work sales and customer service on awareness campaign.
Customer Service Department	• Work with PR to develop material covering the privacy policy for use in the customer service process. • Work on awareness campaign with customers.

Figure 8–1. Assignment of Implementation Responsibilities for the Enterprise-wide Privacy Plan

SETTING TIMELINES
FOR IMPLEMENTATION

Be aggressive when setting the timeline for implementation of the privacy plan. Slowing down when obstacles are encountered is easier than speeding up after people have committed to a schedule. The concept of *now* needs to be embraced. The air of immediacy needs to be recognized by all of the working groups, and management needs to be supportive of the efforts. Implementation of the privacy plan will probably take several weeks to accomplish, and in larger organizations it could take several months. A sample implementation schedule is shown in Figure 8–2.

MONITORING AND EVALUATING
IMPLEMENTATION PROGRESS

The privacy task force needs to monitor the implementation of the privacy plan from beginning to end and evaluate the effectiveness of implementation for all aspects of the plan. During the first two months of implementation, the privacy task force should meet weekly to review progress and make any needed adjustments to the implementation schedule and budget. Each working group should report back to the privacy task force on what implementation has been accomplished, what is pending, and what obstacles have been encountered. Reporting should be done in a uniform manner, and reports should be cataloged for future reference. Each working group should complete a report for each task for which it is responsible, but can group closely related tasks on the same report. A sample *Privacy Plan Implementation Report* is shown in Figure 8–3.

DISTURBING THE PRIVACY
PLAN DOCUMENTS

The privacy plan document needs to be widely distributed in the organization. One of the most economical approaches for distribution is to have the privacy plan document and all related procedures available to employees on the enterprise's Intranet. Publishing on the Intranet in HTML documents makes the privacy plan easily accessible to employees and also both eases and speeds up the revision process.

Distribution of the plan can also be accomplished by using a portable document format (PDF) that can be created from Acrobat software. The Acrobat reader is available to download for free from the Acrobat Web site

Time Frame for Implementation	Examples of Tasks to Accomplish
Week 1	• Assign responsibilities and form working groups. • Establishing a process to monitor implementation.
Week 2	• Working groups propose implementation schedules and budget requirements to the task force. • Working groups that have area specific tasks work on the implementation process. • Distribution of written plan to management level.
Week 3	• Executive level briefings on the privacy policies and procedures. • Development of corporate awareness program. • Development of external communications plan and materials. • Production of training materials. • Training the trainers workshops for all people that will conduct training.
Week 4	• Implement new records management procedures. • Implement new equipment and magnetic media disposal procedures. • Launch internal awareness campaign. • Training all management level staff on privacy policies and procedures.
Week 5	• Privacy task force evaluates implementation progress and modifies timeline as necessary. • Implement new password protection schemes for enterprise information systems. • Implement new physical security procedures and awareness program on procedures. • Training all supervisory level staff on privacy policies and procedures. • Initiate training process for all existing employees. • Initiate training process for all new incoming employees.
Week 6	• Continue training process for all existing employees. • Launch external awareness campaign. • Communicate policies and procedures to suppliers and business partners as necessary.
Week 7	• Announce new information technology product standards and selections. • Continue training process for all existing employees. • Continue internal and external awareness campaigns.
Week 8	• Privacy task force evaluates implementation progress and modifies timeline as necessary. • Continue training process for all existing employees. • Develop procedures to test and evaluate effectiveness of new policies and procedures.
Week 9	• Initiate testing process for new procedures. • Continue training process for all existing employees.

Figure 8-2. Implementation Timeline for the Enterprisewide Privacy Plan

PRIVACY PLAN IMPLEMENTATION REPORT

Date: _____

Work Group Name	Implementation Task
Expected Timeline	Timeline Modifications
Progress Made	Obstacles Encountered
Additional Resources Required	Comments

Figure 8–3. Privacy Plan Implementation Report

(http://www.adobe.com/products/acrobat). PDF documents can be distributed throughout the organization and sent as email attachments to employees who work in remote locations or primarily in the field. PDF documents can also be formatted for easy and neat printing on any laser printer.

During the training process, a copy of the privacy plan should be distributed to all executive-level staff and managers. This training copy may not have to be the entire privacy plan, but could contain highlights and important points that all levels of employees need to understand.

TRAINING FOR PRIVACY PROTECTION

One of the most important steps in implementing the privacy plan is training all employees on privacy policies and procedures. Simply stated, what good is a great plan when no one knows what the plan is? Training of new employees should be done as appropriate for their areas of responsibility. Training of current employees can be divided and prioritized into four types of training, based on employee roles and accomplished in the following order: executive-level training, middle-manager and supervisor training, project-leaders training, and general employee training.

Type 1: Training Executives

Training of current employees should start at the executive level, and all executive staff should be required to attend the training. Executive staff should be trained on these areas of the privacy plan: the work of the privacy task force, the major laws affecting the organization's privacy maintenance requirements, and the enterprise's policies toward suppliers, business partners, and distributors. Recognize that executive level staff often have short attention spans because they are busy on a wide variety of tasks and responsibilities; therefore, this briefing should be limited to no more than two hours. Figure 8–4 shows the detailed training requirements for executive staff.

Type 2: Training Middle-Level Managers and Supervisors

The second training effort should be directed at middle-level managers and supervisors who need to thoroughly understand the privacy policies and procedures to assure that decisions they make during the course of business negotiations and operations management are consistent with enter-

Area of Privacy Plan to be Covered	Desired Outcomes for Training
The Privacy Planning Process and what the task force has accomplished	Understand the effort that has been put forth in developing the privacy plan.
Detailed Table of Contents	Understand the contents of the privacy plan and be able to use it as reference tool.
Disclaimer and instructions as to what to do when a situation arises that the plan does not address	Understand what employees should do when confronted with new situations.
Introduction	Understand and be able to make decisions based on the overall philosophy toward privacy.
Explanation of major laws that impact the privacy requirements of the organization	Understand laws and be able to make business plans that are consistent with legal requirements.
Overview of the types of data for which the organization must maintain privacy	Understand the data assets of the organization as well as the challenge and requirements of maintaining privacy.
Policies and expectations of suppliers, business partners, and distributors	Understand expectations and be able to conduct business negotiations according to privacy requirements.
Appendix of Definitions	Understand how to use the appendix as reference tool.

Figure 8–4. Briefing Outline for Executive-Level Staff

prise policies on information privacy. Middle managers and supervisors should be trained on broader privacy plan content than executive staff. Middle managers and supervisors have more hands-on responsibility for the day-to-day operation of the enterprise and need a far more detailed understanding of the privacy plan than executive level staff. Training topics include the work of the privacy task force, the major laws affecting the organization's privacy maintenance requirements, specific data for which the organization must maintain privacy, and the roles each department plays in maintaining enterprise information and protecting the privacy of that information. This training requires about eight hours, which allows time for discussion and questions and answers. Figure 8–5 shows the detailed training requirements for management and supervisory staff.

Type 3: Training Group Leaders and Project Leaders

A third type of training should be directed toward employees who manage work groups or projects that specifically involve data and information for which privacy must be maintained. These group leaders and project leaders must have a good understanding of the privacy plan as well as a detailed understanding of the specific data, applications, or business processes in which they are involved. Training topics include major laws affecting the organization's privacy maintenance requirements, specific data for which the organization must maintain privacy, the roles each department plays in protecting privacy, and privacy requirements for the specific tasks or projects in which the group and project leaders are involved. This training takes about eight hours, which allows time for discussion and questions and answers. Figure 8–6 shows the detailed training requirements for group and project leaders.

Type 4: Generalized Privacy Training

All other employees should be given at least some basic training so that they understand the overall enterprise policies and philosophy toward privacy. A generalized privacy-training program should be developed to cover the importance of privacy, the laws covering privacy of information in the organization, and what employees should do to help protect privacy. This training should be brief and can be accomplished in about one hour. Figure 8–7 shows the generalized training requirements.

Each employee who attends training should be required to sign and date a statement that acknowledges such training. This signed statement, along with a description of the training and a course outline, should be kept on file. As employees move into different tasks or are promoted to supervisory or management positions, they should go through the training that has been designated appropriate for those positions.

Area of Privacy Plan to Be Covered	Desired Outcomes for Training
The Privacy Planning Process and what the task force has accomplished	Understand the effort that has been put forth in developing the privacy plan.
Detailed Table of Contents	Understand the contents of the privacy plan and be able to use it as reference tool.
Disclaimer and instructions as to what to do when a situation arises that the plan does not address	Understand what employees should do when confronted with new situations.
Introduction	Understand and be able to make decisions based on the overall philosophy toward privacy.
Guidelines for how employees should explain the privacy policies of the organization to customers, clients, or suppliers	Understand the guidelines and be able to implement proper procedures for dealing with inquiries that come to their department.
Explanation of major laws that impact the privacy requirements of the organization	Understand laws and be able to make business plans that are consistent with legal requirements.
Detailed explanation of the specific data for which the organization must maintain privacy	Understand the data for which privacy must be maintained and be able to meet the requirements of maintaining privacy.
Explanation as to the roles each department plays in maintaining enterprise information and protecting the privacy of that information	Understand the role of each department and be able to work with other departments to maintain privacy.
Policies and expectations of suppliers, business partners, and distributors	Understand expectations and be able to conduct business negotiations according to privacy requirements.
Procedures for maintaining information over long periods of time, including on-site and off-site storage	Understand the procedures and be able to meet the requirements of maintaining privacy of long-term information.
Procedures for the proper disposal of data and information in all formats, including print, computer-based, and magnetic storage	Understand the procedures and be able to meet the requirements of maintaining privacy during the disposal process.
Appendix of Definitions	Understand how to the appendix as reference tool.

Figure 8–5. Training Outline for Middle Managers and Supervisors

Area of Privacy Plan to Be Covered	Desired Outcomes for Training
The Privacy Planning Process and what the task force has accomplished	Understand the effort that has been put forth in developing the privacy plan.
Detailed Table of Contents	Understand the contents of the privacy plan and be able to use it as reference tool.
Disclaimer and instructions as to what to do when a situation arises that the plan does not address	Understand what employees should be when confronted with new situations.
Introduction	Understand and be able to make decisions based on the overall philosophy toward privacy.
Explanation of major laws that impact the privacy requirements of the organization	Understand laws and be able to make business plans that are consistent with legal requirements.
Detailed explanation of the specific data for which the organization must maintain privacy	Understand the data for which privacy must be maintained and be able to meet the requirements of maintaining privacy.
Explanation as to the roles each department plays in maintaining enterprise information and protecting the privacy of that information.	Understand the role of each department and be able to work with other departments to maintain privacy.
Task or project specific requirements for privacy maintenance	Understand expectations and be able to execute a specific task according to enterprise privacy management requirements.
Appendix of Definitions	Understand how to use the appendix as reference tool.

Figure 8–6. Training Outline for Group Leaders and Project Leaders

Area of Privacy Plan to Be Covered	Desired Outcomes for Training
The Privacy Planning Process and what the task force has accomplished	Understand the effort that has been put forth in developing the privacy plan.
Introduction	Understand the overall philosophy toward privacy.
How to identify potential privacy problems and what they should do	Understand what employees should do when confronted with privacy-related situations.
Introduction to major laws that impact the privacy require-ments of the organization	Understand laws and the importance of maintaining privacy.
Explanation as to the roles each department plays in maintain-ing enterprise information and protecting the privacy of that information	Understand the role of each department.

Figure 8-7. Training Outline for Generalized Privacy Training

RUNNING THE INTERNAL AWARENESS CAMPAIGN

A strong internal awareness program will inform employees of the importance of the privacy plan and motivate them to learn policies and procedures. Public relations departments are usually very good at managing such
campaigns. However, if the present public relations staff does not have
experience managing internal awareness campaigns, either send them to
training or hire an external consultant to assist in the campaign development. The internal awareness campaign should employ as many methods
as possible to increase the awareness of privacy protection efforts. The following are the methods that can be used in the awareness campaign:

- Attention-getting logos and headlines on the enterprise's Intranet
- Articles in employee newsletters explaining the importance of privacy
  management and the implementation of the privacy plan

- Banners and posters in break rooms and employee cafeterias
- Posters in vending areas
- Posters in restroom and lounge areas
- Banners in parking areas
- Brown bag lunches to discuss the plan
- Pamphlets included in paycheck envelopes
- Direct mailings of pamphlets or letters to employee's homes
- Brief discussions of the plan in staff meetings
- Minitraining sessions at workshops or retreats
- Motivational speakers at large enterprise events
- Celebrity endorsement of campaign goals

RUNNING THE EXTERNAL AWARENESS CAMPAIGN

An external awareness program is more complicated than an internal one because of the many different potential audiences that must be reached. Customers are the most important to reach, but the enterprise must also communicate implementation of the privacy plan to investors, suppliers, business partners, industry analysts, and the media. Each of these target audiences will need different types of information. The external campaign developers should work with appropriate departments to help develop message statements that are relevant to each audience. The external campaign developers should also determine the most effective means of communicating with each target audience.

Reaching customers can be achieved in many ways. Focus on giving a positive message to customers. Do not create an impression that the enterprise is just starting to deal with privacy issues and that privacy had possibly been compromised in the past. The best message is something like "we are putting extra efforts into protecting your privacy." Customers can be reached through inserts in bills, monthly statements, posters or banners at service counters, recorded messages while they are on hold waiting for service, and statements in contracts, on licensing agreements, or on invoices. The message must be positive and should aim to instill confidence in the organization.

While communicating with suppliers, business partners, or product distributors is important, it is especially critical if new policies raise or change expectations as to how these external parties handle data and information. Two approaches should be taken with this target audience. First, a general awareness campaign is helpful and can be achieved through direct mailings, inserts in invoices, or discussions with enterprise liaisons such as sales people or customer service staff. Second, and most important, is a specific awareness campaign that communicates specific messages about the information privacy to specific organizations with which business is transacted. Identifying what type of information exchanges occurs between organizations can be accomplished by reviewing the facts about data use gathered during the privacy-needs audit. Those organizations with which the enterprise exchanges information need to be notified as to new policies and procedures that specifically affect the business relationship.

Communicating with investors and industry analysts about the new privacy plan and renewed efforts to assure privacy protection can help build their confidence in the enterprise. Many dot.com companies have been slaughtered in the press because of privacy blunders. Bad press does not help stock prices, nor does it generally help to convince investment advisors or stock analysts to make "buy" recommendations. Communications with investors and industry analysts should be designed to build confidence. A brief overview of the privacy efforts and implementation of new policies and procedures is what they want to hear. Any communications should be short and to the point. This audience will give you no more than about sixty seconds to get the point across.

Communicating enterprise privacy management efforts to the general media can be very helpful in creating a positive image for an organization. A press release announcing development of a new privacy plan is helpful, but will likely not yield any great results. The best way to exploit the general media is to be prepared to discuss privacy management efforts as opportunities arise. The public debate over privacy will provide ample opportunity to promote enterprise efforts in privacy protection. Several times each week the news covers privacy topics or, in many cases, privacy disasters. The public relations team can exploit these opportunities with a few good media contacts. Once the enterprise has gained some positive coverage, more will likely follow; if people within the enterprise can discuss privacy management, opportunities to do so will become increasingly available because writers always need quotes.

DEVELOPING APPROPRIATE AND COMPLIANT PRIVACY LANGUAGE

The process of developing appropriate and compliant language for contracts, notices, customer agreements, Web sites, brochures, and marketing material is very complex and requires the cooperation of several departments. Legal counsel should have the lead role in this process, but the sales department, marketing department, business units, and customer service should be involved. The complexity of the language and the number of contracts, notices, or agreements will of course vary by the type of business or service in which the enterprise is involved. The number of items that need to be created will also vary by the type of business. In general, these items will fall into one of the following categories:

- Contracts with suppliers and distributors
- Customer agreements
- Web site notices

Safe harbor standards for example, require compliance with several stipulations in order for an enterprise to declare itself as a safe harbor. If safe harbor standards become universal, the task of developing privacy language will likely become easier because references could be made to "safe harbor," or prepackaged language could be adopted. In the case of an industry that must operate under specific laws or regulations, creating privacy statements may be easier. The most complicated language creation situations will occur in environments in which an organization wants to give the appearance of standardized compliance, but still wants to maintain much flexibility in interpreting what can be done with data.

IMPLEMENTING RECORDS MANAGEMENT AND DISPOSAL PROCEDURES

Long-term records management, archiving, and disposal have created a potential privacy nightmare. The process of disposing obsolete or broken computers and used magnetic media is one of the weakest links in privacy protection. Paper records, copies of transaction reports, sales logs, and customer account printouts are routinely thrown into a trash dumpster. Old and inoperative computers are sold by the ton or donated to charity or at times even dumped in back alleys on trash day. As a result of the privacy-needs audit and reviews by the technology subcommittee, most organizations will need to implement new and safer disposal procedures. This is not going to be an easy process. Changing the habits of how people handle their garbage has been a major endeavor for environmentalists, and privacy protectors should expect no less of a challenge.

To achieve change in disposal methods requires at least a two-prong approach. The first is educating employees on how to properly dispose of materials. The second is staffing the facilities management and surplus property departments at a level adequate enough to sort and properly recycle or dispose of paper, computers, and magnetic media. The facilities management, records management, and security departments will need to coordinate efforts to implement more stringent procedures to prevent warehouses and trash dumpsters from becoming privacy hazards. Trash and junk equipment will probably need to be processed in a totally different fashion than they have been for the last three decades. This translates into more staff to deal with garbage and surplus computers and, as a result, a higher cost associated with dealing with the things that organizations don't want. There are few alternatives to increased labor costs. New or revised procedures must be implemented to cover:

- Security of long-term record storage
- Disposal of paper records
- Disposal of magnetic media such as tapes, floppy disks, and removable hard drives
- Disposition, sale, or destruction of used computers

IMPLEMENTING PROCEDURES IN THE CENTRAL INFORMATION TECHNOLOGY DEPARTMENT

As a result of the privacy-needs audit, some procedures in the central information technology (IT) department will need to be changed. In general, older established IT departments are incredibly well-disciplined and professional environments. Most of them, however, lack enough funding for proper computer security. If the technology subcommittee's review revealed that the enterprise was underspending for security, then a new budget and new staffing levels will need to be implemented. If other weaknesses were discovered during the privacy-needs audit or during the reviews of the technology subcommittee, then the IT department will need to develop a plan to address those issues.

At minimum the IT department staff should participate in the highest levels of privacy training offered during the implementation process. Creating awareness of privacy protection among IT professionals is very important to the enterprise's future. Supervisors and project leaders with several years of IT experience are well aware of the need for security and recognize the role of applications developers in security. The IT staff who may need the most training are the least experienced ones, who may certainly be well skilled in computer usage and programming, but may not think in terms of whole systems and relate what they are doing to the needs of the overall system or architecture.

TRAINING FROM THE INFORMATION TECHNOLOGY DEPARTMENT

An important role for the IT department during the privacy plan's implementation is to provide training on the importance of good computer security and the proper password use. In addition, the IT department can help by communicating policies about the use of desktops, laptops, and other devices connected to the enterprise network. IT staff can also work with the public relations department by contributing facts and procedures that can be used during awareness campaigns. This may be a good time to raise the profile of the IT department and have IT staff participate as trainers in the privacy training program. IT staff can participate as cotrainers and do specialized sessions on computer-related issues. Some IT staff might even gain the valuable experience of acting as full-fledged trainers in the privacy training program.

EVALUATING IMPLEMENTATION OF THE PRIVACY PLAN

The privacy task force must constantly monitor the implementation of the privacy policies and procedures. During the weekly meetings of the task force, working groups will report back to the task force and complete the *Privacy Plan Implementation Report* shown in Figure 8–3. This process will be sufficient for fine-tuning the implementation steps, allocating resources, and modifying the timeline. The privacy task force, however, needs to do more than just monitor and receive reports from teams to assure that the privacy plan is actually working. The privacy task force should prepare for the long-term monitoring *and testing* of privacy issues and problems. It should conduct annual evaluations and also perform testing on a regular basis. Chapter 6 of this book, *Evaluating Technology Needs for Privacy Protection*, recommends several procedures to help test privacy protection levels prior to developing the privacy plan. These same tactics can be used to evaluate change and hopefully improvements in privacy protection in the post-implementation environment.

The privacy task force should use the same or similar tests used by the technology subcommittee, who tested information technology security and procedures during the plan development phases. The task force should perform both hard testing, which is designed to identify weaknesses in specific procedures and processes, and *soft testing*, which is designed to illustrate the practical consequences of having security weaknesses that could result in compromised privacy. After conducting the privacy tests, the task force should compare the post-implementation test results with those test results from the privacy plan development process. If the same weaknesses are present in both tests, then more work is required on training, and procedures will need to be tightened again.

RECOGNIZING ACHIEVEMENT AND PREPARING TO SHIFT GEARS

Getting to this point in privacy plan development and implementation can take several months. The privacy task force and the departmental teams have come a long way. The privacy plan is implemented and new procedures have been created throughout the organization. Everyone that worked on the project deserves recognition, which can be done in letters of appreciation and during the employee performance evaluation process. The process of recognizing achievement and effort is important in all types and sizes of organizations. The director of the privacy task force and upper level managers should all participate in the process of recognizing the work done during the development and implementation of the privacy plan.

Once the plan has been implemented, the organization should think about the transition from the planning and implementation process to the ongoing management of information privacy in the organization. Laws that affect privacy are certain to evolve, and the business and operational needs of all organizations change over time. Keeping up with change is critical to protecting the investment that has already been put into the privacy management plan and processes.

9

MANAGING PRIVACY ON THE ENTERPRISE WEB SITE

Regardless of their type of business or activities, enterprises that have Web sites have a unique set of privacy management challenges. Web site privacy issues fall into three major categories: assuring proper use of data collected through a Web site, maintaining the privacy of individuals while they are using a Web site, and protecting data compiled and used by Web applications from outside intruders. All of these issues are addressed in "safe harbor" requirements, and users who are children under the age of 13 are protected by the Children's Online Privacy Protection Act of 1998 (COPPA).

CREATING PRIVACY STATEMENTS FOR THE ENTERPRISE WEB SITE

Creating privacy statements for Web sites has become a complicated business and legal process. Those organizations that fully embrace safe harbor requirements have an easier time creating their privacy statements. Those organizations that attempt to maintain as many loopholes as possible in how they can use data in the future often struggle with ways to keep their privacy statements as ambiguous as possible. Organizations that deal with children under 13 must comply with COPPA requirements or face penalties. To help illustrate how to meet requirements for Web site privacy statements, three examples are shown in Figures 9–1 through 9–3.

Many privacy statements on Web sites are very straightforward. The privacy statement of the White House Web site informs visitors that no personal information will be collected about them unless they choose to provide information. The privacy statement further explains that if White House Web site visitors choose to send personal information in an email

Privacy Policy Statement

At WXYZ.com, we are committed to protecting your privacy. We use the information we collect about you to process orders and to provide a more personalized shopping experience. Please read on for more details about our privacy policy.

The Information We Collect and How Do We Use It?

When you order, we need to know your name, email address, mailing address, credit card number, and expiration date. This allows us to process and fulfill your order and to notify you of your order status.

When you sign up for our Individualized Notification Services we need only an email address that we use to send information you requested.

When you enter a context or other promotional feature, we may ask for your name, address, and email address so we can administer the contest and notify winners.

We personalize your shopping experience by using your purchases to shape our recommendations about merchandise that might be of interest to you. We also monitor customer traffic patterns and site usage to help us develop the design and layout of the site.

We may also use the information we collect to occasionally notify you about important functionality changes to the Web site, new WXYZ.com services, and special offers we think you'll find valuable. If you would rather not receive this information, visit your WXYZ.com Subscriptions Page to change your preferences. Make sure to change your preferences for each account or email address you have left with us.

When you send a greeting through the WXYZ Ecards service, we ask for your email address and that of the recipient in order to complete your request. WXYZ.com will never disclose or send promotional email to recipient addresses provided only to the WXYZ Ecards service.

When you create a "I Want This List," we ask for your name, shipping address, and an optional personal description. We use your name and personal description to identify your I Want This List; we use your name and shipping address to process and fulfill your I Want This List orders. You can also choose to provide email addresses of friends and family with whom you would like to share your I Want This List. We will email the recipients that you choose to tell them about your I Want This List and its contents, and how they can easily access it. WXYZ.com will not disclose or send promotional emails to those recipient addresses provided only to the I Want This List service.

Figure 9–1. Generic Privacy Statement for a Web Site

We have relationships with a group of online stores, and if you shop at these stores by using a link from our store to one of these sites participating in a joint promotion we will receive aggregate or otherwise anonymous statistical information about your shopping trip to these stores. We treat this information with the same care as we treat other information that you entrust to WXYZ.com, and it is fully protected by our privacy policy.

How Does WXYZ.com Protect Customer Information?
When you place orders to access your account information, we offer the use of a secure server. The secure server software (SSL) encrypts all information you input before it is sent to us. Furthermore, all of the customer data we collect is protected against unauthorized access.

What About "Cookies"?
"Cookies" are small pieces of information that are stored by your browser on your computer's hard drive. Our cookies do not contain any personally identifying information, but they do enable us to provide Web site features such as personalized pages. Most Web browsers automatically accept cookies, but you can usually change your browser to prevent that. Even without a cookie, you can still use most of the features in our store, including placing items in your shopping cart and purchasing them.

Disclosure of the Information to Outside Parties?
WXYZ.com does not sell, trade, or rent your personal information to others. We may choose to do so in the future with trustworthy third parties, but you can tell us not to share the information by sending a blank email message to nevergivemyinfo@wxyz.com. If you use more than one email address to shop with us, send this message from each email account you use.

Also, WXYZ.com may provide aggregate statistics about our customers, sales, traffic patterns, and related site information to reputable third-party vendors, but these statistics will include no personally identifying information. WXYZ.com may release account information when we believe, in good faith, that such release is reasonably necessary to (i) comply with law, (ii) enforce or apply the terms of any of our user agreements, or (iii) protect the rights, property, or safety of WXYZ.com, our users, or others.

How Does WXYZ.com Allow Customers to Update or Change the Information It Collects?

You may update or change information related to your WXYZ.com account by accessing your WXYZ.com/Info/ section of the Web site with your email account and password. For other questions related to updating

Figure 9–1. (*Continued*)

or changing your account information, please send email to infohelp@
WXYZ.com.

Summary
We are committed to protecting your privacy. We use the information we
collect on the site to make shopping at WXYZ.com possible and to enhance
your overall shopping experience. We do not sell, trade, or rent your personal information to others. We may choose to do so in the future with
trustworthy third parties, but you can tell us not to by sending a blank
email message to nevergivemyinfo@wxyz.com. If you never want to receive
any announcements or special offers from us, visit the WXYZ.com/Info/
section of the Web site to change your preferences. Remember to change
your preferences for each of the email accounts you have given us.

Your Consent
By using our Web site, you consent to the collection and use of this information by WXYZ.com. If we decide to change our privacy policy, we will
post those changes on this page so that you are always aware of what
information we collect, how we use it, and under what circumstances we
disclose it.

Figure 9–1. (*Continued*)

or on a form submitted through the Web site, then that particular information will be used only to respond to the request. The privacy statement
also explains what information will be automatically collected through the
use of Web technology and how it will be used.

To help organizations get started in writing Web site privacy statements,
a generic privacy statement is shown in Figure 9–1. The generic privacy
statement covers the necessary elements of Web site privacy statements.
This generic model is written for an ecommerce site that sells a variety of
products. The generic statement opens with a basic explanation of philosophy. The statement then explains the information collected and what is
done with that information, how cookies work, the policy on disclosing
information to outside parties, how customers can change their data, and
how customers can limit the use of data collected about them.

In October 2001, the Federal Trade Commission (FTC) will seek public comment to determine whether technology has progressed and whether
secure electronic methods for obtaining verifiable parental consent are
widely available and affordable. Until then, operators are encouraged to
use the more reliable method of parental consent for all uses of children's

personal information. The FTC may bring enforcement actions and impose civil penalties for violations of the required parental consent rule in the same manner as for other rules under COPPA. The FTC also retains authority to examine information practices, including those in use before the rule's effective date, for deception and unfairness. If the FTC has determined that a representation, omission, or practice is *deceptive* it is likely to mislead consumers and affect consumers' behavior or decisions about the product or service. Violators of the law are subject to FTC enforcement action, including civil penalties of $11,000 per violation. The FTC is currently undertaking a number of educational initiatives to promote compliance with COPPA.

Specifically, under Section 5, it is a deceptive practice for a Web site to misrepresent the reason for collecting data on a child's personal identifying information. For example, the Web site claims that the collection of information is to earn points to redeem a premium; however, in reality, the information will be used for another reason, one, which parents, may find objectionable. Section 5 also considers failure to disclose all the reasons for data collection or failure to display the reasons prominently as deceptive practice. In addition, an act or practice is unfair if the injury it causes, or is likely to cause, is substantial, not outweighed by other benefits, and not reasonably avoidable. A generic privacy statement for a Web site that markets to kids is shown in Figure 9–2.

PRIVACY POLICY

Reallybigtoys.com, LLC, a Delaware Limited Liability Company, has created this Privacy Statement to demonstrate our firm commitment to privacy. This statement outlines our information gathering and sharing practices for this Web site.

Information We Collect

When you order, we need to know your name, email address, mailing address, credit card number, and credit card expiration date. This information enables us to process and fill orders and to notify customers of order status.

If you participate in a contest or other promotional feature, we may ask for your name, address, and email address so we can administer the contest and notify winners. We know email addresses and other personally identifying data about visitors to this site only when voluntarily submitted or posted to us.

Figure 9–2. Generic Privacy Statement for a Kid's Web Site

When you complete an on-line survey, we ask for contact information (e.g., your email address) and, sometimes, demographic information (e.g., your age, zip code, and shopping habits). We use contact data from our surveys to send you information and to reach you if necessary. You can opt out of receiving future mailings from us.

How We Use the Information
We do not share any personally identifying data about our guests with anyone outside of Reallybigtoys.com, its parent, affiliates, subsidiaries, operating companies, and other related entities. Information about the activity of visitors to this site is provided automatically when you sign in. We use this information for internal purposes in an aggregate form. We maintain strict security over all the information you share with us and use this information to support your guest relationship with us and improve your shopping experience:

- We personalize your shopping experience by using your information on purchases to guide our future recommendations of items that might interest you. Only Reallybigtoys.com (or people working on behalf of Reallybigtoys.com) will send you these communications.
- We monitor user traffic patterns and site usage to help us develop the design and layout of our on-line store.
- We may use the information we collect to occasionally notify customers of important functionality modifications to the Web site, services, and special offers we think you'll find valuable.

You can opt out of receiving further marketing information at any time. Just tell us when you give us your personal information. Contact Us or call us at (888) BIG Toys.

Important Information About Privacy
You can maintain an on-line account on our site, consisting of your email address and a personal password. Your password is yours and should not be shared with anyone else. If, at any time, you want to change the email address and password we have on file for you, just visit the My Really Big Account page on the Web site.

What About Cookies?
Cookies are small pieces of information stored by your browser on your computer's hard drive. Cookies do not contain any personally identifying

Figure 9–2. (*Continued*)

information. Most web browsers automatically accept cookies, but you can usually change your browser to prevent that. A cookie lets you browse in the store, put items in your shopping cart, and return several days later to continue where you left off, with the items still in the cart. Cookies help us give you a better Web site, by letting us monitor what is working and what is not through Web site traffic analysis. Please be assured that accepting a cookie does not give us access to your computer or personal information under any circumstances.

Your Consent

By using our Web site, you agree that we may collect and use this information. If we change our privacy policy, we will post the changes on this page so you are always informed about what information we collect, how we use it, and under what circumstances we disclose it.

PARENTAL CONSENT POLICY

Children's Privacy—We are committed to protecting the online privacy of children. In accordance with the Children's Online Privacy Protection Act, we will not knowingly collect any personally identifiable information from children under the age of 13 without first obtaining parental consent.

Children Under the Age of 13: Important Notice—Prior to providing any personally identifiable information, either by placing an order for merchandise, setting up an ReallyBigToys account, entering a contest or sweepstakes, or participating in any other activity offered through our site, children under the age of 13 must have their Parent or Legal Guardian complete and return a Parental Consent Form by regular mail to Reallybigtoys.com, 1776 Liberty Blvd., Philadelphia, PA, 99999-9999, or by fax to (999) 999-9999. This consent form states that the Parent or Legal Guardian, by his or her signature, consents to the collection and transfer of the child's personally identifiable information provided. The Parent or Legal Guardian may revoke this consent by completing the Revocation of Parental Consent Form and sending it to the same address or fax number.

For orders placed by children under the age of 13 with parental consent, we will only collect and use information (e.g., email address, mailing address, payment method, and details) to process and fulfill orders and to provide notification of order status.

In the event children under the age of 13 are eligible, with parental consent, to participate in contests, sweepstakes or other activities offered through our site, we will only collect and use information (e.g., email address, mailing address, name, age) to the extent that it is necessary to

Figure 9–2. (*Continued*)

administer that specific activity. We will never require that a child disclose more information than is necessary to participate in an activity as a condition of participation.

Information collected pursuant to this section may also be used for internal review purposes in aggregate. We will not disclose information collected from children under the age of 13 to third parties unless indicated otherwise.

Please contact our Chief Operating Officer at COO@Reallybigtoys.com or call us at 999-999-help with any questions regarding our privacy policy or information we have collected pursuant to this section.

We encourage parents to monitor and supervise the online activities of their children and to consider using parental control tools available from online services and software manufacturers that help guarantee a kid-friendly online environment. These tools can prevent children from disclosing their name, address, and other personal information without parental permission.

We also remind parents to carefully review the privacy policies of all Web sites that their children visit, including those Web sites linking to or from our Web site. Any information provided to these Web sites will be subject to the privacy policy posted at that Web site. The fact that another Web site has established a link to or from our site is not an endorsement of that site's privacy policy by Reallybigtoys.com.

How We Protect Guest Information
When you place an order, access your account information, or send us personally identifying data, that information moves into a secure server. The "Secure Server Software" (SSL) encrypts all information you input before sending it, protecting your information from unauthorized access.

Figure 9–2. (*Continued*)

ENABLING USERS TO CHANGE DATA AND OPT OUT

Safe harbor principles require a Web site to provide the user with the option to change personal data. Both of the generic privacy statements shown in Figures 9–2 and 9–3 inform Web site users about the data collected at the site; they indicate what is done with the data as well as how the user can change or update personal data. Typically a user can go to a specific page on a Web site and access personal data by entering name or email address and a password.

In addition to ensuring that users can change, update, or correct personal data, safe harbor principles also require that people have the right to determine how data can be used. Safe harbor principles are designed for individuals to change their minds about how and when personal data about them can be used. This requires Web sites to provide users with the ability to opt out or opt into a variety of Web site features or marketing approaches. The generic privacy policies in Figures 9–1 and 9–2 both include instructions as to how individual users can control the use of their personal data.

Web sites that use cookies to follow and analyze consumer Web behavior are also faced with allowing users to opt out. Yahoo.com, a search engine that places advertisements on search results and log-in pages, has provided users a list of advertisers using their services. The Yahoo privacy page explains the Yahoo procedure for opting out of third-party ad servers. The policy states that "If you want to prevent a third-party ad server from sending and reading cookies on your computer, currently you must visit each ad network's Web site individually and opt out (if they offer this capability)." Yahoo provides a list of advertising companies that presently includes 24/7 Media, AdMonitor.net, Avenue A, Click Here, and DoubleClick.

Most of these companies make opting out of being tracked and targeted fairly easy for users. Generally speaking, the companies provide an explanation of how to opt out and then require users to read through at least two and sometimes as many as four pages before they are allowed to opt out. This is logical in that the advertisers and advertising service companies would prefer that people did not opt out. The typical language to convince people not to opt out of these kinds of situations is usually not forceful, but it does seem to lack any really convincing power. Figure 9–3 shows a typical opt-out approach for users who do not want cookies from an advertiser.

ASSURING PROPER USE OF DATA COLLECTED THROUGH WEB SITES

One of the most important things to do during the development and implementation of the privacy plan is to make sure that everything is consistent and that everyone in the organization is following the same guidelines. The weakest link in compliance is often the Web team. Web teams want to be a culture within themselves, and in many organizations they have succeeded in thwarting authority and becoming highly independent.

Opt-Out Option

SuperGiganticAds provides an opt-out option that replaces the anonymous SuperGiganticAds identification code in your browser cookie file with an "opt-out" tag. By doing this, the system can no longer recognize your computer as being unique. As a result, SuperGiganticAds is unable to associate you to any profile information.

Please note that SuperGiganticAds is designed to help companies offer you relevant content, ads, and services—without knowing who you are. By opting-out you may:

- Lose some benefits of a personalized Internet experience.
- Experience difficulties linking to a Web site when you click on an advertisement.
- View the same ad multiple times.
- View ads that are not geared to your interests.

NOTE: You must enable browser cookies and exit your browser for the opt&hyph;out cookie to take effect. The opt-out cookies will have the tag hdb7=**00000000000000000000000019009000.**

If you ever wish to reverse the Opt-Out procedure, simply click on the Opt Back In button below. This will delete your SuperGiganticAds Opt-Out cookie and cause SuperGiganticAds to treat you as a new user.

To Opt-Out Click Here

Figure 9–3. Typical Op-Out Option Language

The Web team usually does not ever get fully integrated into the rest of the organization, and this helps them to perpetuate their own culture.

To be in compliance with safe harbor principles, enterprises that collect personal data, including through a Web site, must take reasonable measures to assure that information is reliable for the intended use. Organizations must also make sure that they only process personal information for the purposes for which the information was originally collected. In doing so, an organization is responsible for assuring that information is accurate, complete, and current. In addition, safe harbor requires that organizations must manage how information is passed to third parties. This management means that organizations must assure that third-party uses of data are consistent with the original principles of notice and choice and that third parties take reasonable precautions to protect information from loss, misuse, unauthorized access, disclosure, alteration, and destruction. The Web development and maintenance team needs to be constantly reminded of these principles.

Some Web teams have gone to other extremes in dealing with privacy. Instead of being careless developers who jeopardize the privacy of the data collected on the Web site, they have claimed ownership of the data and the processes and have kept the rest of the organization from benefiting from using the data. The key point, and a difficult part of the organization's privacy maintenance and ecommerce management efforts, is getting the Web team in line and keeping it in line.

Strong management is the best way to manage the Web team and keep it compliant with all of the privacy rules and supportive of the organization. Too many Web teams were established as add-ons to the organization and were first placed in the organization in an ad hoc fashion. The developers should be in the centralized information technology department, where the quality of their work can best be evaluated and supervisors are capable of handling "tech" mentalities. Art, design, and marketing activities belong in their appropriate functional departments where professionals capable of dealing with them can also supervise them with their particular personality types.

The privacy task force or a relevant subcommittee should set comprehensive procedures for the distribution and dissemination of data collected through the Web site. Individuals in the organization must be given specific access to the Web site, and how they use the data must be evaluated. In addition, any affiliates or business partners that are linked to on the Web site, or that are in some manner tied into an electronic Internet-based supply chain system, must also be monitored for proper data usage. This includes fulfillment houses and services that the organization contracts with to package and ship orders for merchandise purchased over the Web site. It also includes organizations with which the enterprise may have some sort of advertising relationships or banners exchanges. Organizations that want to achieve safe harbor status must be very careful about how they build electronic relationships and with whom they build those relationships. The Web team must understand all of these potential problems and should not independently enter into relationships with other organizations or exchange access, exchange Web space, place code on Web pages, or link to other Web pages without management approval. To structure oversight on Web site changes, use the Web site change form in Figure 9–4.

The nature of the World Wide Web is complex and usually a Web site is cross-linked to and from many other Web sites. The enterprise should

WEB SITE MODIFICATION REPORT	
Date: _____	
Web site change (explain changes made to Web site).	Explain ways that the proposed changes could impact privacy protection.
If the proposed changes involve links to or from another Web site list the Web sites involved.	Web Team staff person responsible for report: _____ Date: _____
Privacy committee comments.	Management approval: Yes ____ No ____ Manager's signature: _____ Date: _____

Figure 9–4. Web Site Modification Report

record all the known affiliations and cross-links to and from its Web site. It should also carefully review for potential impact on privacy any marketing or advertising agreements that it has with other entities. Records on file should include signed agreements, management reviews, and Web team comments. In addition, the enterprise should evaluate potential privacy liability issues resulting from relationships with any linking or linked-to Web sites. Files should include all documents pertaining to a relationship with a summary report that is completed by the Web team supervisor and reviewed by the privacy committee. A sample for recording this information is shown in Figure 9–5.

MAINTAINING THE PRIVACY OF INDIVIDUALS WHO USE A WEB SITE

The various types of chat, bulletin board, community, or other participatory functions available to Web site users affect the level of privacy protection that the enterprise needs to provide to users who visit its Web site. The enterprise needs to clearly indicate to users what level of anonymity or exposure they have when using community functions of the Web site. This disclosure sets the tone and the parameters of the privacy contract between the Web site and the user. The level of privacy or anonymity that users are provided is most often determined by the nature of the Web site. Large sites like Yahoo or Planetout.com that provide community services provide high levels of anonymity. Smaller Web sites maintained by professional associations, schools, and universities, may, on the other hand, require that individuals fully identify themselves in order to take place in discussions or post messages to a user group. While the enterprise determines the level of anonymity provided on its Web site, the enterprise should clearly disclose the terms of user participation in activities supported on its Web site.

Anonymity is usually maintained through the use of screen names or *handles*. A Web site using this method allows the user to register and select a unique screen name to use when participating in community functions at the site. The challenge for the enterprise is to provide a process where the selection of a screen name and the creation of a user profile provide a desired level of anonymity and privacy for the type of people that visit and use its Web site. The combinations of subjects, types of participants, and level of anonymity are of course endless. The challenge is to match the people, community rules, and participation approach in a way that attracts users and makes them comfortable in what they are experiencing or achieving at the Web site.

WEB SITE LINKAGE/MARKETING REPORT

Date: _____

Web site linkage or cross-marketing effort (explain the relationship)	Explain ways that the linkage or marketing effort could impact privacy protection.
Privacy committee comments	Web team staff person responsible for report: _____ Management approval: Yes ____ No ____ Manager's signature: _____ Date: _____

Figure 9–5. Web Site Linkage and Marketing Report

PROTECTING DATA COMPILED BY WEB APPLICATIONS FROM OUTSIDE INTRUDERS

A new security threat can be created in the process of allowing users to change data and to opt out as required by safe harbor principles. More features and more interactive opportunities for users also mean more ways for hackers to enter the Web site. Safe harbor principles require that organizations take reasonable precautions to protect information from loss, misuse, unauthorized access, disclosure, alteration, and destruction. Thus Web sites must have added security to assure that only authorized people are getting access to data.

Web site security is often maintained through a combination of technologies, including firewalls, authentication systems, and password systems. The best way to determine whether a Web site is secure is to contract with a computer-security–consulting firm to test the security by conducting intrusion testing. Many Web sites are very vulnerable to skilled hackers, and intrusion testing is the only real way to determine how good security features are working. However, not all intrusions require super hacking skills. Many content- and feature-rich Web sites are just poorly constructed, and persistent intruders sometimes need only wander around the site to find weaknesses and access sensitive data. Intrusion testing teams are skilled in identifying such Web site construction weaknesses. If the enterprise's Web team indicates that the Web site is secure and fails to mention possible weaknesses or to explain how it has determined this security, then intrusion testing should be conducted.

MOVING FROM THE WEB SITE TO THE WEB

Managing privacy on the enterprise's Web site is certainly important, and the sample privacy policies and procedures presented in this chapter act as a guide for the privacy task force and department managers. The Internet and new models of ecommerce go way beyond just having a Web site. Enterprises that participate in supply chain systems or online marketplaces face another set of challenges in managing privacy. Those issues are covered in the next chapter.

10

ΠANAGING PRIVACY oN INTERNET SUPPLY CHAINS

One of the basic approaches to ecommerce is the establishment of relationships among organizations that are capable of providing specialized services, merchandise, markets, or core competencies. An ecommerce company then often offers one-stop shopping, order fulfillment, and shipping services. The company sponsoring the Web site generally does not offer the full array of services but instead contracts out to other companies to supply specific items and to handle packaging, billing, credit card clearance, or shipping services. The buyer actually has no real idea which company is supplying products or delivering the various services available through the Web merchant. Networks of companies that develop such relationships are often referred to as supply chains. These ecommerce practices are prevalent in both Internet-based business-to-business and business-to-consumer operations.

Using supply chain systems, a company that sells flowers over the Internet, for example, can take an order through a Web site and process the order through to the point of shipment without handling paper, making phone calls, or sending faxes. The supply chain, or fulfillment process, for flower sales starts when the order is placed and ends when the flowers are delivered to the intended addressee. The locations and systems could be in different states and even in different countries.

An enterprise that participates in supply chain systems as a consumer of goods or services may pass a customer's personal information on to suppliers or service companies in the process of a transaction. In this case, that enterprise is responsible for protecting the privacy of the data released during the business process. Providers of goods and services, in turn, are responsible for protecting the privacy of information that they are provided during the business process. This chapter covers the following areas related to policies and procedures that supply chain members need to implement in order to protect privacy:

- Implementing safe harbor principles that impact supply chain systems
- Participating in large supply chain systems
- Understanding the data flow in smaller supply chain systems
- Assuring proper use of data by supply chain members
- Monitoring supply chain partners
- Testing the privacy protection in the supply chain
- Taking action when privacy problems in the supply chain are suspected or detected

IMPLEMENTING SAFE HARBOR PRINCIPLES THAT IMPACT SUPPLY CHAIN SYSTEMS

Safe harbor requires organizations to make sure that they only process personal information for the purposes for which the information was originally collected. In doing so, those organizations are responsible for assuring that the information is accurate, complete, and current. In addition, safe harbor requires that organizations manage how information is passed to third parties to assure that third-party uses of data are consistent with the original principles of notice and choice. Organizations who pass data to third parties must also assure that third parties take reasonable precautions to protect data from loss, misuse, unauthorized access, disclosure, alteration, and destruction.

Safe harbor principles also require that enterprises disclose to Web site users, or customers in this case, what types of third parties the information will be disclosed to and how the information will be used. The information, discussed earlier, regarding the purchase of flowers over the Internet, goes through several systems and is possibly seen by dozens of people. To be fully compliant with safe harbor principles, the data flow should be explained to the customer prior to order processing.

As an alternative to meeting general safe harbor requirements, the receiving party must enter into a written agreement with the organization providing the information; this agreement must assure that the receiver will provide at least the same level of privacy protection as is required by relevant safe harbor principles. Such agreements should be executed in writing and considered legally binding. If this alternative is necessary, standardized language should be developed for all such agreements, and counsel should review the written agreement. Management staff of the organization receiving the data should sign the agreement, and the sending organizations should keep all documentation on file.

PARTICIPATING IN LARGE SUPPLY CHAIN SYSTEMS

Numerous large supply chain systems started to emerge in the late 1990s over the Internet. The automotive industry, the chemical industry, and many large conglomerates established supply chain systems. General Electric Corporation invested very heavily in developing a major business-to-business supply chain system that required participants to pay a $1,000 entry fee. Wal-Mart has required suppliers to use Wal-Mart-compliant software in order to sell to the giant retailer, and many other retailers have followed the example of Wal-Mart. Generally speaking, the biggest players in the large supply chain system have considerable investments at stake and recognize the need for privacy protection. The privacy task force, however, should continuously monitor the enterprise's participation in these large supply chain systems to assure that they are meeting safe harbor or other required standards for protecting privacy. Large supply chain systems all appear to support the concept of privacy, but actual adherence to safe harbor principles remains questionable. The following are some of the several concerns about these large supply chain systems and how privacy protection procedures work now and may work in the future:

- To what degree is privacy actually protected compared to the rhetoric and language of privacy protection?
- Are supply chain entrants evaluated or monitored, or is compliance implied based on agreeing to terms and conditions of participation?
- As the supply chain systems mature, will they give greater attention to privacy?
- Is the potential international nature of the supply chain systems a potential liability to privacy protection as entrants come from countries that are notorious for copyright violations or the support of fraudulent activities?
- If a large supply chain system runs into financial difficulties (as many dotcoms did during 2000), will admissions standards become more relaxed and thus enable noncompliant organizations to enter the chain?

- Could information that flows through the supply chain system become a pirated commodity?

The answers to these questions are of course somewhere in the future. However, regardless of the outcome of any of these potential problems, the participating organization that passes data on to another organization, which in turn compromises privacy, will still potentially face consequences under safe harbor principles. The privacy task force or the standing committee on privacy, whichever is active in an organization, should not take information privacy in large supply chain systems for granted. Enthusiasm for new business opportunities and methods should not outweigh the efforts to maintain privacy.

The same scrutiny exercised with individual business partners and internal practices should be applied to participation in large supply chains systems regardless of who sponsors such systems. Thorough documentation on supply chain privacy policies, requirements for participation, and the codes of contacts for participants should be kept on file. If this material is only available on a supply chain Web site, then it should be printed and filed with other documents relating to participation in the supply chain. This documentation could become exhibits in future legal actions or could be used when dealing with investigations by government agencies or when fighting off attacks from advocacy groups.

UNDERSTANDING THE DATA FLOW IN SMALLER SUPPLY CHAIN SYSTEMS

Many supply chain relationships are small and involve very few organizations. In these situations, the privacy task force should set requirements, conduct audits, and monitor compliance as if all the systems were internal to the enterprise. During the privacy-needs audit, all supply chain relationships should be inventoried and documented. In addition, supply chain members should be required to provide documentation on any changes they make in processes or new service providers brought into the chain. A supply chain partner profile should be created and kept on file in the standing privacy committee office. A sample supply chain management report is provided in Figure 10–1. The report is designed to provide a record of supply chain relationships and the status of privacy protection agreements in that relationship.

SUPPLY CHAIN PRIVACY MANAGEMENT REPORT

Date: _____

Internet supply chain relationship (explain the relationship)	Explain ways that the supply chain could impact privacy protection.
Safe harbor status of supply chain member	If supply chain member is not safe harbor compliant provide information on written agreements to protect privacy.
Privacy committee comments	Staff person responsible for report: _____ Management approval: Yes ____ No ____ Manager's signature: _____ Date: _____

Figure 10–1. Supply Chain Privacy Management Report

ASSURING PROPER USE OF DATA IN THE SUPPLY CHAIN

Comprehensive procedures should be set for the distribution and dissemination of data to any affiliates or business partners that are part of a supply chain or Extranet. Such affiliates include fulfillment houses and services that an organization contracts with to package and ship orders for merchandise purchased over the Web site. Organizations that want to achieve safe harbor status must be very careful about how they build electronic relationships with other enterprises, and they must carefully consider with whom they build those relationships. Each supply chain member should be asked to provide a comprehensive report on data usage and, if applicable, data flow to any additional parties. The supply chain member should update this report any time it makes a procedural change that impacts data flow. The privacy task force should audit the status of the data use and data flow at least annually to assure compliance. Figure 10–2 is a sample report that can be used to collect information on data usage and data flow from supply chain members.

Data should be collected from all supply chain members, even those with which the enterprise may not have a direct relationship. If a supplier or service company uses a subcontractor or another supplier or service company, the use of data by those organizations should be tracked and monitored. *The Supply Chain Member Data Usage and Flow Report* requires suppliers or service providers to disclose when data are passed to another organization. *The Supply Chain Privacy Management Report* and a disclosure statement should be completed on that organization to which information is disclosed. If the subcontractor passes data to another organization, a *Supply Chain Member Data Usage and Flow Report* should be completed and a disclosure statement should be required.

MONITORING SUPPLY CHAIN PARTNERS

Organizations that are tied into an Internet-based supply chain system must be monitored for proper data usage. The standing committee on privacy should conduct a regular review of supply chain partners and service providers. The review should include input from customer service departments, sales, marketing, and any other department that have contact with or knowledge of the supply chain member. The standing privacy committee should note any problems encountered with specific supply chain members and then notify appropriate managers of the problems.

SUPPLY CHAIN MEMBER DATA USAGE/FLOW REPORT Date: _____	
Internet supply chain relationship (explain the relationship)	Safe harbor status of supply chain member.
Explain how data used by supply chain member during the business process	List all other parties that data is passed onto during the business process.
Privacy committee comments	Staff person responsible for report: _____ Management approval: Yes _____ No _____ Manager's signature: _____ Date: _____

Figure 10–2. Supply Chain Member Data Usage and Flow Report

If the enterprise encounters a problem with a supply chain member, then that member should be informed of any problems or complaints. If the organization with the problem is a subcontractor to other supply chain members, then the original contractor should also be notified. No matter how much effort an organization puts forth to protect privacy, a supply chain member can cause as much damage and unwanted legal liability as poor internal privacy management. Notifying supply chain members that they will be monitored and held accountable for privacy violations will help to reinforce the seriousness of the issues.

The standing committee on privacy should also monitor the business and ownership status of companies that are sued in the supply chain process. Planners for Internet business should be aware by now that the ownership and corporate health of Internet-related or Internet-based companies can change in minutes. A supply chain member suddenly going out of business is certainly going to be inconvenient, and contingency plans are necessary. However, what could be more disastrous to privacy protection in the supply chain process than that failing company being acquired by competitors in a move toward vertical integration? At that very moment the privacy of data and potential key business intelligence may be at risk. Thus, the enterprise should have written agreements that cover privacy protection if such a circumstance arises; these agreements should be made with all supply chain members.

TESTING THE PRIVACY PROTECTION IN THE SUPPLY CHAIN

One way to test the privacy-management practices and compliance of supply chain members is to regularly create personalities or ghost accounts that place orders for merchandise or services fulfilled through the supply chain. This method was also recommended to test and evaluate internal procedures and practices. If an account is created and suddenly junk mail or marketing materials start arriving at that address, then, likely, somewhere in the supply chain, the names and account information of the ghost account have been compromised. While this testing method may not indicate which supply chain member is responsible for the misuse of data, it will help to identify that potential misuse is occurring somewhere in the chain.

Another way to test the data privacy is to shop for data from the supply chain members in a similar manner to how internal departments and staff were tested. The process is simple and straightforward. An individual with a phone number other than an internal phone number should call the supply chain members and attempt to buy list or other information. Several people within the organization of each supply chain member should be contacted over a period of time to see whether they will sell the information. In addition, these information-shopping tests should be conducted on a periodic basis because managers and staff in the supply chain organizations are likely to change over time.

All test results should be reported back to the standing privacy committee for review and recommendations to appropriate managers or departments. A sample Supply Chain Privacy-Testing Report is shown in Figure 10–3. The report provides space to identify the organization being tested and the nature of the business relationship with that organization. In addition, the nature of the test conducted, the results of the test, and recommendations for further testing procedures should also be reported.

TAKING ACTION WHEN SUPPLY CHAIN PROBLEMS ARE IDENTIFIED

The enterprise should respond very quickly if a test reveals a problem across the supply chain, or if specific organizations are found to be lax in protecting privacy. The enterprise should also take steps if a customer files a complaint about something that happened during the fulfillment process that may result in a privacy violation. Immediately ceasing business with a supplier or service provider in the supply chain can be a very inconvenient, if not an impossible action. To prevent an impossible situation, the enterprise should already have contingency plans for product or service delivery. Contingency planning makes good sense under any circumstances. The financial impact of business disruption can be devastating, and insurance companies are only starting to come to grips with Internet business. The enterprise should not depend on insurance companies to cover losses during a breakdown in the supply chain regardless of the reason for the breakdown. The contingency plan should be well conceived and should be tested annually to ensure that it is still viable.

Rapid change is the basic nature of many Internet companies. An organization could be confronted with changing suppliers or service providers for a multitude of reasons in the rapidly evolving realm of Internet business. In addition to potential privacy problems, business planners in companies using supply chains need to plan for bankruptcies, buyouts, mergers, and acquisitions of supply chain members. In the event that one of these circumstances arises, the enterprise should move very fast and may need to take actions, including, but not limited to, changing business partners.

SUPPLY CHAIN PRIVACY TESTING REPORT

Date: _____

Name and location of organization being tested	Explain the relationship with the organization being tested.
Explain the nature of the test	Explain test results.
Recommendations for further testing	Staff person responsible for report: _____ Date: _____

Figure 10–3. Supply Chain Privacy Testing Report

DEVELOPING A LONG-TERM MANAGEMENT PERSPECTIVE

Working to establish privacy policies and procedures requires considerable effort, and supply chain systems make the development and implementation of privacy policies even more complicated. However, the process of developing and implementing privacy policies and procedures is just the beginning of an ongoing process. The privacy task force needs to establish an infrastructure and process to manage privacy over the long-term. Guidelines for long-term privacy management are covered in the next chapter.

11

MANAGING PRIVACY EFFORTS OVER THE LONG-TERM

Organizations need to constantly evaluate evolving privacy needs. They need to consider the impact on data privacy during business expansion, mergers, or acquisitions. They need to also closely monitor new laws or government regulations that are enacted in any of the countries in which they conduct business. As government efforts intensify, more and more laws will likely be passed that could potentially affect what an organization needs to do to protect the privacy of information in its possession. The global nature of the Internet may well add extra layers of requirements as different countries grapple with regulating the electronic frontier. Laws and regulations will not only influence what an enterprise must do to protect privacy, but also what an enterprise must do to assure that business partners, distributors, and suppliers are compliant.

The privacy task force structure and task force members can have an ongoing role in assuring that an organization stays in compliance with a myriad of laws. The task force should evolve into a *standing privacy committee* that continues the work necessary to maintain privacy over a long period of time. In addition, the privacy task force can act as a clearinghouse for privacy information in an organization and can help to evaluate new technologies that aid in the maintenance of privacy. Really large organizations with thousands of employees may benefit from transforming the privacy task force into a privacy office or bureau. In smaller organizations, the privacy task force is probably the central privacy talent pool and can help guide the organization through the future. The privacy committee or the privacy office will need to deal with the following major areas for ongoing privacy management:

- Organizing for long-term privacy management
- Dealing with new situations such as business expansions or acquisitions
- Monitoring relevant privacy legislation
- Monitoring relevant privacy-related court cases
- Monitoring compliance with privacy policies
- Updating the privacy plan documents
- Becoming proactive as a lobbying force
- Looking for new ways to legally exploit data

ORGANIZING FOR LONG-TERM PRIVACY MANAGEMENT

The development and implementation of privacy policies and procedures is the first major step in dealing with privacy issues. But social conditions change and laws evolve over time. This means that all organizations need to deal with privacy as more than a one-time problem. Privacy management is an ongoing task and requires constant monitoring and reaction to new legislation and the outcomes of various court cases. Deciding the enterprise's best course of action in the long-term management of privacy depends on several factors, including the size and complexity of the enterprise and the type of businesses in which the enterprise is involved. The speed at which privacy requirements are changing in the business sectors in which the enterprise is involved is also a factor. Figure 11–1 shows the factors that influence the best course of action. Enterprises have two basic options when organizing for the long-term management of privacy issues:

1. Evolve the privacy task force into a standing privacy committee that is self-managing. This privacy committee monitors changing needs in privacy management and revises the privacy plan to meet changing conditions.
2. Establish a privacy office or a bureau within an existing division to monitor new requirements, and use the standing privacy committee as a policy body and implementation mechanism.

In option 1, the standing privacy committee has primary responsibility for ongoing management of privacy issues. If this choice is the most suitable, the organization should consider several factors. First, privacy management can be a time-consuming process, and committee chairs must plan on dedicating sufficient time to meet the demands of the task. Second, in

Enterprise Characteristics	Option 1	Option 2
Organizational approaches relevant to enterprise characteristics	Standing privacy committee with responsibility for ongoing management of privacy issues and implement new policies	Privacy office that works with a standing privacy committee to make policy decisions and support implementation
Enterprise size	Small to medium	Large to very large
Diversity of business activities	Single line of business	Multiple lines of business
Geographical disbursement	One or few locations	Multiple locations
Number of countries in which business is done	One or few countries	Multiple countries
Sensitivity of constituents towards privacy	Low sensitivity to privacy issues	Highly sensitive to privacy issues
Speed of changes in privacy laws impacting lines of business	Changes seldom occur	Changes occurring rapidly

Figure 11–1. Selecting the Organizational Approaches for Privacy Management

order to assure continuity, at least one person other than the chairperson should always be fully versed in the privacy plan and the privacy management process. Third, the privacy committee will continue to need administrative and clerical support just as the privacy task force did, and these needs must be planned for in advance.

In option 2 a privacy office monitors evolving needs and works with a privacy committee that makes policy decisions and supports implementation. If this choice is the most suitable, the organization should consider several different factors. First, the privacy office should be staffed with a mid-level manager to oversee operations and work with the privacy committee to coordinate activities and direct ongoing research. Second, the privacy office will also need one administrative or clerical person to maintain documentation and do basic research. Third, the privacy office needs to be trained on new requirements and procedures and should attend workshops or seminars to keep current on new and emerging issues.

HOW THE PRIVACY COMMITTEE SHOULD WORK

The privacy committee should have membership similar to that of the privacy task force. It should have a representative and an alternate from each major department and business unit. The privacy committee will not likely need as much research support from departmental privacy teams as the task force did when developing the privacy plan. The departments may benefit from maintaining a team structure when any monitoring or testing activity falls upon the department or when it has customer service or other external relationship responsibilities. The privacy committee should keep a regimented approach and have regular meetings, review monitoring reports, and update policies and procedures as required.

HOW THE PRIVACY OFFICE SHOULD WORK

If a privacy office or bureau is implemented, the role of the privacy committee will be a little different. The privacy committee should still review, monitor adherence to, and revise the privacy plan and procedures, but it will not have to be self-supporting in monitoring evolving security requirements or in performing administrative and clerical functions. The privacy office should be staffed appropriately to meet the needs of the privacy committee. In addition, the privacy office should be staffed with a research-savvy administrator or with a research assistant in order to facilitate the ongoing monitoring tasks of the privacy committee. The privacy office should also become the distribution point for new privacy-related information that comes into the organization and serve as the repository for all the privacy-related documents created by the privacy task force and the privacy committee.

DEALING WITH NEW SITUATIONS

One of the big challenges in managing privacy is that new situations are constantly arising. Laws and litigation can be monitored through the relatively straightforward process outlined in the next few sections. But new business situations, new business relationships, or specific privacy problems will need to be dealt with as they arise. Also, the variety of circumstances that must be addressed will likely constantly evolve. Department staff will address many of these circumstances by following the policies and procedures in the privacy plan documents. One of the primary purposes of the intensive training, as recommended in Chapter 8, is to equip employees with an understanding of what they should do when privacy issues arise. All employees *must* understand that they need to seek a manager's support in deciding what to do when the privacy plan does not address a circumstance. The manager can decide whether the circumstance should be sent to the privacy committee for review and perhaps for a policy decision. The privacy committee will be challenged to interpret the circumstance and determine whether it fits within the existing privacy policy framework or whether a new policy must be created.

MONITORING PRIVACY LEGISLATION

Every organization needs to devise a means by which it can methodically and routinely monitor privacy-related legislation that may affect operations and the use of information. Watching every piece of legislation in every state in the United States and every country in the world is extreme and will not yield a good return on investment. Once the privacy-needs audit is completed, the privacy task force will understand which type of laws and which regulatory agency have the most impact on the enterprise's privacy management. This knowledge can help to focus legislative monitoring activities in a manner that will be more cost effective. A sample form for tracking legislative activities is shown in Figure 11–2.

The privacy committee or the privacy office should allocate resources to monitor legislative activities. Completing monitoring reports can help

LEGISLATIVE MONITORING REPORT

Date: _____

Government Entity Considering Legislation	Bill Number and Name
Summary of Legislation	
Status of Legislation	Related Laws or Regulations
Expected Outcomes	Position of Lobbying Groups

Figure 11-2. Legislative Monitoring Report

the privacy committee plan for future activities as legislation nears enactment and also plan for future trends in regulatory requirements. Monitoring needs to be methodical, and results of monitoring activities should be recorded and reported back to the privacy committee. Files should be established for related types of legislation so the enterprise's privacy planners can trace the process and plot out potential lobbying activities.

ΠΟΝΙΤΟRING PRIVACY- RELATED COURT CASES

Just as every organization should devise a means by which it can methodically and routinely monitor privacy-related legislation, it should also monitor court cases that may affect operations and the use of information. Watching every court case, like watching every piece of legislation in every state in the United States and every country in the world, is extreme and will not yield a good return on investment. The privacy committee or privacy office should evaluate cases that go to court and then select those to follow. This process narrows the tasks of the staff responsible for monitoring court cases and also provides more meaningful analysis for the privacy committee.

The privacy committee or the privacy office should allocate resources to monitor relevant court cases. Completing monitoring reports can help the privacy committee plan for future activities as court cases unfold. Monitoring needs to be methodical, and results of monitoring activities should be recorded and reported back to the privacy committee. Files should be established for each court case being tracked. A sample form for tracking court cases is shown in Figure 11–3.

ΠΟΝΙΤΟRING COΠPLIANCE WITH PRIVACY POLICIES

One of the major roles that the privacy office or the privacy committee has is to monitor compliance within the organization. The privacy committee should evaluate plan implementation and conduct periodic testing similar to that done during the privacy-needs audit. The testing process can help to identify ongoing weaknesses, and results can be used to fine-tune the training process. In addition, complaints from customers or business partners need to be reviewed for accuracy and corrective action.

The privacy maintenance activities of business partners and distributors also need to be monitored. This should be approached using several

LITIGATION MONITORING REPORT

Date: _____

Court Hearing the Case	Docket Number, Plaintiff, and Defendant
Status of Case	Related Cases
Summary of Case	
Recommended Action	Comments
Recommended Enterprise Actions	Comments

Figure 11–3. Litigation Monitoring Report

different methods. The privacy committee should watch the media for coverage, especially negative coverage, of any business partner or distributor. It should also run soft tests on business partners and distributors to determine how they handle attempts to compromise privacy. In addition, the privacy committee should use some of the same soft testing approaches which were used during the development of the plan and when evaluating implementation. This testing approach differs from information security and procedures testing in that it is not designed to test specific elements or procedures, but rather to illustrate the practical consequences of having weakness in security that could result in compromised privacy. The privacy committee should also prepare for ongoing monitoring of the privacy issues and problems of business partners and distributors. Annual evaluations and testing should be performed on a regular basis.

UPDATING THE PRIVACY PLAN DOCUMENTS

The privacy plan documents and related procedures will need to be updated as laws change and as the privacy policy of the organization evolves. Changes in laws and shifts in business conditions related to privacy will likely continue to occur. The publishing approaches that are recommended in Chapter 8 are loose-leaf binding or HTML to publish documents on an enterprise Intranet. The privacy committee should approve each change in the same manner in which the privacy task force collectively evaluated privacy needs and developed the privacy plan. The committee should discuss, draft, revise, vote, and have a final review of the policy prior to publishing. Clerical staff will be required for the privacy committee to update the privacy plan.

BECOMING PROACTIVE AS A LOBBYING FORCE

Large organizations and even small niche enterprises should become actively involved in attempts to influence legislative actions. This can be done through specific actions on the part of the enterprise or through professional associations or special interest groups. Recognize that advocacy groups are constantly lobbying, and politicians always love to ride the wave of some American apple-pie movement. Privacy has been one of those topics that a politician can't lose by supporting. Just as in a company's internal decision-making process during privacy planning, politicians need to achieve a balance in perspectives if good legislation is going to emerge out of the political chaos that surrounds privacy issues. Direct lobbying is often not as effective as working through professional organizations or trade-related groups. However, educating legislators, especially at the state level, may be easier in small groups or one-on-one sessions.

As the privacy committee or privacy office staff monitors legislative actions, they should also note the attitudes and voting patterns of local legislators or congressional representatives. These politicians may be the easiest to influence because of the organization's constituency membership. The organization should not be shy about approaching legislators and discussing viewpoints on privacy legislation in general, as well as various aspects of specific legislation or regulations. Drastic positions should not be taken in writing because such material will likely be taken out of context and end up being a political liability. The best approach is to publicly advocate a balance between the privacy needs of the individuals and the nature of information and competitive business processes. The best analogy is that of laws to protect the environment, which have shifted from a pro-industrial and complex position, to a pro-environment position, and back to a middle ground of compromise. Now of course the environmentalists may disagree and take a position that modern societies are killing the environment and the government has sold out to big industry, but advocacy has far more to do with positions than it does with facts.

Looking for New Ways to Legally Exploit Data

As regulators and lawmakers clamp down on the use of information, many organizations stand to lose some of the economic benefits of one of their most precious assets—information. The privacy office or privacy committee needs to dedicate time and resources to exploring new avenues to exploit information without running into legal problems. Several alternatives are likely to emerge, including corporations establishing subsidiaries or wholly owned business entities to collect and manage information and handle marketing activities. Cross-marketing programs between affiliated companies are likely to take on new characteristics and could become more important to the long-term stability of groups of business partners. Some alternatives will emerge as industry standards, and others will be created on a proprietary basis.

A monitoring process should be established to help identify new practices and new ideas on how to get the most out of information without being investigated or sued for doing so. Members of the privacy committee and any staff assigned to privacy duties need to get in tune with the trends. As many new methods as possible should be explored and presented to the privacy committee for review and comment and then later distributed to appropriate managers for review.

TAKING CARE OF DETAILS

Managing privacy is an endless ongoing process. Staying on top of privacy issues will take far less effort once the long-term role of the privacy committee is solidified and continuous privacy management processes are put into place. However, attending to details is always required when managing privacy. The next several chapters cover, in detail, many areas of privacy management that organizations should attend to over time. Enterprise storage and information processing issues are addressed in Chapter 13. Protecting the privacy of corporate communications is addressed in Chapter 14. Dealing with problems that could arise when providing employee access to corporate systems with the business desktop, with the road warrior's laptop, and with remote workers is covered in Chapters 15 and 16.

12

PROTECTING THE PRIVACY OF ENTERPRISE STORAGE AND PROCESSING

As more and more enterprise data are distributed across the network, an approach to storage management and to processing privacy must be found that embraces the mainframe, open and proprietary midrange platforms, and PC local area networks. The objective of enterprise open storage, where data are independent of particular operating systems, must be addressed and planned for, despite the high proprietary content of many storage systems. This chapter examines the networked storage and processing privacy problems facing large enterprises, and it provides an authoritative update on the solutions available.

The emergence of the enterprise storage network (ESN) now offers a high-performance interconnect protection and privacy enhancement for storage subsystems. This option, which is being adopted by many of the leading vendors, adds to the many data protection and privacy-enhancing technologies that the data storage manager must consider. The range and complexity of the privacy protection options is expanding almost as fast as the demand for storage. This chapter shows the enterprise's data storage manager how to sort through the privacy protection options (via a checklist) and make the right decisions.

PROTECTING PRIVACY IN THE DATA CENTER

Controlling access benefits an enterprise's data center, which provides and collects information. Controls should be applied over those data center employees, as well as employees within a customer site, who may have access to certain data systems. And, restrictions should be imposed on the uses of attendant data.

So, how should the data center manager respond to the privacy protection issues in an enterprise's data center operations? The following data protection and privacy checklist (see Table 12–1) should be prepared for the data center employees who are responsible for the creation, maintenance, use, and storage of the enterprise's data records that are of a personal or proprietary nature. Such records may include papers, registers, files, documents, photographs, or other data stored in hard copy or electronic form.

Data Protection and Privacy Principles

When completing the *Data Protection and Privacy Checklist for Data Center Operations* (as shown in Table 12–1), the data center's staff members should adhere to the following principles endorsed by the enterprise's privacy committee:

1. *Collection of Data Must Be Lawful and Fair:* Personal and/or proprietary data should only be collected for a lawful purpose directly related to a function or activity of the enterprise.
2. *Informed Consent:* Personal and/or proprietary data should normally be solicited directly from the individual and/or enterprise concerned. At the time the data are collected, the individual or enterprise should be advised that the data are being collected, whether provision of the data is compulsory, and what other parties will have access to the data.
3. *Data Quality:* Enterprises should take reasonable steps to ensure that the personal and proprietary data collected are relevant, accurate, up-to-date, and complete and that they do not intrude to an unreasonable extent upon the personal and/or proprietary affairs of the individual and/or enterprise concerned.
4. *Data Security:* Enterprises should ensure that personal and/or proprietary data are protected by appropriate security safeguards from loss, unauthorized access, and misuse.
5. *Openness:* Any person has a right to know whether an enterprise holds personal or proprietary data and, if so,
   - the nature and source of the data,
   - the main purpose for which the data are used,
   - the classes of persons about whom the data are kept,

DATA CENTER OPERATIONS
Data Protection and Privacy Checklist Form

Date: _____

The Data Center Staff Responsible for Such Information Held by the Enterprise Should Ensure the Following (Check All Tasks Completed):

____ 1. That any personal and/or proprietary data collected by data center staff members or with their authority is done so for a purpose that is lawful and directly related to the function of the enterprise.

____ 2. That any personal and/or proprietary data that the data center staff is seeking should normally be sought directly from the individual or individuals concerned. At the time the data is collected, the individual or individuals concerned should be advised that it is being collected, whether provision of the data is compulsory, and what other parties if any will have access to it.

____ 3. That personal and/or proprietary data to which data center staff have access are not used for a purpose other than that for which it was collected.

____ 4. That personal and/or proprietary data in the data center's possession or control are protected by such security safeguards as it is reasonable in the circumstances to take, against loss, unauthorized access and/or use, modification or disclosure, and against other misuse.

____ 5. When the data is relied on for enterprise purposes, reasonable steps should be taken to ensure that the data are relevant, accurate, up-to-date, and complete.

____ 6. Requests from external persons and/or organizations for access to personal and/or proprietary data held by the enterprise should normally be denied. In particular, personal addresses and telephone numbers of data center staff and all enterprise employees should not be provided unless authorized in writing by the particular employee or staff member, or unless it is permitted or required by law, for example, to police with warrants and to parties as directed by subpoenas.

Table 12–1. Data Center Operations Data Protection and Privacy Checklist Form

- the period for which the data are kept,
- the persons who are entitled to have access to the data, and
- how to obtain access to the data.

1. *Access:*   A person has a right of access to personal and proprietary data held by an enterprise, subject to exceptions provided in the Freedom of Information Act (FOIA) or other relevant law. For example, while the FOIA does cover all government agencies, there are nine exemptions under which documents can be denied. The one the government has the greatest latitude with is the first exemption, the national security exemption. In addition, a second exemption, called the statutory exemption, limits disclosure of material related to the National Security Agency, America's electronic eavesdropping agency. Under the national security exemption, the government does not even have to inform a requester if such documents exist, let alone their descriptions or details. The exemption covers all sorts of national security issues, including operations, foreign government information, sources, and methods of gathering intelligence, whether they are electronic or human.

2. *Correction of Records:*   Enterprises should make any necessary corrections, deletions, and additions to personal and proprietary data to ensure that they are accurate, up-to-date, and complete. Enterprises should, on request, add any reasonable statement a person wishes to see included in his or her record. Other recipients of the data should be informed about corrections.

3. *Ensuring Data Quality before Use:*   Enterprises should take reasonable steps to ensure that data are relevant, accurate, up-to-date, and complete before use.

4. *Using Personal and/or Proprietary Data:* Enterprises should not use personal and/or proprietary data for purposes other than for which collected except with the consent of the person, to prevent a serious threat to a person's life or health, or as required or authorized by law.

5. *Disclosing Personal and/or Proprietary Data:*   Enterprises should not disclose personal or proprietary data to other parties except with the consent of the person, to prevent a serious threat to a person's life or health, or as required or authorized by law.

6. The recipient of the data can only use the information for the purpose for which it is disclosed.

7. *Sensitive Personal Data:*   Notwithstanding principles 9 and 10, data relating to ethnic origin, political opinions, religious or philosophi-

cal beliefs, trade union membership, health, or sexual life should not be used or disclosed by an enterprise without the express written consent, freely given, of the individual and/or enterprise concerned. Criminal history data may only be used and disclosed in accordance with the guidelines endorsed by the enterprise's privacy committee.

ENSURING SECURITY IN ENTERPRISE APPLICATIONS

Privacy versus *security* in enterprise applications is a key topic in enterprise security issues. The widely covered denial of service attacks as well as email viruses have helped raise the visibility of security issues overall. However, privacy and security are really separate issues when it comes to enterprise application management. Privacy is an enterprise-to-consumer issue. More stringent and comprehensive security is required for enterprise-to-enterprise and enterprise information technology.

What's the difference between privacy and enterprise security? A lot of media attention has been given recently to the issue of online privacy, and rightly so. With the proliferation of the Internet and more consumers making purchases online, consumers need to know their privacy rights. In general, privacy involves capturing an individual's personal data.

For example, a 1999 Media Metrix survey revealed that 93.9 percent of Web sites are gathering some type of personal data (name, email address, or postal address) and 57.9 percent are gathering demographic information (gender, preferences, etc.). This has both business and consumer implications. On the enterprise side, this information is worth a lot of money because enterprises engaging in ecommerce can use it to better serve customers, to exchange data with affiliate sites, to better target marketing to customers, and to ultimately drive revenue. Likewise, as the *portal* market continues to proliferate, ebusinesses are gathering even more detailed information about consumer interest, identity, and personal preferences in order to personalize the type of data delivered to a specific individual.

In the United States, the Federal Trade Commission (FTC) has supported a self-regulation approach to privacy issues. However, in a recent survey, the FTC found that only approximately 21 percent of Web sites are meeting FTC standards for protecting consumer privacy. Because of this, the FTC may be recommending that Congress begin to impose rules regulating Internet privacy.

Enterprise security of applications, on the other hand, has to do with a couple of major issues. In the online world, enterprise-to-enterprise transactions involve much more money than an average consumer purchase. Additionally, if a consumer purchases a book from Amazon.com, for example, and uses his or her VISA credit card, most unauthorized purchases have a liability limit of approximately $50.00. This means that VISA (the enterprise) is ultimately responsible for covering what might amount to a large debt that was incurred illegally.

In addition, enterprise applications are of tremendous value and therefore require much more stringent security measures. For example, IBM conducted a research project to calculate the amount of data available in the world. Their research showed that there is approximately 3.6 billion gigabytes of data stored in computer devices on this planet. Now that's a lot of data! From that number, however, 60 million gigabytes of data are stored in strategic enterprise databases. These would be IBM databases, Oracle databases, Microsoft, etc. The market capitalization for those enterprises—and hence, the value of the data—is estimated at $600 billion. The value of enterprise data is staggering. As reported by the recent CSI *Computer Crime and Security Survey,* 43 percent of companies surveyed have calculated the average annual total financial losses due to computer crime to be in excess of $376 million. Enterprises can't afford not to pay strict attention to enterprise computer and application crime.

Identity Theft

Identity theft is also a concern to enterprises conducting ebusiness. As identity becomes more digital, criminals can more rapidly reproduce and take on the identities of others. The Secret Service and private organizations like Citicorp are joining efforts to combat this problem. Strong authentication, especially in an enterprise setting, is critical to preventing identity theft.

So, what should enterprises be doing to protect their valuable data and applications? Because the strategic value of applications in an enterprise is really incalculable, layers of security measures should be in place in order to protect critical assets. Static passwords (far and away the most common security precaution) and firewalls are only preliminary precautions to enterprise security breaches.

To begin with, only strong user authentication, encryption, and access control—where the user must prove his or her identity—provide the level of security that most enterprises would find acceptable. Strong user authentication systems provide protection from both external and internal attacks and can work with passwords and firewalls to provide a much broader form of protection.

ENHANCED TECHNICAL SECURITY INITIATIVES IN ENTERPRISE APPLICATIONS

Technologies designed to protect the data of government and enterprises have effectively deprived private individuals of the power to control their personal information. In addition to facilitating the collection of detailed personal data, enhanced communication technologies have enabled collectors to share data among themselves for a wide range of enterprise applications. Moreover, enhanced security technologies have enabled collection, sharing, and distribution of personal and proprietary data without the knowledge or consent of online users.

Today, most online privacy protection (if it exists at all) takes the form of a lengthy privacy policy. Although these notices purport to protect sensitive private data, many of them contain fine-print provisions that explain how data are, in fact, disclosed and used for other purposes.

Yet enhanced privacy technology can be designed to empower users to make decisions about the collection, use, and disclosure of personal information every time they go online. Some tools developed to protect privacy by cloaking data are likely to reveal identity or to decouple this identity information from the individual's actions and communications. Enhanced privacy technologies, for example, may conceal a user's identity by obfuscating the originator and recipient of a message from points in the enterprise's storage network. Other technical tools allow individuals to browse the World Wide Web without revealing one's identity and to purchase goods with the anonymity of cash.

NOTE: In the end, strong encryption is the backbone of technological protections for privacy. The following section briefly examines the major technical privacy and security concepts and initiatives Platform for Privacy Preferences Project (P3P)

On June 21, 2000, major Internet companies offered the first public demonstration of a new generation of Web-browsing software designed to give users more control over their online personal data and applications. The new products are based on the Platform for Privacy Preferences Project (P3P), a set of software-writing guidelines developed by the World Wide Web Consortium (W3C), the standard-setting body for the Web.

P3P is designed to provide Internet users with a clear understanding of how personal data will be used by a particular Web site. Web site operators will be able to use the P3P language to explain their privacy practices to visitors. Users will be able to configure their browsers or other software tools to provide notifications about whether Web site privacy policies match their preferences. Parents will also be able to set privacy rules that govern their children's activities online. Once Web sites and Internet users can better communicate about privacy, consumers and enterprises will be able to make better judgments about which Web sites respect their privacy concerns.

Proxies and Firewalls

As previously explained, proxies and firewalls are barriers between a computer and the Internet. Communications are only allowed under certain circumstances, and certain types of enterprise communications can be blocked entirely (see Chapter 13, *Protecting the Privacy of Corporate Communications*, for more information). The two main types of barriers are third-party proxies (such as *The Anonymizer* service, described in the next section) and software loaded on the user's computer.

The proxy computer can be set up to block communications such as cookies, junk email, Java, ad banners, the types of communications used by intruders attempting to hack into computers, and others. Several software products allow enterprises to set up personal firewalls that depend on their preferences. For example, an enterprise may set up rules to block all cookies from a certain domain or to reject communications from a specified email server.

Anonymizers

The private sector has developed Internet tools that strip out personal data in order to protect user privacy. One such tool is *The Anonymizer* service, which allows an individual to browse the Internet using an intermediary to prevent unauthorized parties from gathering personal information.

Cookies

An Internet *cookie* is a unique piece of text that a browser saves and sends back to a Web server when an individual revisits a Web site. Cookies contain information such as log-in or registration data, online *shopping cart* selections, user preferences, and Web sites an individual has visited. A major Internet standards body, the Internet Engineering Task Force (IETF), is currently developing two standards of new guidelines for the appropriate use of cookies.

The IETF is considering two complementary *Internet drafts* that would encourage software makers to design cookies in ways that give users more control. These drafts, which lay out guidelines for the use of cookies, suggest that programmers should make sure that

- The user is aware that a cookie is being maintained and consents to it.
- At any time, the user has the ability to delete cookies associated with a Web visit.
- The data obtained about the user through the cookie are not disclosed to other parties without the user's explicit consent.
- Cookie data cannot contain sensitive information and cannot be used to obtain sensitive information that is not otherwise available to an eavesdropper.

EXTENDING PRIVACY PROTECTION TO BUSINESS UNIT APPLICATIONS

Debate over the capacity of self-regulation and market forces to adequately address privacy concerns of business unit applications is common in the privacy and consumer protection arenas. Advocates often take the position that self-regulation is inadequate due to both a lack of enforcement and the absence of legal redress to harmed individuals. Industry often takes the position that self-regulation results in workable, market-based solutions for business unit applications and also places minimal burdens on affected enterprises.

Numerous efforts at self-regulation have emerged, including TRUSTe, the Better Business Bureau's Online Privacy Program (BBBOnLine), and the Online Privacy Alliance. Perhaps more importantly for the long-term, a growing number of enterprises, under public and regulatory scrutiny, have begun incorporating privacy into their business unit applications and have been actually marketing their privacy sensitivity to the public.

PROTECTING DATA ON ENTERPRISE STORAGE NETWORKS

Increasingly, an enterprise's most important records are not *papers* in their data center, but *bytes* stored electronically and held by third parties at distant virtual locations for indefinite periods of time. The Internet and digital technology accelerate the collection of data about individuals' actions and enterprise communications. Enterprise communications, rather than disappearing, are captured and stored on networks as well as on servers controlled by third parties. With the rise of enterprise storage networks and the reduction of physical boundaries for privacy, enterprises must ensure that privacy protections apply regardless of where data are stored. Under the current privacy laws, essentially four legal regimes govern access to electronic data on enterprise storage networks:

1. The traditional Fourth Amendment standard for records stored on an individual's hard drive or floppy disks
2. The Title III-Electronic Communications Privacy Act standard for records in transmission
3. The standard for enterprise records held by third parties. These records are available on a mere subpoena to the third party and with no notice to the individual subject of the record
4. For records stored on a remote server (such as a research paper), or on a university server (such as the diary of a student), or on an employer's server (such as an employee's personal correspondence), the scope of current laws is probably unclear

The third and fourth categories of records are expanding as transactional data collected in the private sector grows and as people find storing records remotely more convenient. The legal ambiguity and lack of strong legal protection for these records is, therefore, growing more significant and poses grave threats to privacy in the digital enterprise storage network environment.

Personal records—records of an individual's reading habits, that individual's online browsing, and all the details of that individual's life that are left behind online and in electronic commerce—should not be treated as mere *business records* available without that individual's knowledge or permission, even at the government's request. For even the most mundane of records can harbor risks and threats to privacy. For example, a couple of years ago, Drug Enforcement Administration (DEA) officials were reviewing records of grocery store purchasing data collected to support *frequent shopper* or loyalty programs. What would DEA officials possibly hope to uncover? According to DEA officials, they were seeking to identify purchasers of large numbers of small plastic bags and baking powder—common grocery supplies used by drug dealers to dilute and package cocaine and other drugs. As businesses intensify their data collection efforts, business managers must take steps to strengthen the privacy protections afforded this information.

Sometimes the equation is flipped; the government has collected the information and the private sector seeks access to it. During the lawsuit brought by several states (including Massachusetts) against the tobacco industry for repayment of state health care costs for smoking-related illnesses, lawyers for the tobacco industry sought access to a Massachusetts database containing records on every hospital visit by every person in the entire state population. While the purpose for collecting the data was to compare what it paid for health care to private insurers, Massachusetts failed to enact privacy protections to limit access to the database. Because the state's argument for repayment was premised on its ability to prove damage to state residents from tobacco products, the tobacco companies wanted to see the data supporting it. Massachusetts acted responsibly, hiring a team of cryptographers to ensure that the data released wouldn't identify individuals; however, the fact remains that the information was not protected by law.

Even enterprise storage networks are vulnerable under today's law. Under the existing legal framework, the same email message would be afforded different privacy protections depending on where and when it was sought: while on the individual's computer; while in transmission; when unread in storage for less than 180 days; or when read, but left on the service provider's server. The differences in protection afforded email depending on whether it is captured in transmission, accessed in storage while unread, or accessed in storage after it has been read, seem unwarranted for the communication. Also, individuals' expectations of privacy remain the same regardless of how the email is captured. In an era where email is more commonly accessed as a stored record than through an interception, the concepts developed for governmental access to paper-based records are an ill fit for access to electronic data in enterprise storage networks and subsequently provide weak protections for individual privacy. The framework for electronic access should reflect individuals' expectations.

PROTECTING PRIVACY IN DATA-WAREHOUSING APPLICATIONS

Financial institutions are using computer systems to gather more information than ever, and they are using it in new ways, activities that suggest that the nature of these institutions may be undergoing a fundamental change with dire consequences for consumer privacy. The traditional banker lived in a culture that valued the confidentiality of customers' financial information. Now, however, banks are hiring people who specialize in target marketing to efficiently market services through *data-mining* and *data-warehousing applications*. These terms refer to software systems that produce a rich harvest of consumer information that allows marketers to concentrate on those who are most likely to buy a product. These systems also produce customer profiles based not only on traditional data (such as information from consumer applications and transactions), but also on lifestyle, demographic, and psychographic data (both actual and implied) that are usually purchased from third-party database sources and then overlaid into the bank's customer marketing databases. By using customer profiles, the bank can most effectively appeal to targeted customers.

In other words, the real value of data warehousing applications in the financial industry, most experts agree, is its capacity for analyzing customer behavior and tailoring marketing strategies appropriately. Data warehousing applications are, therefore, essential in digging deeper to understand and potentially even predict a customer's behavior. Nevertheless, because enterprises are just beginning to collect a massive amount of data, they have to be very conscious about how to ensure the privacy of data they collect.

Privacy in Data-Mining Applications

As previously explained, information is one of the most important assets of enterprises, governments, and research institutions. It is now possible to have fast access; to correlate data stored in independent and distant databases; to analyze and visualize data online; and to use data-mining tools (see the sidebar, "Privacy Threats from Data Mining") for automatic and semiautomatic exploration and pattern discovery.

Privacy Threats from Data Mining

Privacy watchdogs across the country want businesses to offer their customers a bigger say in how information about them is *mined* from computer databases. Data mining, a powerful high-tech technique that can be used to sift through personal data to look for spending patterns and relationships, has become one of the hottest trends in marketing.

Data mining represents a major challenge to privacy because the companies who practice data mining cannot predict what uses the resulting information will have. Informational privacy hinges on companies telling their customers how their personal data will or may be used, but data mining offers few certainties in this area.

The collection of vast amounts of data makes data mining possible and attractive to business. Virtually everything someone does (withdrawing cash from a bank machine, paying with a debit card, renting a video, buying a plane ticket, filing an insurance claim) gets added to a database.

By one estimate, the amount of data in the world doubles every 19 months. The size and number of databases are increasing even faster. Data mining allows businesses with the proper computer software to pull together seemingly unrelated pieces of data from different databases to unearth spending patterns that can help make them better marketers. But putting bits of data together like a puzzle can also reveal a great deal about individuals. Businesses can use data mining to create profiles of the type of person most likely to buy a product. Scanning various databases can then create a list of people who match the profile.

Data mining showed U.S. marketers, for example, that fathers who buy diapers often pick up beer at the same time. The link prompted some stores to stock the seemingly unrelated items on the same aisle so even more dads would reach for a six-pack.

Home Depot adds other customer information (postal codes and the customer's sex and approximate age) to its sales transaction database with an eye to boosting sales. And MasterCard International sells its data warehouse of cardholder transactions to business partners.

Some data-mining connections have ended up with adverse consequences. For example, one database shows that a man who usually buys diapers and family staples like milk and carrots has suddenly purchased wine, oysters, and caviar. Another database shows that, at the same time, his wife has purchased an airline ticket for a business trip. Putting the two bits of information together might suggest infidelity,

The point isn't that someone is really going to be doing detective work on an individual. However, this type of data could reveal more about someone than that person may be aware of or would be willing to share.

The disconcerting thing about data mining is the disclosure of data about someone—the disclosure about larger portions of that person's life as gleaned from relatively innocent, simple data that on the surface appears to have no value or interest to anyone.

Many privacy watchdogs would like to see companies allow customers to say yes or no to the use of their data for data mining. However, some privacy watchdogs don't think that would be helpful because most people don't know what data mining is (a real lame reason not to disclose). Businesses have to act responsibly and adopt a code of fair data practices when dealing with personal data. That extends to and includes data mining.

Data mining creates a thorny privacy issue for business: How does one ask for permission to use data in a certain way when one hasn't yet thought of how that data will be used?

One suggestion is that consumers could be given various choices—not having their data mined at all, only having the data mined in-house, or not having the data mined by other companies. Therefore, consumers should ask how their personal data will be used and ask to see a business's privacy policy.

Knowledge Discovery and Data Mining (KDDM) is an umbrella term describing techniques for extracting information from data and suggesting patterns in very large databases. With the expansion of computer technology, huge volumes of detailed personal data are now regularly collected and analyzed by marketing applications using KDDM techniques. KDDM is also being used in other domains where privacy issues are very delicate. The FBI applied KDDM techniques to analyze crime data and reduce possibilities during investigations into the Oklahoma City bombing, the Unibomber case, and many other crimes. Another example is the application of KDDM for analyzing medical data. While KDDM has many beneficial applications to these domains, individuals easily imagine the potential damage caused by unauthorized disclosure of financial or medical records.

The balance between privacy and the need to explore large volumes of data for pattern discovery is a matter of concern. With that in mind, let's look at three views on privacy: individuals, marketers, and university researchers.

Individuals

Where did you get my name and why? Knowledge discovery in databases that contain personal information has recently become a focus of public attention. For example, in 1989, the Californian Department of Motor Vehicles earned over $17 million by selling the driver-license data of 20.6 million Californian residents. A certain Mr. Brado used this facility to obtain the home address of actress Rebecca Schaeffer, and killed her in her apartment. The sale of driver-license data ended after this tragedy.

In 1990, Lotus Development Corporation announced a release of a CD-ROM with the data on 100 million households in the United States. The information was so detailed that it generated strong public opposition, and Lotus abandoned the project. However, this mostly affected small enterprise, as large enterprises already had access and continued to use

Lotus data sets. At least 500 million credit records, 800 million annual drug records, 200 million medical records, and 700 million personal records are sold yearly in the United States by 300 superbureaus. Among the records sold are bank balances, rental histories, retail purchases, criminal records, unlisted phone numbers, and recent phone calls. When combined, this information provides individuals' data images that are sold to direct marketers, private individuals, investigators, and government agencies.

Surveys in the United States reveal growing concern about privacy. The newest Equifax-Harris Consumer Privacy Survey shows that over 80 percent of respondents (mostly consumers) are against unrestricted use of their medical data for research purposes. At least 89 percent believe that computer technology represents a threat to privacy and that the use of computers must be severely restricted in the future if privacy is to be preserved. At least 87 percent believe they have lost control over their personal data. Time, CNN, and other recent studies reveal that at least 94 percent of respondents believe companies selling personal data should obtain permission from individuals. By contrast, in 1970, Equifax-Harris found only 34 percent considered computer technology as a threat to their privacy.

Marketers
What's the big deal? Marketers often see privacy concerns as unnecessary and unreasonable. Privacy is an obstacle to understanding customers and to supplying better-fitted products.

The existing market of personal data postulates that the gathering institution owns the data. Nevertheless, the attitude of data collectors and marketers towards privacy is significantly more moderate than 20 years ago when marketers believed that there was too much privacy already. The reason for this change, apart from the fact that privacy is under a much bigger threat now, is probably the fear of losing the trust of customers and of gaining massive public opposition. Many data owners acknowledge that a Big Brother aspect in the exploitation of personal data sets, and some measures should be taken to preserve the customers' trust. Others imply that the sinister purpose of data mining is the product of junk science and journalistic excess, but nevertheless believe that marketers should take a proactive stance and work to diffuse the issue before it becomes a major problem.

University Researchers
How can university researchers carry out research based on facts? Researchers feel that privacy regulations enforce inconsistent restrictions on data exploration, and, in some cases, ruin the data.

Personal data are placed on large online networked databases, such as the Physician Computer Network in the United States, with the intent to build and expand knowledge. Data are necessary for informed decision making in the public and private sectors. How could planning decisions be made if census data were not collected? How could epidemics be understood if medical records were not analyzed? Individuals benefit from data collection efforts via the process of building knowledge that guides society. Simply restricting data collection or restricting the use of computer and networking technology cannot achieve the protection of privacy. However, scholars from diverse backgrounds in history, sociology, business, and political science have concluded that the existing privacy laws are far behind developments in information technology and do not protect privacy well. Only 25 countries have adopted, in varying degrees, the recent Organization for Economic Cooperation and Development (OECD) Principles on Data Collection. Twelve nations have adopted all OECD's principles in statutory law. Australia, Canada, New Zealand, and the United States do not protect personal data handled by private enterprises.

KDDM experts offer opposing opinions. Some believe that KDDM is not a threat to privacy since the derived knowledge is only about and from groups. Others who clearly oppose this view argue that KDDM deals mainly with huge amounts of microdata. Some fear different academic standards; statutory limitations that vary from country to country suggest that the practice varies from country to country. Europe has adopted the OECD directives, and investigators across all fields of scholarly research now require the subject's written consent in order to process data. The new privacy laws in Germany have dramatically reduced the number of variables in the census and the microcensus. Some think that subject approval may not be sufficient for data miners to refer or disclose incidentally discovered patterns.

Where do these views coincide? Today, individuals, marketers, and researchers concur that the protection of privacy is urgent. Individuals want recognition that they should have control over records containing information about them. Marketers want to avoid legal consequences, higher costs, and negative public reaction. Researchers want clarity and consistency in regulations. Eventually, a mutually agreeable privacy policy will emerge, but the mechanisms that could enforce it are unclear.

Privacy Issues in KDDM

In the context of KDDM, two privacy issues arise. First, KDDM poses a threat to privacy in the sense that discovered patterns classify individuals into categories and thus reveal confidential personal information with a certain probability. Moreover, such patterns may lead to a generation of stereotypes, raising very sensitive and controversial issues, especially if they involve attributes such as race, gender, or religion. An example is the debate about studies of intelligence across different races.

The second issue is that exploratory KDDM tools may correlate and disclose confidential, sensitive facts about individuals. For instance, a central task in KDDM is inductive learning. This takes as input a training data set and produces as output a model (called a classifier), which is then applied to new, unseen cases to predict some important and perhaps confidential attribute (for example, customer buying power or medical diagnosis). The *classifiers* are typically very accurate when applied to cases from the training set, and they can potentially be used to compromise the confidential properties of these cases.

Also, knowledge of totals and other similar facts about the training data may be correlated to facilitate compromising individual values, either with certainty or with a high probability. For example, consider a data set that has 20 people, including 4 females and 16 males. The data translate into 16 cases of disease A, where none of the females has disease A. If it is known that Mr. Jackson's information is part of the data, it is possible to infer that Mr. Jackson has disease A.

While Issue 1 in the preceding falls in the sociological, anthropological, and legal domain, Issue 2 is a technical issue. The technical problems were anticipated in the early 1980s, well before widespread acceptance of KDDM. Despite this fact, and the apparent interest in this issue as part of the enterprise and marketing community, little has been done in terms of finding a technical solution to the problem. Approaches for privacy in KDDM have only recently been considered. However, none have been applied seriously for KDDM. All the privacy protection methods proposed for KDDM are well known and applied in the context of statistical databases. Therefore, methods have been developed to guard against the disclosure of individual data while satisfying requests for aggregate statistical information. Removing identifiers such as names, addresses, telephone numbers, and social security numbers is a minimum requirement, but is insufficient to ensure privacy. Reidentification based on remaining fields may still be possible, and, if so, removing identifiers should never be used on its own. As a simple example, note that early geographical analysis of medical records replaced personal addresses by latitude and longitude coordinates. Today, electronic city maps allow individual homes to be identified.

Traditional methods in database security do not solve these problems; for example, KDDM may allow the identification of specific patterns that significantly narrow possibilities. Finding associations about buyers of milk near a needle-exchange program are the kinds of inferences that might point to an infringement of privacy.

The technical challenge is to provide security mechanisms for protecting the confidentiality of individual information that is used for knowledge discovery and data mining. More specifically, enterprises need to develop techniques for replacing original data with data that approximately exhibit the same general patterns, but conceal sensitive information. In addition, enterprises need to develop mechanisms that will enable data owners to choose an appropriate balance between privacy and precision in discovered patterns. That is, the new methods balance the level of privacy and the plausibility of generated hypotheses.

Such techniques and mechanisms can lead to new privacy control systems to convert a given data set into a new one in such a way as to preserve the general patterns from the original data set. This will allow for balance between privacy and the precision of general patterns.

RESPONDING TO PRIVACY ISSUES IN DISTRIBUTED APPLICATION DEVELOPMENT

Enterprises recognize a limited window of opportunity to ensure that open technologies and competing implementations continue to drive distributed application development toward more functionality and performance at lower cost. Now is the time for industry to ensure that consumers, enterprises, and governments will profit from the efficiency and effectiveness that can be achieved through an open, secure infrastructure for distributed application development. Delay could easily result in point solutions that are isolated and proprietary; serious divisions within the electronic marketplace; consumer confusion and distrust; very serious problems with security and privacy; and the loss of U.S. leadership in this economically critical technology.

Security and Payment

In a recent ecommerce industry survey, a majority of respondents fingered privacy as the main reason—above cost, ease of use, and the morass of unwanted marketing messages—that they're staying off the Net. Consumers need forms of electronic payment that they can understand and trust. Enterprises need secure and efficient distributed application development methods to reduce paperwork and enable the consumer to buy more things more quickly. Enterprises and consumers need forms of personal identification that are reliable and convenient.

Privacy

The consumer may want to limit the collection of detailed personal data such as buying habits and financial resources. The consumer may also want access to the personal data that have been collected, or may want to maintain a personal record and analysis of what personal data could have been collected. Consumers may also want the means to become more adept at hiding or manipulating personal data.

Thus, security and privacy services provide authentication of other parties, role-based access control, protection of privacy, assurance of data integrity, nonrepudiation of transactions, and assurance that mobile or shared objects have not been corrupted. Examples include cryptographic algorithms and their software or hardware implementations.

In other words, security and privacy services must be based on well-understood, reliable theory and efficient implementations. Security and privacy may be extremely important. As noted in the previous reference to the results of the industry survey, many consumers will participate in electronic commerce only if they are confident that personal data will be protected. Enterprises must have acceptable privacy policies and demonstrable technologies to ensure that they are enforced to protect distributed application development.

Distributed Application Development Research and Technology

Industry sees two areas for opportunities for major economic benefits from distributed application development investment: Public Key Infrastructure (PKI) and multiapplication smart cards.

PKI is needed to provide effective and efficient security and privacy for the development of distributed applications. Industry has good ideas for developing consortia and technologies that will provide the institutional and technical infrastructure for the following:

- Key management, certification, etc.
- Improving the efficiency of encoding and decoding large volumes of data
- Very large scale, cooperative demonstrations to ensure scalability, user confidence, etc.

Multiapplication smart cards can provide convenient, secure, and private services to support distributed applications like electronic billing; digital cash; role-based access control; access, manipulation, and storage of personal records on the Web; and, verification of identity. Very large scale, cooperative demonstrations will be needed to determine factors such as the following:

- Integration with existing or envisioned infrastructures (PKI, credit cards, debit cards, ATMs, cash, microcash, etc.)
- Appropriate identification of the owner (PIN, signature, biometrics, etc.)
- Determination of which applications are of most interest to users
- Assurance of user confidence and acceptance
- Assurance of scalability

Distributed application development could drive the unification and simplification of Web technologies. It could also make them more complex and dangerous if enterprises do not develop the proper technologies for evaluating and protecting data. Consumers could develop adverse reactions; they could reject an electronic marketplace that was too complex; they could (and should) develop a distrust of unevaluated data, unreliable payment mechanisms, and a loss of privacy.

Whether most enterprises are aware of it or not, and whether they like it or not, distributed application development is a limited reality today with great potential for tomorrow. A limited window of opportunity exists for developing simple, ubiquitous, and efficient distributed applications to technical or perceptual problems such as simplification of the user interface, security, and privacy. Advanced research programs and new technology providers will be very important in ensuring that enterprises develop interoperable technical solutions. The alternative is the development of proprietary point solutions that are globally inefficient and unreliable for both people and their information technology systems. Industry and government partnerships are particularly important to encourage the development of new technologies that may involve very high risk.

UNDERSTANDING INDUSTRY-SPECIFIC ISSUES

Why is the continuing development of information technologies that impinge on personal and proprietary privacy a continuing struggle in contemporary advanced industrial societies? One important line of explanation focuses upon changing social conditions in which many modern enterprises deal with enormous clienteles. Environmental factors such as social mobility and distributed computing improvements, however, cannot completely explain the diversity of surveillance technology used across industries and even between enterprises. Enterprises link the adoption, use, and impact of new distributed computer technologies for large-scale record keeping to a set of social practices they refer to as *data entrepreneurialism*. Data entrepreneurial explanations focus on the active attempts of coalitions within enterprises to organize enterprise production in a way that takes advantage of changes in society and information technology. The internal structure of enterprises has been transformed by the rise of professional management, who are trained and rewarded to pursue managerial strategies that depend upon data-intensive analysis techniques. This internal structure is an important institutional explanation of modern society's push to increase the surveillance of indirect social relationships. These data entrepreneurial practices are tied to key policy debates about the impact of distributed computing on privacy, with examples of commercial uses of surveillance technology that illustrate the ramifications of data entrepreneurialism for changes in public surveillance.

Finally, while this chapter showed the enterprise's data storage manager how to sort through the privacy enhancement protection options and make the right decisions, the next chapter outlines the issues that must be addressed in crafting a balanced policy for protection of critical corporate communications. Topics covered in the next chapter include, but are not limited to, vulnerabilities of the wired organization, Intranet security threats, vulnerabilities created by Extranets, email privacy and vulnerability, email attachment risk factors, privacy issues in data sharing with business partners, and privacy problems in global business data infrastructures.

13

PROTECTING THE PRIVACY OF CORPORATE COMMUNICATIONS

The vulnerability of critical corporate communications and the unique risks associated with networked computing have been recognized for some time. But the issue was given new urgency recently by recent cyberattacks on corporate communications privacy.

One of the more troublesome recommendations of the President's Commission on Critical Infrastructure Protection (PCCIP) was for the establishment of an early warning and response capability to protect government and private sector telecommunications networks against cyberattack. The PCCIP recommended that such a capability should include a means for near real-time monitoring of the telecommunications infrastructure, the ability to recognize and profile system anomalies associated with attacks, and the capability to trace, reroute, and isolate electronic signals that are determined to be associated with an attack.

Also, the PCCIP recommended the adoption of key recovery encryption in which decryption keys would be surreptitiously available to the government. Key recovery of this kind, which introduces vulnerability into computer security systems, had been opposed by privacy advocates and had achieved little acceptance in the marketplace. Just recently, the PCCIP substantially revised its encryption policy and has now ceased using the export laws to promote key recovery. Nonetheless, the PCCIP's embrace of key recovery illustrated how the critical infrastructure issue could become the vehicle for other agendas having nothing to do with infrastructure protection. In this case, the PCCIP was pushing its ongoing desire to guarantee the success of wiretapping and computer evidence seizures in investigations unrelated to critical corporate communications. Other proposals from the PCCIP included more intensive background checks of employees in critical infrastructures and the use of more secrecy to protect information about critical infrastructures from public disclosure.

This chapter outlines the issues (via checklists) that must be addressed in crafting a balanced policy for critical corporate communications protection. Let's begin the analysis by accepting two key premises—that the critical corporate communications identified by the government are vital and that they are subject to new vulnerabilities because of their reliance on cybersystems.

UNDERSTANDING THE VULNERABILITY OF THE WIRED ORGANIZATION

How would an act of terrorism affect an organization's foreign or domestic operations? A recent US. State Department report cites 644 deaths and 5,985 people injured in 2000 due to terrorist attacks. Anti–U.S. attacks accounted for one quarter of those incidents. Sixty-five percent of the attacks were directed against the wired business organization.

Protecting the Vulnerable Wired Organization

The preceding paragraph was not meant to scare the reader, but merely to wake up wired organizations, operating both domestic and internationally, to the reality that cyberattacks and violence operate hand-in hand. Cyberattacks with a "twist of violence" will be the status quo for the rest of this century. (See the sidebar, "Privacy and Physical Security for Corporate Communications.") Wired organizations must learn how to protect their corporate communications in order to keep up with the ever-increasing cyberterrorism that promises to bring down the critical infrastructure that is the foundation of the global free market society.

Privacy and Physical Security for Corporate Communications

Let's look at how physical security can support the security needs of corporate communications centers and data centers. A brief note about windows is in order:

Don't put windows in the corporate communications center (CCC) and data center. A computer room should not have outer walls, let alone windows. Windows are physically weak, with weak frames, and they allow people to see how an organization's CCC has laid out their equipment, including their security equipment.

Recently, for example, a security threat expert investigating a manufacturing company reported that a company's site had floor to ceiling windows in the computer console room. The expert looked through windows into the room and stared at a 5-meter banner on the wall. The banner had huge numbers printed on it. "That's not the main modem number, is it?" he asked. It was. So much for dial-in security!

If the Security Administrator (SA) cannot get approval to remove the windows in the computer room, the SA should install vertical blinds and keep them closed all the time. The SA should also install security glazing (shatterproof, metal-reinforced glass) and perhaps gratings securely attached to the walls. In addition, the SA should install breakage sensors and connect them to the building's main alarm system. Aim motion sensors and closed-circuit television cameras at the windows. Move equipment away from the windows, out of view. Install a few dummy security cameras and motion sensors just to keep spies and intruders guessing.

High-security sites do not permit windows in their CCCs and data centers for a couple of other reasons. Most obvious is that external windows offer opportunities for attacks on individuals. More subtly, windows vibrate when people talk; using laser interferometers, spies could measure those vibrations and reconstitute the sound waves. An exterior window provides an easy way for industrial or other spies to eavesdrop from another building. However, don't try to persuade the SA's top officials to give up their corner offices—some advice is just too unpleasant to bother presenting to upper management when the risks are low. Instead, the SA should suggest that an office with several windows is perhaps not the best place to discuss top-secret strategic plans. Discussing make-or-break information should be conducted in sealed rooms with no windows. The key is to be reasonable and not to apply security rules without thinking.

Protecting Important Corporate Communications Information

Many U.S. companies operating domestically and internationally are threatened daily by foreign information-collection efforts. The National Counterintelligence Center (NACIC) reports that U.S. industries have been the targets in most cases of economic espionage. Other foreign collection activities include biotechnology; aerospace; telecommunications; computer hardware and software, advanced transportation and engine technology; advanced materials and coatings; energy research; defense and armaments technology; manufacturing processes; and semiconductors. Foreign collectors target proprietary business information such as bid, contract, customer, and strategy information, as well as corporate financial and trade data.

Of all of the new information vulnerabilities facing U.S. companies domestically and internationally (see the sidebar, "Sources of Corporate Communications Threats"), corporate communication vulnerabilities appear to be the most significant. For example, the NACIC concluded that specialized technical operations (including computer intrusions, telecommunications targeting and intercept, and private-sector encryption weaknesses) account for the largest portion of economic and industrial information lost by U.S. corporations.

Sources of Corporate Communications Threats

Foreign intelligence operations target key U.S. businesses. For example, two former directors of the French intelligence service have confirmed publicly that the French intelligence service collects economic intelligence information, including classified government information and information related to or associated with specific companies of interest. Foreign intelligence agencies may break into facilities, such as the foreign offices of a U.S. company or the hotel suite of a U.S. executive, and copy computer files from within that facility. The files are usually copied from a laptop computer in a hotel room or from a desktop computer connected to a network in an office. Having attained such access to hardware as well, they can also insert malicious code that will enable future information theft.

For example, according to a report from the National Communications System, countries that currently have significant intelligence operations against the United States for national security or economic purposes include Russia, the People's Republic of China, Cuba, France, Taiwan, South Korea, India, Pakistan, Israel, Syria, Iran, Iraq, and Libya. All of the intelligence organizations of these countries have the capability to target telecommunications and information technology systems for information or clandestine attacks. The potential for exploitation of such systems may be significantly larger.

Another source of communications threat can occur from within an organization. A disgruntled or disloyal employee may collude with outside agents. Threats involving insiders are particularly pernicious because insiders are trusted with critical information that is not available to outsiders. Such information is generally necessary to understand the meaning of various data flows that may have been intercepted, even when those data flows are received in the clear. The threat from within was recently demonstrated by Wen Ho Lee, the former Los Alamos scientist allegedly accused of spying for the People's Republic of China.

Corporate communication (network) hackers and electronic vandals can cause destruction of intellectual property without the intent of theft. Cyberterrorists may threaten to bring down an information network unless certain demands are met; extortionists may threaten to bring down an information network unless a ransom is paid. Disgruntled customers seeking revenge on a company also fall into this category.

Thieves may also attempt to steal money or resources from businesses. Such individuals may be working for themselves or acting as part of a larger conspiracy (in association with organized crime). The spread of ecommerce will increase the opportunities for new and different types of fraud, as illustrated by the large increase in fraud seen as the result of increased electronic filing to the Internal Revenue Service. Even worse, customers traditionally regarded as the first line of defense against fraud (because they check their statements and alert the merchants or banks involved to problems) may become adversaries as they seek to deny a signature on a check or alter the amount of a transaction.

The prevalence of such threats is difficult to determine because many companies do not discuss for the record specific incidents of information theft. In some cases, they fear stockholder wrath and losses in customer confidence more than they fear security breaches; in others, they are afraid of inspiring copycat attacks or revealing security weaknesses. In still other cases, they simply do not know that they have been the victims of such theft.

Finally, only a patchwork of state laws applies to the theft of trade secrets and the like (and not all states have such laws). No federal statute protects trade secrets or addresses commercial information theft. Federal authorities probing the theft of commercial information must rely on proving violations of other statutes, such as wire and mail fraud laws, interstate transport of stolen property, conspiracy, or computer fraud and abuse laws. As a result, documentation of what would be a federal offense if such a law were present is necessarily spotty. For all of these reasons, what is known on the public record about economic losses from information theft almost certainly understates the true extent of the problem.

Because they are so easily accessed and intercepted, corporate telecommunications (particularly international telecommunications) provide a highly vulnerable and lucrative source for anyone interested in obtaining trade secrets or competitive information. Because of the increased usage of these links for bulk computer data transmission and email telecommunications intercepts are cost-effective for intelligence collectors. For example, foreign intelligence collectors intercept facsimile transmissions through government-owned telephone companies, and the stakes are large—approximately half of all overseas telecommunications are facsimile transmissions. Innovative hackers connected to computers containing competitive information evade the controls and access companies' information. In addition, many American companies have begun using electronic data interchange, a system of transferring corporate bidding, invoice, and pricing data electronically overseas. Many foreign governments and corporate intelligence collectors find this information invaluable.

Why is electronic information so vulnerable? The primary reason is that it is computer readable and thus much more vulnerable to automated search than are intercepted voice or postal mail transmissions. Once the information is collected (through an existing wiretap or a protocol analyzer on an Internet router), computers can relatively easily search streams of electronic information for word combinations of interest (e.g., *IBM*, *research*, and *superconductivity* in the same message). As the cost of computing drops, the cost of performing such searches drops. Therefore, at the root of this nongovernmental demand for security is the threat posed by automated search, coupled with the sensitivity of certain communications that are critical for nongovernmental users.

A Glimpse of Cyberterrorism

At first, the urgent phone call from the U.S. Transportation Department confounded Cheng Wang, a Long Island-based Webmaster for Falun Gong, the spiritual movement that has unnerved Chinese authorities. Why did the department think his computers were attacking theirs? The answer turned out to be startling. The electronic blitz hadn't come, as it seemed, from various Falun Gong Internet sites. Rather, someone had lifted his electronic identities. Computer sleuths followed a trail back to the XinAn Information Service Center in Beijing—where an operator identified it as part of the Ministry of Public Security, China's secret police.

Web hacking, it seems, isn't just for amateurs anymore. While the recent rash of cybervandalism against some of ecommerce's biggest names has garnered headlines, the vandalism is only part of the story. From Beijing to Baku, governments and their surrogates are using the Internet to harass political opponents and unfriendly neighbors, to go after trade secrets, and to prepare for outright warfare. Burma's military junta, for instance, is blamed for targeting the *Happy 99* email virus at opponents who use the

Net to advance their causes. Dissidents describe the attacks as inept proof, perhaps, that dictatorships are still behind the hacking curve.

Hack Attack

But Burma is not alone in trying. In January 2000, hackers from Azerbaijan with names like *The Green Revenge* and *Hijack* tampered with dozens of Armenian-related Web sites, including host computers in the United States. Experts suspect involvement or support from the Azerbaijani government, which imposes tight controls over Internet use within its borders. Relations are tense between Azerbaijan and Armenia, which fought a war over the disputed territory of Nagorno-Karabakh, so before long the Armenians retaliated in kind. It is the first precedent of a physical battle going online.

In Cheng Wang's case, his computers in Hauppauge, NY, were among Falun Gong sites around the world hit by a barrage of hacking attempts and email bombs with attachments that coincided with a physical crackdown on the group's practitioners in China. Several of the hacking incidents were traced to the mysterious XinAn office.

Tracking down who is to blame is often difficult. But for networked Americans, who own 46 percent of the world's computing capacity, such electronic conflict should be unsettling. True, the scariest scenarios dreamed up by experts, such as a hostile government disrupting financial markets, haven't come to pass yet. But more than a dozen countries—among them Russia, China, Iraq, Iran, and Cuba—are developing significant information-warfare capabilities. A senior CIA official cited a Russian general who compared the disruptive effects of a cyberattack on a transportation or electrical grid to those of a nuclear weapon. China is considering whether to create a fourth branch of its armed services devoted to information warfare with an estimated 30 million Chinese hackers. The Pentagon isn't sitting still either. Recently, the U.S. military's offensive cyberwarfare programs were consolidated at the U.S. Space Command in Colorado.

Nearly as worrisome as a cyberattack to experts is electronic espionage. From March 1998 until May 1999, intruders broke into computer systems belonging to the Pentagon, NASA (which has virtually no security or security monitoring to speak of), the Energy Department, and universities, making away with unclassified, but still sensitive, data. One of the worst computer security breaches in U.S. history, it spawned an investigation, named Moonlight Maze, which pointed to a Russian intelligence-gathering operation.

Successful cyberwar is likely to—have no exploding munitions to tell an organization it's under attack. Tapping into an adversary's command-

and-control system could yield a gold mine of data about enemy plans. The longer a cyberspy conceals his or her presence, the longer the intelligence flows. Or, false information about troop locations and battlefield conditions could be inserted into enemy computers, so that leaders would end up making decisions based on bogus information.

During the Kosovo bombing campaign in 1999, the Pentagon set up a high-level information-operations cell. All the tools were in place, according to an internal briefing prepared by Adm. James Ellis, NATO's No. 2 military commander during the war. But the United States mostly held back. By the time Pentagon lawyers approved cyberstrikes against Serbia, events had overtaken the need for them.

Double-Edged Sword

Cyberwar raises a host of unprecedented legal questions. The line between fair-game military sites and civilian infrastructure may not exist. There is collateral damage in cyberspace. If someone diddles with somebody's control mechanisms, how assured is anyone that it would stop right there? The United States, more dependent on corporate communications than anyone, might lose the most in legitimizing cyberwar. Some countries, including Russia, have proposed what might be called *electronic arms control*. But the obstacles are daunting: Verifying a treaty would make counting Russian nuclear missiles look easy.

Among the sites hacked in the Caucasus Web war was one belonging to the DC-based Armenian National Institute, which studies the 1915–1918 Turkish genocide of Armenians. Logging onto http://www.armenian-genocide.org in late January 1999, one would have been redirected to a site offering information on Azerbaijan's president.

The Austin, Texas–based InfoGlide Corp., which makes powerful search software for such uses as insurance-fraud investigations, has its own rules on these matters (see the sidebar, "Calling Tech Support! Calling Tech Support!"). The company will not license the technology to nine countries and three U.S. government agencies because of the potential for privacy abuse. That hasn't stopped at least one of those countries from trying. Two years ago, a company tried to buy rights to the technology. It turned out to be a front for the Chinese government.

Calling Tech Support! Calling Tech Support!

After years of surveillance, Tokyo police thought they'd seen everything about Aum Shinrikyo, the high-tech doomsday sect behind the 1995 nerve-gas attack on that city's subway system. But even the cops were surprised after raiding cult facilities recently and finding evidence that Aum had developed software programs for at least 20 government agencies, including the Defense Ministry, as well as some 90 Japanese firms. With their identities hidden behind a web of front companies and subcontractors, Aum engineers sold as many as 110 systems ranging from databases for clients to an Internet messaging service.

Although no evidence has yet emerged that Aum installed so-called *trapdoors* to secretly gain access to its clients' data, authorities have reason to worry. In the mid-1990s, sect members burglarized and stole secrets from Japan's top defense contractor and its top semiconductor maker—part of an extraordinary campaign to develop biological agents, laser guns, and other high-tech weapons. Until now, Japan has shown an almost unbelievably low sense of its need for cybersecurity. That may soon change.

NOTE: Solutions for coping with information-age vulnerabilities may well create new responsibilities for businesses. For example, businesses may have to ensure that the security measures they take are appropriate for the information they are protecting, and/or that the information they are protecting remains available for authorized use. Failure to discharge these responsibilities properly may result in a set of liabilities that these businesses currently do not face.

PROTECTING THE INTRANET FROM SECURITY THREATS

Most readers of this book are probably aware that an Intranet's security and privacy takes many forms. Security includes hardware, the location of the Intranet's physical components, antivirus software, firewalls, data encryption—even preparation for what to do in the event of a natural disaster. That list is only a representative sample of the concerns security administrators (SAs) must bear in mind every time they make a decision concerning the Intranets placed in their charge. Administering an Intranet is a difficult, time consuming, and challenging task on a good day. Wait until an organization's Intranet is affected by an event with a "negative outcome," the term used by people who want to obfuscate what they're really saying.

When the subject of Intranet security arises, most Information Technology (IT) managers and professionals seem to focus on sophisticated technology rather than good, solid IT management controls. IT management controls provide a great deal of protection. They are the foundation for productive use of more sophisticated technological controls.

Although the focus here is on Intranet security, clearly many of the concepts are drawn from a broader application of "security and privacy." First, though, what does *Intranet security* mean? Intranet security means protecting information assets from accidental or intentional—but unauthorized—disclosure, modification, or destruction, including temporary unavailability. This definition creates a broad range of concerns for IT management and the Intranet security and privacy specialists. Also, sensitivity to one of these threats does not imply sensitivity to the others. For example, information that would damage the organization if it were destroyed may or may not be at all sensitive to disclosure.

The publicity received by hackers and computer viruses has propelled the issue of protection of information on computers to public attention. Although this attention has been focused on the malicious external threat, the greater threat lies with mistakes. In other words, it lies with errors of omission and commission by employees whose honesty is not in question and who have authorized access to the information as part of their jobs.

The Risk Takers

Even with a realistic understanding of the threats—external or internal, deliberate or accidental—an enterprise still needs to know what actions to take and whether those actions are justified. Protection from threats involves risk, and evaluating that risk is a key first step in determining what action to take.

The following list of risks was originally based on a U.S. government study of government agencies conducted more than 14 years ago. No clear-cut recent data exist, so the range of percentages (representing monetary loss) are, of necessity, broad, although recent studies that address pieces of the list support the conclusions:

1. Errors and omissions are, first and foremost, estimated to be 60 percent to 85 percent of aggregate financial loss. Stressed, poorly trained, ill-supervised employees, even if honest, are clearly the primary concern.

2. Dishonest employees are next (26 percent to 41 percent). Accidental action benefiting an employee, frequently discovered through an error and undetected by IT management, can provide a great temptation. IT management controls put in place to detect and prevent errors and omissions can also serve to detect and prevent acts by the dishonest employee.

3. Fire and natural disasters account for 20 percent to 25 percent of aggregate financial loss.
4. Disgruntled employees, at about 10 percent to 25 percent, are fourth in priority.
5. Water, not directly from natural disasters, is less than 15 percent.
6. Other, which includes everything else, is 2 percent to 4 percent, according to some consultants. Consensus puts it at no more than 6 percent. This category covers external threats and strangers, including hackers.

The major threat, then, is from employees, whose honest mistakes not only cost the most, but are also the training ground for the dishonest and disgruntled. The stranger or hacker, frequently commanding great attention, is the lowest threat. Controls for errors, incidentally, usually control both the employee and the stranger. Of course, the threats for any specific organization can vary significantly from the preceding list, depending on the type of threat, the environment, and the nature of the applications and data.

The sequence or priority of the concerns is the important issue. It continues to be empirically validated by security professionals and consultants observing organizations over a broad spectrum of size and type.

As security controls are introduced, the aggregate cost of those controls, of course, rises. At the same time, the cost of expected losses logically decreases. The objective is to spend no more money on controls during a given period than would be expected in losses, had no action been taken. In dealing with risk, one is dealing with probabilities of occurrence. The lack of reported losses does not make predicting potential loss easy. Nonetheless, administrators should attempt to minimize the combined costs to those for expected losses and for the controls to be put in place.

The cost of controls, on the other hand, is somewhat easier to determine. Some basis for decision on expenditures is necessary, although *sleepability* (how comfortable one is with one's security given adequate knowledge about risks and controls) should not be totally discounted. Also, some estimating techniques are recommended here to introduce as much rationality and objectivity as possible. Due to lack of firm input data, more sophisticated mathematical approaches are probably not much more accurate overall and are certainly more expensive and time consuming. Three options are available for handling risk:

1. *Avoid it:* This is putting security controls in place. Most of what is discussed in this part of the chapter fits into this area. When con-

sidering the suggested approaches, SAs should keep in mind that those approaches should be measured against the attempt to minimize overall costs.

2. *Assign it to others:* This approach is usually insurance, such as business interruption insurance.

3. *Assume it:* If the expected cost of loss is lower than the cost to correct the exposure, taking no action is the lower cost alternative. SAs are cautioned to ensure that all potential costs, including things such as the embarrassment from bad publicity, have been considered before accepting the risk.

Organization and Policy

Naturally, Intranet security doesn't come about by accident. SAs have to plan for it, formulate an Intranet security policy, let everyone in the organization know what that policy is, and have the staff to enforce it. Also, to select the best security solution for the SA's particular environment, an organizationwide evaluation panel should make recommendations.

Formulating an Organizationwide Policy

After assessing risk, the SA's next step (and the single most important action the SA can take to begin an information security program) is formulating an organizationwide policy for protecting information. This policy should be signed by the chief executive officer and should apply to all employees. This policy not only sets direction and gives broad guidance, but it also demonstrates top-level executive support, which is crucial to further action across the organization. This policy should be short—one to four pages— and should be distributed to all operating units. Out of the policy will flow documents such as standards, guidelines, and procedures.

The policy should contain the organization's definition of information security. It should include a statement regarding applicability to all the organization's information, regardless of the media on which it resides. The policy should spell out the consequences of noncompliance. It should specify the requirement for ownership, classification of information, and the individual responsibilities of IT management, owners, suppliers of services (information technology), custodians, users, and security staff. The policy should not be technical, but should include broad statements regarding individual identification, password control, and access by least possible privilege.

Security Staff Function

The Intranet security officer (ISO) should have a coordination function. He or she should be responsible for guidance, assistance in audits and systems design, publishing security-related materials, and developing awareness programs. This staff function sometimes reports to a high-level IT manager who has responsibility across the entire organization. However, that approach is not usually appropriate. Many opinions exist regarding specific reporting. Some companies have successfully placed the function in areas such as audit, legal, or security. The IT function, of course, would have one or more people working in this specialty, at least part-time, but not for the entire enterprise. The responsibility for Intranet security, however, rests with line management, and the policy should state this clearly.

The Owner

The *owner*, a specific individual, is responsible for making and communicating decisions regarding the use, classification, and protection of assigned information. The owner has the *property rights* interest in an information asset for the organization. Other names have been used by different organizations, but the concept is the same: Who is responsible? All information in the organization should be accounted for in the ownership program. The information technology function is ordinarily not the owner. The real owner is usually the manager of the business unit supported by the application or the remote user in a time-sharing environment. The owner approves application controls and authorizes access to the information. The owner participates in risk assessment, risk acceptance, and contingency planning associated with the information. Ownership also involves two other roles:

1. The *custodian* has authorized possession of the information and is responsible for following owner-authorized controls. Frequently, this is the IT department (the supplier of services).
2. The *user*, on the other hand, has only authorized access and is responsible for simple and standard rules.

Awareness and Education Program

Unless all employees are aware of the security policy and other organization rules regarding privacy, the security program cannot function effectively. Lack of an awareness program can even affect an organization's legal position in case of theft (for example, if employees do not understand the meaning of classification markings). Individuals must clearly understand which assets they are responsible for and the privacy protection those assets are to receive.

IT management periodically needs to advise all employees of their responsibilities regarding asset protection. An education program is recommended, with seminars, films, and publications depicting the value of information and why protection is needed. Posters and bulletins can remind them of the need to protect information. New employee orientation is an important part of the information protection awareness program because the new person is more impressionable. Signed certification that the employee has read and understands the security and privacy policies is highly recommended. This should be done for new employees at the time of employment and annually for all employees. Not only does this certification focus attention on the subject, but it provides some legal protection as well. Finally, security staff and line management who have heavy information security and privacy responsibility should be encouraged to attend classes and seminars hosted by professional groups, consultants, and educational institutions.

Formulating a security and privacy policy is time consuming, but the ISO can speed up the process with multiplatform policy-construction kits. If the ISO wants to take matters into his or her own hands, such a kit is probably the best way to go.

Nothing that comes right out of the box will fit an organization's Intranet security and privacy needs exactly. The ISO must customize every such security awareness and security-training effort, at least to some degree. If the ISO expects a perfect fit as soon as the package is opened, the ISO should also expect disappointment.

In addition, after the ISO customizes the security policy and software, the ISO's job isn't finished. Eventually, the company's security needs will change, which means the ISO must come up with a new or revised security policy. And a revised policy means that the ISO must retrain the employees. If the ISO uses computer-based training, the program must have the flexibility to change when the ISO security requirements change. The ISO should be able to use the same computer-based security training materials as before without having to go back to the vendor.

Having Access to Information

The ISO is undoubtedly concerned about security and therefore also needs to be concerned about which employees have access to which information. The ISO cannot, of course, give every employee access to all the company information. Talk about temptation! Only certain employees need access to read or manipulate the company's financial records, for example. The idea here is *access control*. The first thing the ISO needs to be concerned with is physical security: Keep unauthorized people away from hardware. In addition, make decisions concerning data classification, identification, and authentication of users, data access, and dial-up controls—each of which is covered in this part of the chapter.

Physical Access

Although the focus of this part of the chapter is not on traditional physical security, if the physical protection of the information is not adequate, more sophisticated data protection methods may be wasted. Good physical control is the backbone of all security programs.

For computer facilities at a central site, restrict access to personnel working on the shift to which they are assigned, as well as to escorted authorized visitors. In facilities planning, segment areas so no more than 8 to 10 people are in the room at one time. This is based on the theory that with greater numbers, additional people are less likely to be noticed or recognized. Use a combination of limited entrances: locks, badges, and security personnel to restrict access to sensitive areas. Also, with the proliferation of personal computers, security officials must pay special attention not only to protecting the information by locking it up when not in use, but also to protecting the PCs from theft.

Classifying Information

Although information should be classified for all three areas of concern (disclosure, modification, and destruction), the first of these usually requires the most attention. In all three areas, classification is simply a label that tells people in the organization what type of controls are required based on that organization's privacy policy and specific rules; hence, the importance of education. The alternatives to an information classification policy are to protect everything or protect nothing, both of which are too costly.

Some data, particularly some programs, are especially sensitive to modification. Some organizations call these *fraud-sensitive programs*. Other information is especially sensitive to destruction; without it, the organization may have difficulty continuing in its mission. One name frequently used for this type of information is *vital records*. Some organizations have created more than one level of vital records based on the time and cost to re-create them. Keep in mind that these two classification groups, along with classification based on sensitivity to disclosure, are generally mutually exclusive. Just because a record is vital does not necessarily make the data confidential also. For example, accounts receivable of some organizations may be vital, but not confidential.

Classification regarding sensitivity to disclosure requires multiple levels, each with a different level of protection. The names of the classifications and rules about them are, of necessity, dependent on the organization. Four levels of classification exist in addition to "unclassified": (1) internal use only, (2) confidential, (3) confidential restricted, and (4) registered confidential. Deciding which classification to use is based, among other criteria, on factors such as (a) time until an event, such as an announcement, (b) data combinations, (c) data reduction or level of summarization, and (d) specifics of conclusions, as opposed to raw data.

The classification is assigned by the owner, whereas the custodian or service supplier carries out the requirements, which may require decisions. The user should be able to follow a simple set of rules set forth by the owner.

Individual Authentication and Identification

Identification to the level of the individual must be made to support other aspects of the security program, such as auditability, ownership, and classification. *Authentication* is verification that the individual is who he or she claims to be. This means user identifications (user IDs) and passwords cannot be shared.

Magnetic stripe cards are increasing in use, especially with a password or personal identification number (PIN). The use of these and other tokens appears to be growing. Biometrics techniques—that is, physical or behavioral characteristics, or "who" someone is—are gaining in interest. These techniques include technology such as hand geometry, fingerprint identification, signature verification, and voice recognition.

Although these forms of authentication other than password or PIN are being marketed, they do not have widespread use so far, with the exception of bankcards and physical access. It appears that passwords will continue to be the primary means of authentication for the time being. In addition to prohibiting password sharing, the passwords themselves should not be trivial or easy to guess, and they should be changed regularly. They should be protected as confidential, and therefore, should not be written down on or near the terminal or on access cards. Password protection should be part of the ongoing awareness program.

Data Access
Policies and controls for data access are the only methods available to enforce the individual auditability requirements discussed previously. The

best policy for access is one of "least possible privilege." In other words, the user has access only to the information necessary to do the job. For information classified as confidential (or equivalent) and higher, "need to know" should be kept current by periodic revalidation. At some level (at least registered confidential or the equivalent), a complete audit trail of access and change must be maintained. Procedures should exist to determine accountability for all changes to data and programs. A mechanism should be in place to detect unauthorized attempts to access resources such as data and programs. The owner of the resource, the user's manager, and the security staff should all be notified of potential violations to prevent collusion.

Access-control software provides the facilities to control information at this level. Experience has repeatedly shown, however, that installing access-control software without the prerequisite policy, ownership, awareness, and classification has not only been frustrating and sometimes traumatic, but usually falls short of the original objectives for its use.

Dial-Up Controls

Most organizations today are past the point of prohibiting dial-up into or among their computers. Some major companies, such as banks, securities brokers, and retailers, are already allowing dial-up from customers' home computers. Furthermore, the technology to connect a dial-up line to a local- or leased-line circuit without knowledge of the central site is relatively inexpensive.

Systems with a significant number of dial ports require controls that reach beyond those for nondial lines. Do not publish or post telephone numbers. Dial-back facilities provide protection from many of the risks by requiring preidentification to access the system prior to login. The incoming call is received, authenticated, and then disconnected. The dial-back device then initiates the connection to the authorized remote location. Call forwarding is a potential threat, although a small one, because the perpetrator must have physically accessed the remote telephone to initiate it. Other approaches involve terminal identification when access has been initiated, such as Synchronous Data Link Control (SDLC), smart tokens, and cryptography.

Cryptography

Cryptography can protect both the secrecy and authenticity of information. Secrecy is maintained by encrypting the entire message or file. Authentication is validated by encrypting a tag. It uses all the information that is verified by the receiver for later use. Also, it not only validates where all the information originated from, but also that nothing has been altered. Cryptography is the only known protection for privacy and authenticity of information transmitted from satellites. Also, the nature of the Data Encryption Standard (DES) is that the algorithm is public knowledge; only the key must be secret. The identical key must be used to encrypt and decrypt; otherwise, the result is worthless.

Privacy of Information

Security is all about maintaining the privacy of information on an organization's Intranet. The ISO may be able to use firewalls to keep outsiders from gaining access to that data, but how does the ISO protect that data from unauthorized people within the organization? The ISO needs a means of ensuring the privacy of data while it is on an Intranet server or while it is being transmitted from the server to a local PC.

When the Intranet administrator (IA) has access rights to all the data on the server, nothing can stop him or her from looking at data kept on that server—except a lack of time, of course! Just in case an organization's Intranet isn't that busy, one can avoid any temptation to pry by using software that prevents the IA from accessing the information.

By encrypting any sensitive data on the server (company financial records or employee medical information, for example) and then transmitting it (again, encrypted) to and from a local computer on the Intranet, the IA can ensure that no one will be able to read the data. Encrypting data during transmission prevents someone from intercepting usable data in transit because encrypted data are worthless without the key. Therefore, the data are protected at all times.

Maintaining privacy, then, partly revolves around using encryption. In the best situation, even IAs rarely should have access to all the company data. The IA should, nonetheless, investigate all the encryption options available. Some will work better in a situation than others will. The IA should also find the encryption software that provides the type of data security that an organization's Intranet requires.

Sign-On and Sign-Off

If the IA happens to be one of those unlucky souls with permission to access all sorts of data on the Intranet, the IA may appreciate the problem many people face: signing on. Sure, it doesn't sound like a big deal, but if the IA has to know a great many passwords just to do the job, the IA can appreciate another bit of software geared toward one goal: simplifying the sign-on process for Intranet users while maintaining password security.

Many people work for organizations that use an Intranet that requires different passwords to gain access to various resources. These people may have trouble just getting to the information they need to do their work every day. The more passwords a user must remember, the more likely that individual will take shortcuts by writing down the passwords. These people are probably thinking several things:

> They want to do their work everyday, and they have to be able to get all the information they need. That information is on the Intranet, but they have to use 12 different passwords to get it all. And if they forget one or two of them, they won't be able to get all the data they need. And if they can't get all the data they need, they can't do the work. And if they can't do the work, the company may go under, and they'll lose their jobs, as will coworkers. Everyone suffers, including families, all because the passwords were forgotten. Reading the passwords off a sheet of paper is a whole lot easier than remembering them.

The exact mental scenario varies from person to person, although not by much. Actually, the solution is the same in each case: Simplify the sign-on process. A primary means of simplification lies in passwords.

Look at the situation from the other side. The IA in charge of assigning or overseeing security and passwords has enough of a headache just making sure everyone in the organization has an appropriate password and the correct access rights. For a company with hundreds, or even thousands, of employees who need Intranet access, maintaining passwords and user IDs may be monumental.

What happens then, when Intranet security is compromised because an employee writes down a password, which is then stolen by an unauthorized person? "No big deal?" "It's only one password." But think about it for a minute. First, consider that the theft of that one password could conceivably lead to the loss of sensitive, private, or even secret company data. Where might that information end up? In the hands of a competitor, perhaps?

As explained earlier in the chapter, industrial espionage is rampant these days. What will all of those out-of-work Cold War spies do if they're still relatively young and their pensions don't pay them as much as they need or want? Their skills may come in handy for spying on entities other than governments.

Suppose, though, that the person who steals the password doesn't intend to sell the information to anyone else. That individual merely enjoys the thrill of pretending to be a spy, or of having access to information that most of his or her colleagues don't, or of knowing things other employees don't know. No harm done, right? Possibly, but security administrators (SAs) and their companies can't take that chance. Maybe the thief will face a financial crisis one day and decide the only way out is to sell the information. As unlikely as that scenario may be, SAs must reckon with the possibility. After all, their jobs consist of considering all the possibilities (not just probabilities) and then preparing for them.

Second, what if several dozen employees write down their passwords and this same scenario (theft of passwords) is played out with each one? The time "wasted" in continually issuing new passwords mounts up quickly when it is added to the time consumed by routine password-management responsibilities. This is especially true for very large organizations.

The key to solving the problem is simplification. If an organization's Intranet includes software that enables employees to access applications automatically (with fewer passwords required), the employees will be less likely to feel the need to write down their passwords. If they need to remember 4 or 5 passwords (or even fewer) instead of 12, compliance with security policy is far more likely. SAs may still have problems with the occasional user who simply refuses to memorize the passwords and writes them down instead, but the necessity to require new passwords should drop. More time is freed up for routine password management.

Audits

Sometimes the SA is not the only person interested in how well the organization's security policy functions. Banks are just one example of organizations whose security policies interest others. The government has a vested interest in a bank's security policy and its execution. That brings up the topic of audits.

IT Management Controls

Using good, fundamental IT management controls is the most effective step in developing and maintaining a good security and privacy program. IT management's control over processing information, whatever the media is, must be at least as good as the controls in the organization's mainline function. For example, if a company is a financial institution, the controls over the information technology systems must be as good as those over the financial records. Table 13–1 lists some specific tasks that the IT management staff should follow.

IT MANAGEMENT SECURITY AND PRIVACY CONTROLS CHECKLIST FORM

Date: _____

The IT management staff responsible for such information held by the enterprise should ensure that the following tasks have been completed (check all tasks completed):

____ 1. Separate duties to determine individual responsibility.

____ 2. System changes should be independently originated and approved.

____ 3. Span of control should be consistent with the complexity and similarity of the function to be supervised.

____ 4. IT should be separate from its principal users to retain its independence.

____ 5. Controls should exist to ensure that all work is processed in accordance with procedures.

____ 6. Controls should exist for the timely detection of errors.

____ 7. Sensitive functions, such as error correction, recovery and restart, and IPL procedures, require special controls.

____ 8. Personnel procedures, such as job rotation, hiring, and termination practices, should be reviewed for their data security impact.

Table 13–1. IT Management Security and Privacy Controls Checklist Form

IT Management Reviews

In addition to internal and external audits, a program of self-assessment and peer review has been found very effective. In other words, they are conducted as a "friendly audit" to bring exposures to the attention of the IT management responsible for fixing the problems, rather than reporting to top management.

Formal audits should include information security. Some audits should focus on it, including both physical and logical access controls. Unannounced, independent control testing should be performed. Penetration testing of systems should be part of this process, but only after controls are in place. Audit of offsite "vital" records should be done periodically. Both internal and external audits are the primary means for top management to ensure that their directives are properly implemented.

Application Development Controls

Application programs should do what, and only what, they are intended to do. Achieving this goal usually involves major changes to the way applications are developed in most organizations. Some requirements are as follows:

Applications are developed in a structured environment using programming techniques such as phase reviews, walk-throughs, inspections, complexity limits (such as number of paths, none crossing), and scope limits (such as no more than fifty lines of code).

The owner, user management, maintenance management, and auditor are involved in the development and phase review processes.

Changes to programs are independently authorized by owner management and approved by development management under a structured change control system, fixing accountability for all changes to a single IT manager.

Programmers never have access to live data or operating programs.

Contingency Planning

Security also involves preparation for disasters. Contingency is the general term for the unexpected, and a disaster certainly qualifies as a contingent event. Needless to say, IT management is intimately involved in contingency planning.

Documented Contingency Plan

A concise, documented contingency plan should be in place to provide for continuation of critical applications in the event of a catastrophic event. The plan cannot be restricted to the IT function. A disaster or catastrophe may affect many parts of the organization; thus participation of all of those potentially affected is important. The focus of the plan should be on critical functions (those necessary to keep the organization running) even in the event of a required move to another location. The plan should be distributed to executives and relevant IT management and should be accompanied by instructions to keep contingency plan copies offsite.

When developing the contingency plan, list individual responsibilities in detail. The focus should be on personnel privacy issues, because the effect on them will likely be greater than that on the buildings and equipment. Include listings of personnel, computer equipment, software, communications equipment, vendors, and forms (with sample copies). Although major disasters are infrequent, short interruptions or specific equipment outages are common. Take steps in the plan to provide for these small "disasters," to keep them from becoming major ones. To be complete, the plan should cover the emergency situation. This is the period during which the disaster is in progress. Also, the plan should cover back-up processing, which is the interim period until recovery is in place and the primary responsibility of the user. It should also cover recovery operations, which are the responsibility of IT staff and include provisions for possible long-term processing until permanent operations are restored.

Private Records Program

Records designated as *private* (that is, records sensitive to destruction) under the organization's classification program must be backed up and rotated offsite on a regular basis. Take care to choose offsite storage that is not susceptible to the same disaster. The offsite storage location should provide for protection against fire, water, and variations in temperature and humidity. Consider maintaining highly critical data in more than one offsite location. Procedures should be in place to audit the offsite information for currency on a periodic basis.

User Responsibility

The user or user department must have a plan to operate temporarily without the IT function. This is based on the premise that, in a crisis, IT will be focused on restoring service. Alternative procedures may mean using a manual system or a commercial computer service, such as an Intranet facility. The user's documented plan should also include those functions that are not automated. Although the responsibility is the user's, IT should remind user management of the responsibility they have and cooperate with them in developing their plans.

Regular Testing

To be effective, regularly test all parts of the plan. Test emergency plans by drills, exercises, or third-party reviews. Consider testing back-up and recovery plans by simulations or walk-throughs. Use offsite data to test the appli-

---

IT MANAGEMENT SECURITY AND PRIVACY PROGRAM CHECKLIST FORM

Date: _____

The IT management staff responsible for such information held by the enterprise should ensure that the following tasks have been completed (check all tasks completed):

___ 1. Create and publish the security and privacy policy (the key to the entire program is creating and publishing the security and privacy policy. This document serves as the support for the remaining activities).

___ 2. Create an awareness program. This is important because it informs and reminds employees of their security and privacy responsibilities.

___ 3. Carry out the security and privacy program. Although security is a line management responsibility, a security staff can be instrumental in carrying out the program.

___ 4. Create an ownership program. An ownership program is vital to any data access control system, ensuring that all assets are accounted for.

___ 5. Create a classification program. A classification program is important to prevent overprotection or underprotection, either of which can be expensive.

___ 6. Create a data access policy. A data access policy is essential to limit access to sensitive resources to those who have a "need to know." It must also state who may change or delete data.

___ 7. Install system software. Installing system software can facilitate implementation of the access control policy. Variances can be quickly noted, and action can be taken to limit unauthorized activity.

Table 13–2. IT Management Security and Privacy Program Checklist Form
Note: Both internal and external audits are the primary means for top management to ensure that their directives are properly implemented.

cations' portability should a move to another location be necessary. To minimize disruption and expense, plan all tests well in advance. Test results should be documented, accompanied by recommendations made for changes in procedures when necessary, and then reviewed by upper management.

Recommendations

The tasks indicated in Table 13–2 should be followed by IT management to initiate an organizationwide security and privacy program.

IT management reviews and audits are essential to test the effectiveness of controls and to initiate changes when necessary. Thus, the topics discussed in this part of the chapter are primarily management related and can be effectively carried out through an active security and privacy program.

CONTROLLING VULNERABILITIES CREATED BY EXTRANETS

As previously mentioned, the *Intranet* is a familiar concept: an internal communications system that uses technology developed for the Internet. Often beginning with electronic mail, organizations eventually add scheduling and collaboration applications to create an organization that extends beyond the constraints of buildings and walls—an organization built on communications as much as material production. When the move outward includes customers, suppliers, and trusted partners, the resulting communications structure is described by a new buzzword: the *Extranet* (see the sidebar, "Extranet Security").

Extranet Security

Extensive Extranet implementation plans by companies mean nothing if the Extranet creates security and privacy vulnerabilities or does not offer security at all. Confidential or private information must remain just that—for the integrity of the site and to ensure the enforcement of a joint defense privilege. Although no security measure can be labeled foolproof, Web-based solutions have developed to dramatically decrease the likelihood of a breach of security. Internet Service Providers with experience in security issues can implement layers of protection by using techniques such as IP filtering, IP tunneling, Secure Socket Layers (SSLs) client/server key encryption, and server-resident username and password restrictions. In many cases, good ISPs are able to configure their networks so that they can follow access trails down to individual computers in offices. Currently, privately disseminating Web-based information through Extranets is not necessarily secure and will only become more vulnerable if technology fails to improve.

While not every company has extensive Extranet plans, most look for faster private corporate communications among trading partners (for data sharing with business partners), the ability to spread information throughout the organization, and closer ties with customers, suppliers, and partners.

What do organizations get from Extranets? Quick private communication with customers and partners is an advantage in the market. Getting input from key customers on product features before introduction is important. Extranets are supposed to make a company more effective. And, the person who creates information should be instantly available to the person who's using the information. The feedback loop hits real time. That real-time cycle of response to new products, which gives engineers direct access to customer ideas for improving products, is an important ingredient in a strategy to dramatically shorten product cycles.

Having engineers and customers talk to each other may speed product development, but it also fundamentally changes the way information moves through an organization. Sharing information between such departments as marketing and engineering will make corporate data ubiquitous, providing information to individuals who formerly were denied access because they lacked a need to know.

So what are the major technologies involved? How are the high-speed promises of the Extranet to be realized? The Extranet rests on four technologies: the Web, the Internet, groupware applications, and firewalls. It's possible that Intranets and Extranets would have developed without any one of the four, but highly unlikely.

The Web's major contribution to Extranets is freedom from specific platforms. If a company has a client/server application for vendors, deploying that with a traditional client/server isn't practical from an installation or support perspective. A significant limitation of the traditional client/server development approach is the requirement that each workstation execute the same software. Developing applications with a Web-based interface solves the software development and support problem, but not without cost. Companies may have to retrofit applications for the Web environment, leading to multiple versions of a supposedly standard application. The Internet is the conceptual incubator of both Intranets and Extranets, and universal connectivity has liberated private corporate communications practices. But the success of the Internet has carried a price, and the Internet has issues from the manageability standpoint. The tools a company has in which to manage the Web are fairly immature. In other words, the tools used to manage an Intranet generally make unrealistic assumptions about the nature of the systems on the Intranet; this situation results in certain types of hardware and software remaining invisible to the manager's screen. Also, Intranets usually lack powerful directory services. One can find a lot of the good solutions for management—a proprietary structure for directories and even for digital signatures.

Access and management may mean little to a corporate executive. For most companies that are installing Extranets, protection against unwanted intrusion is made up of products centered on a *firewall*, which is a device that examines incoming or outgoing data to stop any unauthorized transmission of or access to information. Two principal types of firewalls are in use: packet-level and application-level firewalls. *Packet-level firewalls* are good enough for most situations because they tend to be thorough, but they can also be slow and inexact. But when an individual is connecting to another Intranet, an *application-level firewall* is needed because the other company's applications might make legitimate requests of the corporate communications network that are different from those that an independent user might make.

So Why Do Corporate Executives Worry?

Many vulnerabilities issues surround Extranets, and executives should be aware of a few of the major ones. The first, not surprisingly, is security. Most IT directors protect themselves against *prank* intrusions, but Extranet experts say that disgruntled employees or businesses lacking ethics may pose even more significant threats. Some experts suggest using a multilevel approach to protect against the outside attacks that can infiltrate any casual protection.

In other words, security is a function of several things: The various servers one could get to from a Web server can be protected by name. But, even if one could find the server, it's password protected. If an individual managed to hack a way in, that individual could see only what the company's hacked account would let the perpetrator see. And, finally, if an individual could get past that, the company could use RSA Security's (Rivest, Shamir, & Adleman (public key encryption technology)) encryption methods or other encryption to hide the information inside a safe stream.

Another significant vulnerability issue affects those whose lives and livelihoods may be affected by a new way of working. Many barriers, most driven by the desire for power, hinder the adoption of Extranets. People-controlled information silos are in the past. Now the discussion is about eliminating that control—eliminating the power base for some people—and one can hit a lot of resistance with that thought. One, however, has to make allowances for the fact that it's very threatening to some people.

Legal issues are also a concern. Companies and individuals are now *doing* through a system what was previously done face to face, and things that were not written down before may now be written and stored. As a result, an individual may be able to capture information that was never captured before. However, that individual may discover legal implications if subpoenas are issued. In this environment, guidelines on purging materials become important.

Finally, even when everyone in an organization supports the initiative to develop an Extranet, the magnitude of the change should not be underestimated. In other words, the enterprise must focus on the right measures of success when an Extranet is created. The natural tendency for management is to be interested in automation for more transactions. If IT management doesn't handle the change correctly, a vendor or customer *touch* declines, and the organization loses something. Therefore, how much *touch* can an organization afford to lose without losing the crucial interactions? If the organization drives transactions two times their previous rate but loses the contact with the customer, is it a loss they can afford?

The creation of an Extranet, therefore, can be placed in the same category of a large-scale organizational change that includes privacy reengineering. In other words, any time an organization takes the Intranet outside the company, it must view that effort as a privacy-reengineering project. The organization must carefully consider privacy and cultural issues and resistance to change when adopting an extranet.

UNDERSTANDING EMAIL PRIVACY AND VULNERABILITY ISSUES

If the boss isn't reading an employee's email, the company computers might be doing it for him. The market for email monitoring software, which lets companies search for harassing letters or leaks of trade secrets, will explode by an estimated 15 times over the next five years, from $73 million in sales to $1.1 billion in sales, according to a new study from International Data Corp. of Framingham, Massachusetts.

Content Technologies of Bellevue, Washington, a top maker of such software, funded the study. Sixty-five percent of American companies currently monitor employees' Internet use and 49 percent save and review employees' email, according to a survey done in 2000 by the American Management Association.

Nearly 45 percent of those companies aren't telling their employees they're doing it. (See the sidebar, "Should Employees Be Notified? That Is

The Question!") Having a program sort through dirty words, trade secrets, and harassment in email is a lot better than the alternative—where humans are rummaging through things.

Should Employees Be Notified?
That is The Question!

Recently legislation was introduced in Congress to require employers to notify workers if they're monitoring their electronic communications at work. Rep. Bob Barr, R. -GA., and Rep. Charles Canady, R. -FL, sponsored the House version of legislation that would force employers to tell employees if they scan or read their email, monitor their computer keystrokes or Web use, or eavesdrop on their telephone conversations. Sen. Charles Schumer, D. -NY, introduced a companion bill in the Senate.

The American Management Association reported in an April 2000 survey that 84 percent of major U.S. firms record and monitor their employees' phone calls, Internet connections, and computer files. One of three companies reported that they had fired employees for misuse of telecommunication equipment.

A Real Protection Racket

Employers may have good reason for their electronic searches. They are being held legally responsible for harassing email sent within companies. In almost every case where someone allegedly harassed an employee, the email record is subpoenaed. Some companies, such as banks and securities firms, are legally bound to keep email records to protect against charges of financial misdealing or insider trading.

In 1999, the *New York Times* fired 34 workers for sending distasteful jokes through email. The company said the firings were necessary to maintain a harassment-free workplace. At a subsidiary of Chevron Corp., offensive chain letters sent through email were used as evidence in a successful sexual harassment suit in 1995. That has companies scared. Certain types of email liability can be dramatic: discrimination lawsuits and harassment lawsuits.

Automatic Censors

Products like Content Technologies' MIMESweeper suite use lists of keywords and sophisticated grammatical rules to filter through corporate mail, searching for potential liabilities. The word *breast*, if it's in reasonable proximity to *chicken*, is probably no problem. If it's in reasonable proximity to other words, it might not be so good.

Automatic censors like MIMESweeper can even scan nontext documents, like compressed Zip files, spreadsheets, and graphics, for offensive phrases. For example, MIMESweeper doesn't actually look for dirty pictures—it looks for offensive filenames and text that are often embedded in the images. If text is associated with an image, that image can pretty much be identified based on the text. MIMESweeper's *recursive disassembly* system takes apart emails bit by bit, looking for files zipped within attachments buried within other files.

The Perils of Privacy

Employees have few privacy rights in the office. Many companies ask employees to sign away their rights when they're hired. But recently employees have been fighting back with suits based on a 1986 privacy law. The result has been a confusing legal climate.

The few cases that have addressed the issue of privacy with respect to email have been spotty at best. But companies taking action on personal information (medical conditions, for example) found in supposedly private email would be liable to employment-discrimination suits.

The key is for companies to clearly inform their users about how much privacy to expect. The companies who spy on email without clearly informing their workers make themselves vulnerable to privacy lawsuits.

Lovers and thieves who pay attention to their language will always be able to avoid content-surveillance software. An employee who knows that the surveillance software is there can always figure out a way to communicate in such a way that the software won't be able to block it.

CONTROLLING THE SERIOUS RISKS FROM EMAIL ATTACHMENTS

Few businesses would let complete strangers run rampant through their corporate headquarters without the least bit of inspection. The same should be true with regard to who companies invite into their corporate communications systems.

But, as many businesses learned recently with the worldwide rampage of the "Love Bug" computer virus, casual attitudes toward email file attachments can be as dangerous as leaving the front lobby unattended. That's because email attachments are the vehicle of choice for those responsible for planting computer viruses.

Email attachments are like keys that open a computer system's front door. An attachment is simply a program, and anytime the user loads a program, all the gates to a company's computer are basically opened, which gives any potential virus a license to wreak havoc inside a company's hard drive.

As soon as the program is launched, the virus starts doing dirty work throughout the computer. A virus spreader theoretically could implant a virus that activates in email without the need for an attachment. However, most antivirus software programs probably would catch it before it does any real damage.

Using an email attachment helps a virus fly under the radar screen. More accurately, it gets the recipient of the email to turn off the radar altogether.

As a precaution, therefore, email users should consider the legitimacy of any email attachments before opening them. If an email message is unexpected or seems out of place, don't open it, even if the email comes from a familiar source; many viruses now, as Love Bug victims discovered, forward themselves to those listed in a computer's email address book. The Love Bug spreads to hundreds of thousands of computers worldwide and destroys graphics and other files.

A contaminated email attachment is often disguised as something users want to open, like the Love Bug, which came with the message heading "I LOVE YOU." If an attachment has a picture or a nice message, then it's more likely to get opened.

Think of what might have happened had this person sent the "I LOVE YOU" virus on Valentine's Day. It could have brought people and corporations to their knees.

RESPONDING TO PRIVACY ISSUES IN DATA SHARING WITH BUSINESS PARTNERS

Two aspects of the privacy issues with regard to data sharing with business partners require comment. First, the kind of data sought must be well understood. What the government wants to know from business is hard to determine with specificity. Clearly, the government seeks data about computer attacks on critical infrastructure cybercontrol systems. Virtually all such attacks are also crimes, and the FBI can be expected to seek a wide range of data necessary to determine damage and assess blame. Both inquiries of this kind and assistance the National Infrastructure Protection Center (NIPC) might render in improving security after the fact could involve the government's acquisition of information deemed sensitive business secrets by the companies from which they are obtained (see the sidebar, "National Infrastructure Protection Center (NIPC)"). If this is so, businesses will expect the FBI to provide clear assurances that the confidentiality and privacy of such data can and will be well protected. The FBI is developing a security regime to provide such assurances. To be effective, it must be well understood publicly and rigorously applied.

National Infrastructure Protection Center (NIPC)

The National Infrastructure Protection Center (NIPC), located in the FBI's headquarters building in Washington, DC, brings together representatives from the FBI, other U.S. government agencies, state and local governments, and the private sector in a partnership to protect U.S. critical infrastructures. Established in February 1998, the NIPC's mission is to serve as the U.S. government's focal point for threat assessment, warning, investigation, and response for threats or attacks against our critical infrastructures. These infrastructures include telecommunications, energy, banking and finance, water systems, government operations, and emergency services.

On May 22, 1997, President Clinton announced two new directives designed to strengthen U.S. defenses against terrorism and other unconventional threats: Presidential Decision Directives (PDD) 62 and 63. PDD-62 highlights the growing range of unconventional threats that are faced, including *cyberterrorism* and chemical, radiological, and biological weapons, and creates a new and more systematic approach to defending against them. PDD-63 focuses specifically on protecting the nation's critical infrastructures from both physical and *cyber-attacks*. These attacks may come from foreign governments; foreign and domestic terrorist organizations; and foreign and domestic criminal organizations.

The NIPC is a part of the broader framework of government efforts established by PDD-63. Under the PDD, the NIPC serves as the national focal point for threat assessment, warning, investigation, and response to attacks on the critical infrastructures. A significant part of its mission involves establishing mechanisms to increase the sharing of vulnerability and threat data between the government and private industry.

Second, in cases with no ongoing investigation, the FBI will seek voluntary provision of data from business. The nature of this data is still not clear and is variously described in the National Plan. A better definition of this category of voluntarily provided information and, most importantly, clear justification for its collection is urged. The private sector will wish to know to whom the information will be disseminated, how it may be used, and how it will be protected from unauthorized use. Only the government can provide the necessary representations. Without them, its policy will be ineffectual.

The FBI should provide more data concerning the operation and especially the business secrets confidentiality aspects of INFRAGARD, its rapidly expanding pilot project with some businesses in voluntary data sharing for critical infrastructure protection. Similarly, any protocols developed to assure confidentiality and privacy would put meat on the bones of the government's proposals for cooperation.

The Financial Services Information Sharing and Analysis Center (FS/ISAC) seems to offer a much more promising model for sharing of data. Under the FS/ISAC as announced by the Administration in October 1999, data sharing on risks, attacks, and responses will occur among the private sector members of the financial services industry, not between industry and government. The FS/ISAC is a private-sector nonprofit corporation formed to facilitate the sharing of data on threats, incidents, and vulnerabilities in cyberspace. It was developed by the financial services industry, at the prompting of Treasury Department officials, but the government is not a direct participant in the system. Data will be shared among member firms and can be shared in a form that does not even identify the originating institution. No personally identifiable data will be shared, and data will not be forwarded routinely to the government.

UNDERSTANDING PRIVACY PROBLEMS IN GLOBAL BUSINESS-DATA INFRASTRUCTURES

Government descriptions of privacy protection plans for critical global business-data infrastructures put some emphasis on the use of indirect, market-based incentives, rather than legislative mandates, to encourage the development of best practices and appropriate data security and privacy standards. These mechanisms include the measurement of industry adherence to new data security and privacy standards by insurers when writing liability coverage, incorporation of such standards in accounting evaluations, and the influence such standards will exert on the price of corporate financial instruments.

The government's asserted intent to avoid mandates should be applauded, but whether its concepts will bear fruit as anticipated remains unclear. The key element in all such schemes is data security and privacy standards, an area where the private sector may well be ahead of most government agencies. Insurers, accountants, lenders, and investors already understand the importance of data security and privacy, but until widely accepted standards are established, they cannot play a role.

This observation only underscores the earlier point concerning how such standards will be developed. The government should both encourage and cooperate with an industry-led approach to standards, but must avoid using the standards-setting process as a proxy for government mandates. If such a process is to succeed, it cannot be driven by a government prescription, nor handled from the government end as was the CALEA process, nor can it be required to meet artificial deadlines.

NOTE: CALEA stands for Communications Assistance for Law Enforcement Act (1994 "CALEA" or the digital telephony law). CALEA ordered telecommunications carriers to ensure that their systems can continue to accommodate law enforcement wiretaps notwithstanding the introduction of new technologies and services.

Government can best serve such a process by continuing to seek consensus among business, Congress, and the public about the need for the privacy protection of critical global-business data infrastructures. The increased research and development spending sought for fiscal year 2001 can also be directed in ways that aid the standard-setting process; however, the extent to which industry associations or groups were consulted in setting priorities for this spending is unknown.

RESPONDING TO INDUSTRY-SPECIFIC ISSUES

Three policy questions dominate the issue of privacy protection for global-business data infrastructures: how limited should the government's role be; what is adequate infrastructure security and how will appropriate standards be determined; and, what information does the government need from business and why? None of these questions seem fundamentally settled if only because policy continues to develop. More questions than answers remain. Nonetheless, a few basic principles are emerging that should guide infrastructure privacy protection efforts:

- General or centralized monitoring of communications need not and should not be a chief or central component of the government's response to computer security and privacy. Other activities (notably the identification and closing of existing vulnerabilities) should be given higher priority.

- Authority for increased monitoring of information technology systems is not required and should be rejected. Rather, the underlying laws for monitoring corporate communications systems and accessing stored data should be strengthened.
- The role of the FBI and the NSA in computer security and privacy should be carefully limited. Their surveillance agendas trump their protective missions, and their activities are often so cloaked in secrecy as to generate understandable suspicion.
- Oversight of infrastructure protection should be institutionalized within the Executive Branch and should be accessible to the public. The Executive Branch should establish appropriate mechanisms for oversight of computer security issues and should involve both industry representatives and privacy advocates.
- Congress must follow this issue carefully and should insist upon periodic reports on the status, scope, and effectiveness of critical infrastructure activities. Special focus should be given to initiatives on monitoring and intrusion detection and to the protection of privacy.
- In summary, while the government needs to participate, especially in educating society about what is at stake, the government's role in privacy protection within the private sector infrastructure should be limited and largely advisory. The private sector should set data security and privacy standards, and the government should clearly define and limit what data it seeks from businesses and how that data will be used.

A New Window of Exposure for Corporate Communications

Finally, every season yields a bumper crop of corporate communications privacy and security stories: break-ins, new vulnerabilities, and new products. But this season has also generated a crop of stories about computer security philosophy. There has been resurgence in opposition to the full disclosure movement—the theory that publishing vulnerabilities is the best way to fix them. In response, defenders of the movement have published their rebuttals. And even more experts have weighed in with opinions on the DeCSS case, where a New York judge ruled that distributing an attack tool is illegal. What's interesting is that everybody wants the same thing; they're just disagreeing about the best way to get there.

When security vulnerability exists in a product, it creates a window of exposure. This window exists until the vulnerability is patched and that patch is installed. The shape of this window depends on how many people can exploit this vulnerability and on how fast it is patched. What everyone wants is to make this window as small as possible. A window of exposure has five distinct phases:

1. **Phase 1** is before the vulnerability is discovered. The vulnerability exists, but no one can exploit it.
2. **Phase 2** is after the vulnerability is discovered, but before it is announced. At that point, only a few people know about the vulnerability, but no one knows how to defend against it. Depending on who knows what, this could either be an enormous risk or no risk at all. During this phase, news about the vulnerability spreads (slowly, quickly, or not at all) depending on who discovered the vulnerability. Of course, multiple people can make the same discovery at different times, so this can get very complicated.
3. **Phase 3** is after the vulnerability is announced. Maybe the person who discovered the vulnerability in Phase 2 makes the announcement, or maybe someone else who independently discovered the vulnerability later makes it. At that point more people learn about the vulnerability, and the risk increases.
4. In **Phase 4**, an automatic attack tool to exploit the vulnerability is published. Now the number of people who can exploit the vulnerability grows exponentially.
5. Finally, the vendor issues a patch that closes the vulnerability, starting **Phase 5**. As people install the patch and resecure their systems, the risk of exploitation shrinks. Some people never install the patch, so some risk remains, but that risk decays over time as systems are naturally upgraded.

In some instances, the phases are long, and sometimes they're short. Sometimes Phase 5 happens so fast that Phases 3 and 4 never occur. Sometimes Phase 5 never occurs, either because the vendor doesn't care or no fix is possible. But this is basically the way things work.

The goal of any responsible security professional is to reduce the window of exposure as much as possible by taking one of two basic approaches: (1) limit the vulnerability data made public or (2) limit the time of vulnerability by quickly issuing a patch.

The first approach is to reduce the window in the space dimension by limiting the amount of vulnerability data available to the public. The idea is that the less attackers know about attack methodologies, the harder it is for them to get their hands on attack tools, and the safer networks become. The extreme position in this camp holds that attack tools should be made illegal.

This approach might work in theory, but unfortunately is impossible to enforce in practice. A continuous stream of research in security vulnerabilities is occurring, and most of this research results in public announcements. Hackers write new attack exploits all the time, and the exploits quickly end up in the hands of malicious attackers. Any one country could make some of these actions illegal, but doing so would make little difference on the international Internet. In some isolated incidences, a researcher has deliberately not published a discovered vulnerability, but public dissemination of vulnerability data is the norm because it is the best way to improve security and privacy.

The second approach is to reduce the window of exposure in time. Since a window remains open until the vendor patches the vulnerability and the network administrator installs the patches, the faster the vendor can issue the patch the faster the window starts closing. To spur the vendors to patch faster, full-disclosure proponents publish vulnerabilities far and wide. Ideally, the vendor will distribute the patch before any automatic attack tools are written. But writing such tools can only hasten the patches.

This also works a lot better in theory than in practice. In many instances, security-conscious vendors have published patches in a timely fashion. But just as many times security vendors have ignored problems or network administrators have not bothered to install existing patches. A series of credit card thefts in early 2000 was facilitated by vulnerability in Microsoft IIS that was discovered, and a patch released for, a year and a half earlier.

The problem is that for the most part, the size and shape of the window of exposure is not under the control of any central authority. Not publishing a vulnerability is no guarantee that someone else won't publish it. Publishing a vulnerability is no guarantee that someone else won't write an exploit tool, and no guarantee that the vendor will fix it. Releasing a patch is no guarantee that a network administrator will actually install it. Trying to impose rules on such a chaotic system just doesn't work.

And to make matters worse, dozens and hundreds of vulnerabilities exist, all with overlapping windows. One vulnerability might be shrinking while another 10 are growing. It's like the little Dutch boy, plugging leaks in the dike with fingers while other leaks spring up nearby.

Vulnerabilities are inevitable. As corporate communication networks get more complex and more pervasive, the vulnerabilities will become more frequent, not less. Every year brings more security holes than the previous one. The only way to close the window of exposure is to make it not matter. The only way to do that is to build security and privacy systems that are resilient to vulnerabilities.

The most relevant issue in this debate is detection and response. Most computer-security products are sold as prophylactics: firewalls prevent network intrusions, PKI prevents impersonation, encryption prevents eavesdropping, etc. The problem with this model is that the product can either succeed or fail; either the window of exposure is closed or it is open. Good security includes not only protection, but also detection and response. An Internet alarm system that detects attacks in progress, regardless of the vulnerability that was exploited, has the ability to close the window of exposure completely.

The key to Internet detection and response is vigilance. Attacks can happen at all times of the day and night and any day of the year. New attack tools appear all the time; new vulnerabilities become public all the time. Without out-sourced detection and monitoring, everyone is at the mercy of all the hackers and product vendors and security professionals.

Those advocating secrecy are right that full disclosure causes damage, in some cases more damage than good. They are also right that those who build attack tools should be held liable for their actions; the defense of "I just built the bomb; I didn't place it or set the fuse" rings hollow. However, secrecy cannot be enforced. Information naturally disseminates, and strategies that go against that are doomed. Those advocating full disclosure are right that rapid dissemination of the data benefits everyone, even though some people make ill use of that data. Everyone would be in a much worse position today if vulnerability information were only in the hands of a privileged few.

Neither full disclosure nor secrecy solves computer security; the debate has no solution because no one solution exists. Both sides are missing the point. The real issue, how to close the window of exposure, is subtler. IT management has to stop thinking of software security as an end state—that fixing the bugs will somehow make the software perfect. Security and privacy vulnerabilities are inevitable, as is a window of exposure; smart security solutions will work regardless.

Finally, while this chapter outlined the issues that must be addressed in crafting a balanced policy for critical corporate communications protection, the next chapter will discuss privacy issues for corporate desktop application development technology. Topics covered in the next chapter include, but are not limited to, privacy and security issues for corporate desktop applications; desktop and the internal security threats; training end-users on privacy; security issues and procedures; and monitoring desktop users for privacy violations.

14

PROTECTING CORPORATE DESKTOP PRIVACY

Desktop application development via the Intranet is still being conducted in many corporations. Using Net technology, most of the corporate desktop applications (groupware, electronic form distribution, human resource postings, and travel reservations) are becoming Web enabled. These Web servers are providing real-time and dynamic content to legacy systems. Proprietary client applications (SAP, PeopleSoft, and DBMS) are being replaced with Web browsers (the universal client). However, this change is severing the security provided by the tightly coupled client. Data security and privacy are *not* being addressed properly because of the infancy of the Web technology and the fundamental differences between the Web applications and the traditional client-server applications. This chapter will discuss privacy issues for the development of corporate desktop applications and raise the level of consciousness of desktop data security and privacy.

PRIVACY AND SECURITY ISSUES FOR CORPORATE DESKTOP APPLICATIONS

Web technology is experiencing widespread growth as an effective platform for deploying corporate desktop applications. Web technology also allows for heterogeneous browser platforms and write-once, run-anywhere applications. Most of the computation in corporate desktop applications is performed on the server. The desktop receives HTML pages or small-embedded software and scripting information from the server. Instead of being distributed for remote execution, code executes in the place that it lives—the server—and either exports its user interface or exports its object interface for remote use on the desktop. If the application functionality

211

changes, the Web server is updated, not each user's desktop. The IT department does not have to distribute client-side software or configure users'
desktops. The desktop administration savings alone justify using Web technology for internal application deployment.

Desktop Security Shortcomings

Since most computer security statistics show that insiders commit over 90
percent of all computer-related fraud, the desktop threat is higher than any
threat from the Internet. A properly administered commercial firewall with
a stringent security policy and some ancillary products will combat most
desktop threats (such as hacking, denial o-service, and virus software). The
real security problem with most corporations is *inside/man-in/* the firewall.
Insiders often have a motive to strike against a company. Insiders often have
direct physical access to the computer and familiarity of the resource access
controls. The principal threat at the application level is the abuse or misuse of authority by authorized personnel. The main threat at the network
level is the *man-in-the-middle attack*, in which an insider has physical access
to the LAN that allows viewing sensitive data as it traverses the network ().

Although insiders cause more damage than hackers do, the external
hacker problem remains very serious and widespread. Common Gateway
Interface (CGI) scripts or HTTP scripts written in interpreted rather than
compiled languages, such as Practical Extraction and Reporting Language
(PERL) or shell scripts, are particularly vulnerable to hacking because they
can be fed misleading statements. By submitting unanticipated input data
to a CGI script, hackers can get the server to mail them password files, set
up Telnet sessions to secure resources, or gain access to useful configuration data. The WWW security problems are summarized as follows:

- Controlling access to the WWW files
- Eavesdropping
- Misusing the CGI scripts executed on behalf of the browser
- Privacy

NOTE: CGI scripts may be written in scripting languages (like Perl or
TCL) or in any other programming language (like C, Pascal, or Basic).
On some HTTP servers, these CGI programs are stored in a directory
called *cgi-bin*, and so they are also sometimes called *cgi-bin scripts*.

Desktop Web technology is ideal for giving users quick, easy access to internal documents and data. The openness of the technology means that special care must be taken to ensure that the wrong people don't get into unauthorized information or applications. The Web technology does not provide the adequate mechanisms to control access to corporate data. This is due largely to the stateless nature and lack of security mechanisms to perform proper access control delegation (end-to-end security). The Web server is not acting on behalf of the user, but as a single superuser to access backend legacy systems.

Comparison of Client-Server and Web Applications

Traditional client-server development environments can rely on persistent connections between clients and servers. Web communications that use HTTP are intermittent, meaning that they are constantly being established, torn down, and reestablished as the browser requests pages and objects over the network. Therefore keeping the connection state between requests is next to impossible. Alternative methods like cookies and modified URL links are all that technology offers at the present time. This lack of a constant connection state is a major security limitation with HTTP.

Currently, the HTTP protocol only supports basic authentication (cleartext username with an uuencoded password). HTTP roots are from the Internet; therefore HTTP offers no more security than the current suite of Internet applications (FTP, TELNET, and SMTP). Each time that access to a Web page requires authentication, the Web server performs an authorization check. If an empty authorization header field is sent (status code 401-Unauthorized), the user is prompted for a username-password pair. The browser caches the authorization information locally for each given URL realm. This allows users to authenticate once for a given resource. Most modern client-server applications (such as SAP, Novell, and NT Server) use encrypted passwords and strict access-control binding.

Delegation of Authority

Delegation of authority is the process of transferring authority to a given principal in order to perform a certain action that requires access control. Authorization specifies the resources that are to be accessible to a principal, which can be a user, process, role, or job title. A *resource* could be a transaction, account, menu, or something one wants to protect. The user or process that requests access to a resource is defined to be a *principal*. An access control list (ACL) is associated with each resource. An ACL lists the individuals (or principals) authorized to access the resource; it also provides the access rights authorized (such as query, debit, and trade). An ACL manager processes the request from the principal and compares it to the resource's ACL.

Currently, WWW technology does not address authorization in a standard fashion. Most authorization is performed at the operating system level (file and directory) and at the DBMS level (tables). This approach requires desktop application developers to develop specific security code to provide a finer granular access to corporate resources. The benefit of an authorization standard is to provide desktop application developers with a common authorization Application Programming Interface (API) that will allow them to get the same security level without writing specific code. This standard approach will allow an application to get to market quicker—with ease of maintenance.

Most authorization decisions are based on a relationship with a given principal name. This name could be part of a role (group) for a given job title within an organization. In most cases, access to resources is not performed from a principal name, but from a job title or role name. Associative access-control mechanisms consist of resource ACLs or user-capability lists, which identify the resources to which a user has access. This access decision is based on the permission (credit, debit, etc.) that is derived from the intersection of the resource and role pair. An ACL consists of roles and permissions for a given object. Conversely, a capability list consists of resources to which a role has access.

Logical access control is based on the accumulation of a given action over a period of time (thresholds, sequences, or some logical combination). An associative check should be performed before the logical. This will allow organizations to limit a principal's access based on credit or trade limits, or based on necessary sequences to complete a transaction (such as bank authorization before a purchase is completed).

Active Content Problems

Remote distribution and execution of software on the desktop is less risky than on the Internet. Java, JavaBeans, and ActiveX have paved the way for this technology. Most of the security concerns with this technology stem from source code authentication and verification. The Internet poses a major problem because trusting sites one doesn't control is difficult and most of the code is largely anonymous. Since most firewalls filter inbound traffic only, this poses a big problem for corporate communications networks. If some rouge software infects a browser, then all of the keystrokes and data associated with that browser could be sent outbound over the Internet. Java now supports source code authentication.

ActiveX is a binary object code based on OLE that runs inside the browser. ActiveX is not constrained by the browser. Once enabled, it can perform any operation that an OLE-based application can perform. The differences between executing client applications and ActiveX are negligible. ActiveX runs a lot faster than Java, but nothing protects it from wrecking havoc on one's desktop. For example, an ActiveX control called Exploder can shut down Windows 95.

Desktop Security Solutions

A corporate security policy is the foundation upon which all desktop data security–related activities are based. In order for a security policy to be effective, it must receive senior management approval and support. The security policy must keep the technological pace of the information technology system, which allows access to corporate communication resources. The corporate communications security policy must balance the organization's operational requirements with state-of-the-art security solutions. Since both of these are under constant change, the policy must stay current.

Before it can protect corporate communications resources, the corporation must first understand what is being protected and why. The *what* is derived from data classification of corporate proprietary data (very confidential, confidential, internal, and public). The *why* is based on how important (value) the data are to the corporate officers, and what would be the cost and effect of data loss. All data security plans should encompass four major aspects of data security:

1. Physical, including physical and procedural controls to corporate resources
2. Network, including network isolation (or firewalls) and packet encryption
3. Platform, including intrusion-protection and compliance-monitoring tools
4. Application security, including strong authentication, privilege management, and electronic commerce

HTTP

HTTP proposes two major changes: persistent connections and digest authentication. *Persistence* is accomplished by modifying the connection header field to allow for a keep-alive attribute. This keep-alive attribute will allow the browser to form a persistent connection and perform multiple requests without the overhead of opening and closing connections. In addition, stronger authentication mechanisms, such as security tokens, can be employed.

Digest *authentication* is based on a simple challenge-response paradigm using a nonce value (Keyed MD5). This will alleviate the eavesdropping threat that troubles basic authentication.

Secure Socket Layer (SSL), proposed by Netscape, provides a low-level encryption scheme used to encrypt packets in higher-level protocols such as HTTP, TELNET, and FTP. SSL includes provisions for server authentication—verifying the server's identity to the client—and for encryption of data in transit. SSL also includes an optional client authentication that verifies the client's identity to the server. The key pair used for client authentication will also be used for secure email, that is, by using S/MIME Secure/ Multipurpose Internet Mail Extensions (S/MIME).

NOTE: S/MIME is short for Secure/MIME, a new version of the MIME protocol that supports encryption of messages. S/MIME is based on RSA Security's public-key encryption technology. It is expected that S/MIME will be widely implemented, which will make it possible for people to send secure email messages to one another, even if they are using different email clients.

Authorization

To properly design authorization into an enterprise, one has to employ some basic security concepts of separation of duties, least privilege, and individual accountability. *Separation of duties* is the practice of dividing the steps in a critical function (such as monetary transaction approval, audit reviews, wiretap approval) among different individuals. The *least privilege* principle is the practice of restricting a user's access (to data files, processing capability, or peripherals) or type of access (read, write, execute, delete) to the minimum necessary to perform the job. *Individual accountability* consists of holding someone responsible for his or her actions. Accountability is normally accomplished by identifying and authenticating users of the system and subsequently tracing actions on the system to the user who initiated them. The problem is integrating the security mechanism into the existing desktop design.

Active Content Solutions

The browser must control all active content processing. This includes regulating the download, enabling ActiveX controls or external plug-ins, and executing ActiveX scripts and Java. Browsers must also control from whom and where they accept software—which should be from trusted sites and software publishers. The browser exerts this control by storing the public keys of the sites and by digitally signing the active content before it downloads. If code is not signed, the browser by default should not download it.

Browsers protect themselves from Java using a strict applet sandbox-style security measure that resides in the Java virtual machine. The enforcement happens after the code is downloaded, verified, and instantiated by the class loader. The applet security manager takes over monitoring all operations from this point. The applet security manager is established at startup, and it cannot thereafter be replaced, overloaded, overridden, or extended. Applets cannot create or reference their own security manager. Applets are also prevented from reading and writing files on the client file system, and from making network connections except to the originating host.

Microsoft's Authenticode addresses this risk by identifying who published the software before it is downloaded, and by verifying that no one tampered with it before or during the download process. This approach still does not solve the problem of malicious code, such as a virus or Trojan horse, being introduced into the browsers. Be on the lookout for an on-line virus scanner for ActiveX controls. Other than the aforementioned techniques, the only way to control ActiveX is through procedural means such as security awareness training.

Network Security Controls

Desktop application security must be robust enough to thwart network sniffing. Due to the infancy of Intranet desktop technology and its roots from the Internet, a network topology can be constructed to alleviate some of the risk. Some of the options include desktop firewalls, Ethernet-switching hubs that support a virtual LAN, and partitioned LANs. Placing firewalls at strategic points between a department's access to Web pages can effectively limit Web-based desktop applications between departments. Most networking equipment vendors are offering hubs and routers that have firewall-like capabilities, expressly for enhancing Intranet desktop security.

Security Requirements for Desktop Applications

Table 14–1 lists tasks to complete for possible mechanisms that a data security administrator can use to protect desktop applications from threats. The list is a snapshot of the state of the art in security requirements for desktop applications.

CORPORATE DESKTOP SECURITY AND PRIVACY CHECKLIST FORM

Date: _____

The IT management staff responsible for such information held by the enterprise should ensure that the following tasks have been completed (check all tasks completed):

- ___ 1. Desktop application security and privacy policy (least privilege access).
- ___ 2. Program policy (initiate a desktop application security and privacy program and staffing).
- ___ 3. Initiate security and privacy awareness training and education program.
- ___ 4. Senior management approval and organizational support of the security and privacy policies and staff.
- ___ 5. Protection of data (risk assessment).
- ___ 6. Data classification definition/methodology (what are you trying to protect and how important (value) is the data (cost and effect of loss).
- ___ 7. Examples of proprietary data by classification.
- ___ 8. Responsibilities for implementation of this policy.
- ___ 9. Marking and handling procedures by classification.
- ___ 10. Standard access definition document.
- ___ 11. Description of organization's data assets.
- ___ 12. Organization's employee responsibility/function identification.
- ___ 13. Implementation requirements (separation of duties).
- ___ 14. Standard access definition matrix (access request forms).
- ___ 15. Properly administered Internet firewall and ancillary products.
- ___ 16. Firewall policy configuration/backup management procedure.
- ___ 17. Compliance management and intrusion detection tools.
- ___ 18. Intruder escalation process.
- ___ 19. Utilize HTTP's persistent and digest authentication functions.
- ___ 20. SSL for transport privacy for sensitive information.
- ___ 21. All sensitive data folders require an SSL label.
- ___ 22. SSL v3.X for client authentication using public/private keys.
- ___ 23. A physically protected certification authority server.
- ___ 24. A policy addressing multiple certificate authorities (delegation).
- ___ 25. Fine grain authorization promoting least privilege and user accountability.
- ___ 26. The ability to grant access to abstract objects (screen, menu, field).
- ___ 27. Browser capable of controlling active content download, enabling, and execution.
- ___ 28. A certified Java Applet security manager and verifier.

Table 14-1. Desktop Application Security and Privacy Checklist

UNDERSTANDING PRIVACY, DATA MINING, AND THE DESKTOP

Suppose that the statement "Helen subscribes to a certain magazine" is a fact. Can Helen lay claim to this fact? Does she own this fact about herself? She knows she subscribes to the magazine; the friends she tells about her subscription know; employees of the magazine know; the postman knows; others who might see the magazine in her mailbox know, etc. Suppose further that the publishers of the magazine have entered this fact into their computers. Helen's name now appears on a list of all subscribers. Do the publishers have the right to reveal to others that Helen is a subscriber? Do the publishers have the right to sell a list with Helen's name on it?

No one can lay claim to facts that are available to all. Facts in this sense are public and not private in that the individual appropriation of facts does not deprive anyone else of them. Everyone knows the date of the discovery of America, or that $5 \times 5 = 25$. Such knowledge on the part of one person does not prevent others from knowing these facts. Moreover, if individuals cannot own facts, then they cannot own facts about themselves, any more than they can own other kinds of facts. Facts about them do not belong to them.

While no one can own the fact of Helen's subscription, others can own data representing this fact. The publishing company has the exclusive right to manage data entered into their computers; the right to the income from the use of the data; the right to replace or erase the data; the right to keep the data indefinitely; and the right to transfer the data to other computers. In short, the publishers have the right to sell the list, unless selling the list to an advertiser or another magazine for promotional purposes would somehow harm or threaten Helen. An increase in the amount of mail in Helen's mailbox, however, does not constitute harm. Helen may suffer an inconvenience, but she is not harmed or threatened.

Should data privacy extend to data about Helen of the sort "Helen subscribes to a certain magazine"? The strong version of data privacy (called *strong privacy*) entails that it does.

Strong privacy cannot be right. Helen does not own facts about herself of the sort "Helen subscribes to a certain magazine." However, the publisher can own this fact as data. So long as owners of data cause Helen no harm or threaten no harm, then data they own are theirs to use as they wish. They do not violate Helen's data privacy by selling a list with her name on it without her knowledge or consent. Of course, it would be a different matter if Helen subscribed to the magazine on the condition that the publishers do *not* share her data with others. In the case of facts like this, however, she must explicitly opt out.

Now, suppose that the statement "Helen had an operation last October" is a fact. Just as Helen cannot own the fact of her subscription, she cannot own this fact either. Jill knew she was in the hospital; the physicians, nurses, and allied health professionals in attendance knew; the billing staff at the hospital knew; employees of her health maintenance organization knew; the friends and family she told about the operation knew, as did anyone else Helen told. However, although no one owns the fact that Helen had an operation, her operation is not properly common knowledge like the distance between Philadelphia and Washington, DC. Nor does the statement that no one can own facts mean that others have a right to know this fact.

Our society recognizes certain areas of privileged communications. Physician/patient confidentiality, lawyer/client confidentiality, and priest/penitent confidentiality are all instances of privileged communications. Facts revealed in such disclosures are confidential. If society did not respect the privacy of certain personal communications, this would seriously impair the practice of medicine, law, etc., in well-known and documented ways.

Suppose further that billing clerks have entered the fact of Helen's operation into her HMO's database. The HMO would then own the data representing the fact of Helen's operation. Limits to the use of such data come not only from liability for use, but also from the strictures of confidentiality. Even though Helen's HMO owns the fact about her operation as data, the HMO does not have the right to use the data any way they want. Helen's HMO may own the data in the sense that they have the right to exclusive use of the data as put into their desktop computers, but they cannot use the data in ways that would harm or threaten harm. The HMO cannot, for example, violate the confidentiality of the physician/patient relationship. Data are the owners to use as they wish, so long as they harm no one and threaten no harm.

Suppose Helen's HMO wants to engage in outcomes measurement to improve the quality and efficiency of the delivery of care. Outcomes measurement (a form of data mining) involves the examination of clinical encounter information, insurance claims, and billing data to measure the results of past treatments and processes. Helen's HMO wants to share its studies to help providers cut costs and improve care by showing which treatments statistically have been most effective.

The ethical issue concerns the extent to which the HMO must secure Helen's consent to use and disseminate data on her operation. Should medical data privacy cover all facts about Helen's operation stored as data, or can Helen's HMO use and disseminate some data without her consent?

In outcomes measurement, Helen's HMO would need to secure her consent only for use and dissemination of inner-circle data. The confidentiality of patient data protects both inner-circle facts and data. Consequently, the strong version of data privacy does apply to inner-circle data. Individuals and organizations should not automatically have access to these sorts of data. Also, Helen should be able to exercise a substantial degree of control over all inner-circle data.

However, Helen cannot lay claim to intermediate-circle facts any more than she can lay claim to other kinds of facts. On the other hand, her HMO does own the facts of her operation stored as data. The HMO has a right to the exclusive use of these data, so long as such use and dissemination does not harm Helen or threaten harm. By definition, intermediate-circle data are cleansed of personal communications. The HMO does not, therefore, violate Helen's right to privacy when it uses such data in outcomes measurement without Helen's knowledge and consent. In short, medical information privacy ought not to extend to intermediate-circle data.

The use or dissemination of data about individuals without their knowledge and consent is not necessarily a violation of their data privacy. Thus, the data mining of medical records is not by its very nature intrusive and threatening. Nevertheless, the right to exclusive use of data does not confer on owners a right to harm or threaten harm to others. Limits to use and dissemination of data stem not only from liability for use, but also from the structures of confidentiality. Simply because no one can own facts does not mean that everyone has a right to know all facts. Although individuals may not own facts about themselves, they also have no general obligation to make known personal facts about themselves. When individuals make personal facts known to others in confidence, they have the right to insist and expect that they will be kept confidential. Owners of data, therefore, have an obligation to determine that confidential records are secure.

On the other hand, those of us living in this information age ought to be aware of the distinction between facts and data, between what is properly public information and what is private. Some facts about individuals stored as data are facts that are available to all. Organizations can therefore use and disseminate these data without the individuals' knowledge and consent. While individuals may have a right to correct errors and rebut false statements, the property rights of the owners of data may limit their rights to privacy. Ethical and legal analysis in the future will undoubtedly focus on the categories that distinguish kinds and types of data. Such analysis ought to sort data according to whether it is inner, intermediate, or outer circle in order to delimit the private and the public.

ADDRESSING INTERNAL SECURITY THREATS TO THE DESKTOP

The average bank robbery usually nets the perpetrator around $2,100. The average computer break-in causes $470,000 in loss or damage. Most every financial institution across the country (and probably throughout the world) has a detailed plan for what to do in case of an in-person robbery. However, fewer than 4 percent of financial institutions worldwide have developed an internal security policy that specifies the steps to take when suspicious activity is detected with regard to the institution's computer systems and desktops. (See the sidebar, "Rising Internal Threats")

Rising Internal Threats

Increased use of the Internet is a boom to ecommerce and a danger to internal security. This is the belief of IT executives responding to a recent International Data Corporation (IDC) survey of 400 commercial U.S. companies with revenue over $200 million.

The increased use of the Internet is clearly seen as both heaven and hell—heaven because ecommerce can boost revenues and lower costs; hell because it opens up networks and servers to external and, more significantly, internal attacks. IT executives are dealing with these challenges and opportunities by radically increasing spending on firewalls, encryption, antiviral software, intrusion detection, single sign-on, public key infrastructure and certificate authority, and other security management software.

Sixty percent of the IT executives whom IDC surveyed said that they believe the number of security threats to their organizations will increase 30 percent per year. Nevertheless, most of the respondents expressed confidence in their current system security and even more confidence in future system security. This confidence is a result of the increasing number of security technologies they expect to implement and the organizational commitment they perceive backing their security requirements.

Corporations back their commitment to security products with dollars. IDC found the worldwide Internet security software market grew 100 percent from 1999 revenues of $4.5 billion to 2000 sales of $9 billion. Revenues continue to grow to an estimated $4.2 billion per year. Moreover, this market will reach $17.4 billion in 2002 and $29.6 billion by 2005.

IDC splits the overall Internet security software market into several submarkets, including firewalls, encryption software, antiviral software, and authorization, authentication, and administration software. Firewalls, which enforce security restrictions and restrict inappropriate access, will experience the fastest growth. Worldwide revenues in this market will increase 50 percent compounded annually through 2003, compared with an overall market growth rate of 40 percent.

Antiviral software will be the largest market by 2003, with revenues approaching $4 billion. Data from IDC's Internet security survey clearly show that virus attacks are extremely costly to organizations in terms of lost productivity and downtime. The average site in the survey reported 92 incidents of virus infections in a 12-month period. Typically, the viruses affect 23.4 percent of all users, and each user spends 77.2 minutes repairing the problem and damage. IT staff members spend 80.2 minutes on each viral infection. Antiviral software that reduces or eliminates infections is extremely cost effective for IT personnel and users alike.

IT executives in IDC's survey indicated that high costs and lack of integration are the top two obstacles impeding security development. Issues of cost and integration are within the power of security technology suppliers to overcome. Resolving these issues could enlarge the security technology market.

A limited number of people have the capability to rob a financial institution in person. However, potentially millions of people have the capability to cause mischief by computer. Break-in software programs and guidelines can be obtained on the Internet.

Everyone pictures the greatest threat to computer systems and desktops as the archetypal computer hacker: the 14-year-old boy sitting in his basement causing mischief. But keep in mind that a lot of money is at stake in computer crime. The trade in sensitive data about a corporation's customers—such as social security, credit card, and account numbers; balance information; and spending patterns—is lucrative; so lucrative, in fact, that organized crime currently poses the fastest growing threat to an institution's computer security.

And hacking (or an attack to computer systems from outside the institution) does not pose the only or even the greatest threat to an institution's systems. Even if an institution does not have an active link between its Internet server and the institution's backend system, the institution's systems are still vulnerable. Over 90 percent of the threat to an institution's systems come from its own employees: current, former, and contract. So, while an institution may have minimal threat from terrorists, competitors, and organized crime, they still have considerable exposure within the institution itself.

Well, can't the institution buy and implement software or hardware that will keep its computer system safe? Yes and no. There are stand-alone computers whose sole job is to monitor networks and critical machines. There are autonomous software agents, or *autobots*, that roam the system looking for suspicious activities. But no system is completely safe. As has always been the case, security technology and criminals are in a never-ending race, each trying to outsmart the other.

So, where does that leave the security administrator (SA) and the institution? Where the SA has always been: making sure that the institution is as safe as can be. And the single most important factor in assuring that safety is to develop an internal security plan that addresses the institution's computer systems and desktops.

What is an internal security plan for an institution's systems? It is the detailed plan that the institution creates to deal proactively with everything from identifying weaknesses in the systems to damage control in case of a break-in. An internal security plan should address at least four issues:

- *Risk identification:* Knowing the systems well enough to know where their weaknesses are
- *Break-in prevention:* Developing a strategy for addressing the systems' weaknesses by *plugging the holes*
- *Break-in recognition:* Being able to tell when a breach has occurred
- *Damage control:* Minimizing the damage in the event of a breach or disruption

In addition, the plan should outline specific steps for how the institution will go about repairing the system if a break-in or disruption occurs. The plan should state exactly what the institution plans to do when a red alert is sounded.

Most importantly, the plan should name one person as the plan's administrator—one person who is ultimately responsible for the system and its safety. Only one person should act as administrator for two main reasons. First, if a crisis should occur, one person should have the authority to act immediately without having to call a committee together or wait for approval from someone else. Second, one person should be ultimately responsible for clearing employees for various levels of security. If too many people are making security clearance decisions, then the security of the entire system is jeopardized.

Finally, the plan should rely on the expertise and experience of the institution's employees for success. The SA may have hardware and software in place to help monitor security, but the employees who use the system are the ones who ultimately know its weaknesses. Consider pay incentives for employees who help identify and fix weaknesses in the system and for those who help catch break-in attempts. If IT management turns their employees into the system's police force, with real rewards for doing their jobs well, IT management will help transform them from the biggest threat to the institution's security to its greatest protective force—turning the institution's greatest security liability into its greatest security asset.

TRAINING END USERS ON PRIVACY AND SECURITY ISSUES AND PROCEDURES

Education and training programs are critical to an organization's attempt to protect privacy and data security. Formal training programs seek to educate a system's end users about existing policies and proper procedures so that they can incorporate them into everyday behaviors. At their most effective, training programs help employees internalize the value of privacy. Training end users before allowing them access to sensitive data reinforces how seriously committed management is to protecting data privacy. Both formal and informal training programs can help workers understand their responsibilities for protecting information and learn the procedures they must follow to do so. A variety of education tools and policy instruments, such as confidentiality agreements, can serve this role.

Training Programs

Most organizations have formal classes or programs to educate employees about privacy and system security. Many provide such training in an orientation session before giving an employee access to sensitive data. Similarly, refresher courses serve to remind long-time employees about existing policies, to update them on changes, and to discuss strategies for real-life situations that they may encounter on the job. An employee transferring to a different job also needs training to understand how the new position changes his or her responsibilities with regard to privacy and security.

Training should be provided on a regular basis at both the organizational and departmental levels in order to convey general policies as well as the particular requirements of a department. To make the abstract message more concrete, a special effort should be made to discuss specific circumstances encountered in particular departments that might involve or threaten privacy. Interdepartmental workshops or in-service sessions should also be held to discuss practical applications of the confidentiality policy. Because some participants may have scheduling limitations, training options often include flexible delivery formats, widely varying schedule choices, and contingency plans that may include one-on-one sessions for extreme cases.

Training end users to use the information technology system and to safeguard data privacy or security poses special challenges for a number of reasons. In addition to their busy schedules, end users often have a variety of relationships (they may be employees of competing organizations or contractors and/or subcontractors) with other organizations that may compromise data privacy or security of the IT system.

Most sites that use a standard training module (lecture, handouts, and commercial film) for new employees report that such modules are not at all effective in either capturing interest or imparting lasting information. To help spark end-user interest in the importance of data security, a different form of system training is needed for some end users. Innovative training methods have been evaluated in studies on changing behaviors and may be of use for training in confidentiality and security as well. Among the types of techniques that might be incorporated in confidentiality and security training is the use of grand rounds in health provider organizations. With grand rounds, cases or vignettes involving inappropriate disclosure of health information are examined in detail and adjudicated by the medical staff. No matter which training techniques are developed for end users, IT management must help develop the training and act as champions of and models for privacy.

Informal Training

Often the most effective training occurs in spontaneous or unintended ways. Rather than stressing orientation and training programs, some organizations rely more on socializing new employees into an organizational culture that stresses the highest moral, ethical, and legal standards. Nevertheless, this practice can backfire unless the organization has taken care to develop a culture that values privacy and security as much in practice as on paper. New employees seeking to fit in emulate their coworkers, but senior employees who have fallen into bad habits may pass their habits along to others.

In addition to the training and education employees receive in their day-to-day responsibilities, they need to participate in organizational learning. Organizational learning refers to the willingness of employees, both individually and collectively, to examine policies, procedures, and resulting behaviors for their effect on privacy (such as patient privacy in health provider organizations). Organizational learning happens only in organizations where the dominant culture stresses the importance of employee involvement in policy development and procedural evaluation. Similar to efforts toward total quality management, organizational learning involves a constant process of questioning the underlying goals of a policy, whether the resulting procedures appropriately guide policy into practice, and whether actual behavior reflects procedures and, if not, why not. In health provider organizations, managers and employees individually and collectively take responsibility for asking whether patient needs (in terms of both health care delivery and privacy) are being met and what changes would more effectively support those goals.

The cultural environment supports organizational learning by either valuing questions or discouraging them. A medical organization may deny the probability of breaches of patient privacy on the grounds that nobody here would do that. By failing to acknowledge that individuals can (either through accident or malice) fail to protect patient privacy, the organizational culture thus inadvertently ensures that changes in policy and practice are unlikely to occur. These organizational defensive routines are patterns of behavior that prevent employees from having to experience embarrassment or threat (confrontation over behavior that led to breaches of patient privacy). At the same time, these defensive routines prevent employees from examining the nature and causes of that embarrassment or threat. In the absence of mechanisms to the contrary, new employees are likely to emulate the conduct of experienced personnel—whether or not that conduct is in compliance with established organizational policy.

Educational Tools

A variety of tools may be developed to support or enhance formal training programs. These educational tools include attractive pamphlets, computer system enhancements, self-study modules available for use in the computer-training center or to take home, and posted reminders in elevators and cafeterias.

An organization's IT system may be designed to educate end users as to possible breaches of confidentiality. One option is to make a confirmation screen appear whenever an end user accesses sensitive data. The screen should contain text reminding the end user that sensitive data is about to be accessed and asking the end user if the action is justified. Another common option is to display an abbreviated version of the confidentiality policy every time an end user signs onto the IT system. Unless organizations change the appearance of these screens on a regular basis, however, they are unlikely to be effective. For example, changing the presentation or the content will catch an end user's eye.

Self-study computerized modules may offer additional opportunities for informal training. These could be offered across departmental desktop machines or at a central location such as the human resources department.

IT management should also develop a special pamphlet to present the organization's confidentiality and security policies. The pamphlet should be short and visually attractive to capture end user attention in a way that a chapter in a larger policy manual could not. With the word *confidentiality* prominently displayed on the cover, the pamphlet should include the following information:

- *A summary of the organization's confidentiality philosophy and reference to the policy:* End users should be referred to specific sections of the main policy manual for further details related to what information is to be considered confidential, procedures to follow for ensuring confidentiality, and disciplinary actions that would follow breaches of policy.
- *References to relevant statutory and regulatory requirements:* A synopsis of relevant law should be referenced to reinforce the organization's policy and emphasize that confidentiality is not simply an organizational requirement.
- *References to specific functions of the IT system designed to reinforce policy:* The pamphlet should describe how user ID and password combinations constitute legal signature. It should inform end users of the existence of audit records and remind them they will be held accountable for the files they access. It should also describe a function that allows end users to look up access to their own compiled employee records.
- A reminder to end users about privacy rights and responsibilities.
- The pamphlet should be distributed to new end users during orientation and should be readily visible in work areas. The organization should stress that a person's record exists in several formats, including the electronic one. In specific reference to the IT system, the pamphlet should read as follows:

1. The end user's computer key (identification and password) is considered equivalent to his or her signature.
2. An audit trail may be kept when the end user's key is used to access data from the computer.
3. The end user could be contacted for any concern over why his or her key accessed a particular file. The self-audit lookup feature of the IT system makes end user privacy a high-visibility issue and creates an organizational ethos that is not observed at other organizations. The privacy of end user's electronic records should also be personalized.

Additional measures can be implemented to reinforce policy manuals. Organizations should also develop a video to reinforce key concepts of the organization's policies on end-user privacy and security and help make them stand out from data on benefits, recycling, and cafeteria hours. New employees should watch the video during orientation and before a system ID and password are issued. Unlike a commercial product with anonymous actors, the video should demonstrate management's commitment to the confidentiality of information by having senior executives in the organization introduce policy concepts. The video should also include examples that help personalize violations to employees. Actor-employees in the video should re-create instances where privacy has been breached. The video should be initially innocent, reinforcing the message that even good intentions can lead to unintended consequences. Actor-employees should be shown being disciplined for accessing another employee's electronic record to obtain a mailing address for a get-well card. The organization will be successful in delivering the message if it presents examples to which employees could relate.

A key factor in reinforcing organization policy is the practice of retraining every year. Annual installments should remind employees that policy is in place to guide their behavior. Annual training sessions also should allow an organization to educate employees about changes that have resulted from statutory or regulatory changes, procedural changes, and changes in the threat environment. Sections should be marked off on the employee performance review form to record the employees' attendance at training and viewing of the confidentiality video.

In addition to a formal policy guide, periodic memos and newsletters should be circulated to employees in order to provide regular reinforcement and to make a tangible addition to the employee's knowledge base. Information on changes in the data system should be distributed routinely, and the ongoing policies should be regularly reinforced.

User Confidentiality Agreements

In addition to informing employees of the organization's expectations with regard to keeping data confidential, organizations need to hold them responsible for their behavior. Organizations should require any individual accessing the IT system to sign a form verifying that he or she had read, had understood, and was committed to the organization's confidentiality policies. In keeping with other ongoing efforts, employees should be required to sign this agreement during the initial orientation session and annually thereafter at the time of their performance review. Confidentiality agreements may also be used for nonemployees who have access to data; these can include contract workers, vendors, office staff, students, and temporary workers.

MoNiToRING DESkToP USERS FoR PRIVACY VioLATioNS

The past several years have shown a growing trend among employers to monitor the actions and performance of their workers (desktop users). Concerns about employee productivity, privacy violations, quality of work, employee theft or misuse of company property, unlawful drug use, and other factors potentially affecting employee productivity, combined with technological developments, have increasingly led employers to use new ways to monitor employee performance. Recently, an industry survey of 1,000 businesses found that about 33 percent of the businesses have searched employee computer files on their desktop, voice mail, email, or other networking communications. The percentage jumped to 40 percent for businesses with 1,700 or more employees. This part of the chapter discusses the legality under federal law of various forms of technological surveillance of employees or users for privacy violations.

Federal Wiretap Statutes

Although often referred to as "wiretap" statutes, federal laws on this subject cover much more than tapping onto telephone lines. They also include eavesdropping on oral conversations and intercepting or accessing phone or electronic communications for privacy violations. Employers considering technological methods of monitoring employee communications should first carefully examine whether the contemplated actions would be lawful under these statutes. The complexity of both statutes makes this task difficult.

Telephone Conversations

Under the federal statute, telephone conversations constitute *wire communications* since they are *aural* (containing the human voice) and are transmitted over wire, cable, or similar facilities. With certain exceptions, it is unlawful to *intercept* private wire communications. The term *intercept* is defined to mean the acquisition of the contents of the communication through the use of any *electronic (desktop), mechanical, or other device*. It is also unlawful to use or disclose the contents of any private wire communication that was unlawfully intercepted. The statute's definition of *electronic, mechanical, or other device* excludes telephone equipment furnished by the provider of the communication service (the phone company) or by the user for connection to the facilities of the service and used in the ordinary course of business. This is commonly referred to as the *business phone extension* exclusion. Numerous court decisions have addressed this exception, some finding it applicable and others not. However, two decisions by the Tenth Circuit Court of Appeals, which is the federal court of appeals for Colorado and several other states, have found employer monitoring of phone calls *lawful* under the business extension exclusion.

Oral Conversations

Federal law also provides protection to *oral communications* that are not transmitted over phone lines. As with *wire communications*, federal law prohibits only unlawful *interception* (or use or disclosure of contents of a communication that was unlawfully intercepted), and *interception* must involve the use of an electronic, mechanical, or other device. Furthermore, federal law defines protected *oral communications* as including only those uttered by a person exhibiting an expectation that such communication is not subject to interception under circumstances justifying such expectation. Consent is also a lawful basis for interception. Thus, if an employer wishes to eavesdrop on an oral conversation, under federal law it must do one or more of the following actions:

1. Avoid the use of any electronic, mechanical, or other device.
2. Only eavesdrop in situations where the people engaging in the conversation could not reasonably expect not to be overheard.
3. Obtain the consent, express or implied, of one of the parties to the conversation.

Video Surveillance

Surveillance limited to video images, without sound, would not be subject to federal wiretap statutes if the surveillance does not acquire the *contents* of any communications. The term *contents* is defined to include any information concerning the substance, purport, or meaning of a communication. If a hidden video camera observed two employees speaking and then exchanging cash for drugs, it might possibly be considered to have intercepted some of the *contents* of the communication. However, an argument could also be made that it only observed an act and did not acquire the contents of what was spoken. An *interception* would definitely occur if the video images were actually used to acquire a communication through lip reading, or perhaps even if it were feasible to do so. If video surveillance were found to have acquired the contents of communications, it would likely be unlawful unless there were implied *consent* by virtue of an announced policy of video surveillance in specified areas.

EMail

Email and other electronic communications that do not include the human voice constitute *electronic communications* under the federal wiretap statutes. The 1986 amendments to the federal law added a new chapter that prohibits, with certain exceptions, accessing wire or electronic communications that are in electronic storage. Because the exceptions under this chapter differ from those in the chapter that prohibit intercepting communications, and because the legal remedies for a violation are not as broad, some commentators have questioned whether accessing email messages would constitute violations of both chapters. Accessing email messages while stored electronically does not constitute an *interception*, and the legality of that action will be determined only under the 1986 chapter of the law addressing access of electronically stored communications.

That chapter of the federal law contains a broad exception, which provides that accessing stored electronic communications is not unlawful if authorized by the person or entity providing the wire or electronic communications service. This exception should allow employers free access to email messages stored on email systems that it provides; however, the lawfulness of access to email messages may be questioned if they are delivered to the workplace through an independent service such as AOL. In order to establish implied consent to email access on the part of employees, a cautious employer will publish a policy informing employees that the company reserves the right to access and monitor all email messages stored on its computer system, regardless of the messages' origin or content. In addition, an employer who obtains the written acknowledgment or consent of its employees to such a practice should have even greater protection.

If an employer also wishes to intercept email messages while in transit, the interception chapter provides an exception for a provider of a wire or electronic communications service to intercept communications as necessary to the rendition of the service or the protection of the rights or property of the provider. If that exception is not broad enough to cover the desired scope of email interception, the employer should take all necessary steps to publish its policy of intercepting messages while in transit and thereby obtain implied consent of employees. The business extension exclusion for voice communications over telephones, discussed previously, presumably would not apply if the interception were not accomplished through use of telephone equipment used in the ordinary course of business.

The reading or copying of an *electronic communication* is defined by federal law to be the transfer of data by electronic, or photooptical means, and does not include electronic storage of such communications. Copying, reading, recording, or taking an electronic communication while it is in transit would constitute wiretapping, however, unless it is with the consent of one of the parties to the communication, or unless it is necessary for the providing of the service or to protect the provider against fraud.

Therefore, it is safer for employers to access stored email messages than to intercept them while in transit. Access to stored internal email messages on a company's computer system should be lawful. For extra protection, or if interception of email messages in transit is desired, employers should publish a policy of monitoring email messages.

Voice Mail

A voice mail message containing the human voice is a *wire communication*, not an *electronic communication*. Under the chapter of federal law governing access to electronically stored wire or electronic communications, the legality of accessing electronically stored voice mail messages would be the same as discussed previously for email. Unlike the definition of *electronic communication*, however, the definition of *wire communication* includes such communications while in electronic storage. Therefore, the chapter of federal law that prohibits intercepting wire communications would also appear to apply to acquiring electronically stored voice mail messages, unless the business extension exclusion discussed previously in the section concerning phone conversations applies. To avoid being held liable for an unlawful *interception*, the cautious employer should publish a policy sufficient to satisfy the requirements for valid implied consent.

Desktop Computer Files

Desktop computer files that do not contain the human voice cannot be *wire communications*. The definition of *electronic communication* is limited to any transfer of signs, signals, writing, images, sounds, data, or intelligence of any nature transmitted in whole or in part by a wire, radio, electromagnetic, photoelectric, or photooptical system. Therefore, computer files that are created and then stored on a desktop computer would generally not constitute *electronic communications*—those computer files involve no transfer or transmission. If that is the case, the federal wiretap statutes do not restrict access to desktop computer files. To the extent that a desktop computer file is a transferred communication, for example, a computer file attached to an email message, the analysis in the preceding concerning access to or interception of email messages would apply.

Computer Tracking Systems

Computerized systems that track, for example, the number of keystrokes or errors by an employee, or the number and duration of customer service phone calls handled, would not be subject to the federal wiretap statutes— such systems do not acquire the content of any communications.

Employee Monitoring

Technological monitoring of employees in the workplace presents both practical and legal issues. On the practical side, employers should consider exactly what they need or expect to gain through monitoring, and what alternatives may exist. Many commentators and organizations claim that employee monitoring may be counterproductive by resulting in lower morale, increased job stress, and perhaps even lower production. Horror stories on this subject include testimony before the Senate concerning an express-mail company employee whose computer logged the length and frequency of her trips to the restroom; the employee was reprimanded for using the restroom four times in one day. Nevertheless, employers should be aware of the possibility of future legislative action and the negative fallout that can result from employee monitoring.

   Employers should consider the expense of litigation, even if no specific law appears to have been violated. Another action is still pending in federal court in New York by an individual whose voice mail messages to his lover were accessed and then played back for his wife. Recently, a West Virginia jury awarded three employees $125,000 in a case involving video surveillance in locker rooms; the surveillance commenced after the employer heard rumors of illegal drug transactions. The court in that case also issued a permanent injunction against video monitoring in locker rooms, showers, bathrooms, and other areas where there is a high expectation of privacy. The lesson is fairly simple: the further an employer goes in monitoring employees or in disclosing information obtained through monitoring, the more likely a lawsuit will be filed. An employer who chooses to proceed with some form of employee monitoring as discussed in this chapter should consider the following points:

1. Identify the business purpose for the monitoring, and confine the extent and manner of monitoring to what is reasonable to accomplish that purpose.

2. Avoid recording all communications or otherwise monitoring personal communications, unless a strong reason to do so exists and unless employee consent is first obtained.

3. Unless covert monitoring is both necessary and lawful, inform employees in writing of the company's policy concerning monitoring. Specifically identify what types of communications may be monitored (phone calls, voice mail, email, computer files, etc.), which job positions or other categories of employees are subject to monitoring, what means are used for the monitoring (live monitoring of calls, tape recording, random review of email, etc.), and whether monitoring may include personal as well as business communications. Consider obtaining from each employee a signed acknowledgment that the employee is aware of the company's policy. Also consider obtaining from each employee a signed consent to monitor the phone calls, email, voice mail, etc.

4. Consider adopting and publishing a policy that monitored phone lines and company voice mail, email, and computer equipment are to be used only for business purposes. Inform employees that they should not expect privacy with respect to communications over these systems.

5. Inform employees that any employee passwords for company systems do not guarantee privacy and may be overridden by the company. Consider requiring employees to notify a designated administrator of their passwords to facilitate any necessary company access to these systems.

6. If continuous monitoring or tape recording of customer service phone lines is necessary for quality assurance or other compliance purposes, consider a recorded message announcing to outside parties that calls are monitored.

7. Carefully control the dissemination of information obtained through monitoring.

The preceding suggestions and attention to the other points in this chapter should reduce the risk of litigation and legal liability for employers who choose to utilize technological monitoring techniques in the workplace.

RESPoNDING To INDUSTRY-SPECIFIC ISSUES

Longstanding tensions between consumers' right to privacy and the legitimate business needs of financial service providers came to a head in 1999 when Congress passed legislation addressing privacy issues. It was inevitable that Congress would act. Consumers have legitimate interests in privacy. Financial service providers have an equally legitimate need to gather and use information, not only to prevent fraud, but also to expand consumer options.

In its first direct response, Congress in 1999 addressed privacy issues as part of the Gramm—Leach—Bliley (GLB) Act, which achieved comprehensive reform of laws governing financial services. Title V of GLB put in place the most far-reaching set of privacy safeguards pertaining to financial information and certain personal data ever adopted by Congress.

Regulatory agencies must still complete the critical task of writing the detailed rules that will dictate how the new statute will be applied. But the major mandates of Title V are clear enough. The following requirements apply to all covered institutions, including banks, credit unions, thrifts, insurance carriers, brokerage firms, credit card issuers, and electronic funds transfer (EFT) services:

- Businesses may not disclose a customer's account number for the purpose of marketing appeals by a third party.
- Businesses must develop practices to protect information from unauthorized access by outsiders—hackers, for instance.
- Companies must inform customers in a clear, timely manner of their policies concerning the sharing of information with unaffiliated third parties.
- Customers must be informed of their right to opt out of that arrangement—that is, to refuse permission for the dissemination of certain types of data.

GLB: Just the Beginning

Despite the historic nature of the legislation, passage of GLB has not satisfied the most ardent privacy advocates. Drafts of federal agencies' regulations to implement Title V were still works in progress when efforts began to enact even more stringent legislation at the national and state levels. Providers of financial services thought that the early months of 2000 would be a time for refining the fine print of detailed federal rules. Instead, the providers and the public they serve face the threat of additional legislation, most likely at the state level, that would further circumscribe (possibly in destructive ways) what companies can do with information about their customers.

The new statute and the quest for more legislation at the federal and state levels create uncertainty in all sectors of the industry. There is good reason for the concern felt by banks, credit unions, thrifts, insurance carriers, brokerage firms, credit card issuers, and electronic funds transfer (EFT) services. As they consider appeals for yet another round of privacy legislation, policymakers would do well to consider the following points:

- Even a few states imposing disparate versions of privacy requirements would amount to a recipe for chaos.
- Additional restrictions would make compliance efforts by institutions not only cumbersome, but also expensive and confusing for both employees and consumers.
- At a time when U.S. authorities are attempting to reconcile policies here with privacy principles adopted by the European Union, adding new, different standards would complicate that process and may also slow it down.
- With enforcement agencies refining regulations to implement Title V and service providers striving to improve their voluntary privacy safeguards, logic dictates that systems now being honed should be given a real-world test before yet new policies are even considered—let alone enacted.

The public and policymakers alike need to understand that at least some of the additional privacy measures would have the unintended consequence of damaging consumers' interests. To that end, this chapter has examined the implications of the ongoing policy debate and put it in context.

Reasonable outcomes—that is, addressing consumers' concerns without forcing service providers into a straitjacket—will be more likely if the effort to impose new statutes is better understood. This reality places a new premium on informed decision making and accurate media coverage that provides factual information to help offset the often emotional arguments of those who seek still more onerous laws.

The Dynamic in 1999: How Everyone Got Here

Though several earlier laws (such as the Fair Credit Reporting Act and the Electronic Fund Transfer Act) dealt with certain privacy concerns, there was a growing sense of unease over the issue among consumer advocates and some members of Congress as GLB moved toward passage in 1999.

Given the landscape, it was hardly surprising that privacy advocates used the bill as a vehicle for their agenda. But the pressure to act was not solely the result of energetic consumer advocacy efforts.

Privacy experts have also stressed the crucial contribution of enhanced information exchanges in providing better service to consumers at lower cost. That includes additional choices as to how and from whom customers get the services they want. But many of these benefits remain in the development stage, and others have only begun to be available to the public. Because the benefits lack immediacy for many consumers, privacy advocates wanting to impose new restrictions can more easily exploit fear of the future and limited negative experience.

The ability to exploit an isolated, but compelling incident was illustrated recently when Minnesota authorities accused a major bank of selling customers' personal information to a marketing firm. The bank consented to cease the practice and to pay a fine.

While no evidence showed that the Minnesota case represented a widespread practice, that case gave the advocates of statutory policing (as opposed to self-regulation) a timely talking point. It also fed a belief that business organizations viewed private financial information as a commodity to be sold for profit rather than as a tool to benefit their customers.

Meanwhile, the privacy issue has gained greater currency through pervasive discussion of the related issue of security of online information. The Federal Trade Commission (FTC), having laid out a set of principles for Internet information practices, periodically reports to Congress on the degree of voluntary compliance by the operators of commercial sites. In 1999, the FTC reported that only 30 percent of the 200 most frequently used Internet sites were complying with all of the FTC's principles. The FTC's principles stipulate that users should be informed about how personal information might be used, that they have an opportunity to consent to that use, that they can access data concerning them, and that the Web site operator has provided security measures against improper scrutiny by other parties.

Anxiety about Internet security is heightened by individual anecdotes that become horror-story metaphors. While these may be atypical, the

industry (as it shapes practices and public affairs policies) should understand the emotional appeal of these accounts.

According to widespread public sentiment, many Internet service
providers are reluctant to meet privacy concerns. In other words, ISPs don't
view privacy as a critical issue and thus have lax security on their sites. An
annual survey of consumer sentiment carried out by three universities and
AT&T Labs showed in the spring of 2000 that many Americans shared that
view. According to the research, 88 percent of Internet users fretted about
threats to their privacy, up from 82 percent the previous year. While this
poll focused on use of the Internet, ecommerce can easily be associated
with all commerce in which computers play any significant role and where
privacy issues can arise.

The Rush to Legislate

The pressure to legislate has not abated with enactment of GLB. For elected
officials, crusading for tighter privacy laws is a politically savvy move that
shows them delivering an ostensible benefit for the average citizen without levying new taxes or spending large sums. That is an enviable posture
for a political leader, particularly in an election year and in an environment
in which many voters believe industry has assumed the Big Brother role
that George Orwell had assigned to government.

Whatever the motivation, elected politicians across the nation are now
racing to surpass the federal rule makers, creating a privacy pile on. Issues
at hand include the following:

- Legislators in at least 18 states are promoting bills aimed at imposing
  constraints more rigorous than those in GLB. This raises the threat of
  a hodgepodge of restrictions that would constitute an operational nightmare, particularly for any service provider operating across state lines.
- New federal legislation with bipartisan backing, now pending, would
  toughen GLB's privacy regime.
- A bipartisan Privacy Caucus has sprung up on Capitol Hill to promote
  additional restrictions on the use of financial information. Senate Democ-
  rats have formed a separate Privacy Task Force for the same purpose.

The irony is that Title V, as it now stands, goes further than anyone
would have imagined a few years ago in terms of privacy protection. It
requires service providers to give customers extensive explanations of their
information-sharing policies. Companies must also notify patrons of secu-

rity measures to prevent the theft of personal information. These disclosures must be distributed at the outset of a business relationship and annually thereafter.

Preexisting business relationships are also covered by the new disclosure requirement. Based on this disclosure, customers have the right to *opt out*, or prevent their service provider from transferring nonpublic, personal information to an unaffiliated third party. Individuals can opt out at any time during their business relationship with the company.

Perhaps the most serious threat of privacy overkill comes from those who would replace the *opt-out* approach with *opt in*—an approach that requires consumers to actively accept the disclosure practices of financial institutions.

As discussed in more depth next, experience in other fields shows consumers regard *opt-in* requirements as a burden, and they fail to take the active step of *opting* in even when it is to their clear benefit. In many instances, the failure to *opt in* to disclosure policies would deprive consumers of clearly beneficial services to which they have grown accustomed.

A provision of GLB that would allow state law, in some instances, to supersede the new federal rules heightens the potential impact of any new state measures. Title V, as it now stands, contains a number of common sense exceptions that allow certain information transfers, even if a customer opts out. These exceptions are designed to facilitate a variety of routine transactions, such as verifying bank balances and enabling use of credit, ATM, and debit cards. But new state rules might exclude some or all of the federal exceptions, thereby creating obstacles that would reduce convenience, add costs, and weaken fraud-prevention measures.

Combined with an opt-in rule, elimination of such exceptions could unintentionally deprive consumers of access to services that they prize because many services cannot exist without the data sharing excepted by Title V. Until customers realized that they must exercise an opt-in document to receive services, the financial institution could not provide the service. Thus, customers would unwittingly lose conveniences to which they have grown accustomed.

Indeed, shared financial information is critical to beneficial innovations, including fraud reduction initiatives and expanded payment options. For example, databases operated by third parties rely on shared information from institutions across the country to verify account existence and availability of funds in order to help reduce check fraud. While the data are comprehensive, they contain no personal information; all identifiers are *scrubbed* by the participating financial institutions and only numeric information is shared.

Consumers also benefit from antifraud programs that use artificial intelligence to identify unusual or unexpected changes in an individual's credit card spending—a common tip-off of credit card theft. Such programs, which rely on the sharing of up-to-date information, could be placed at risk by unwise state regulations. Also, state measures may encourage a flood of class action lawsuits against financial institutions over alleged privacy violations.

Holes in the Case for Additional Regulation

The case for additional regulation can be rebutted with hard facts. For one, the examples of actual harm to consumers because of privacy abuse are rare. Moreover, existing law covers many familiar privacy problems:

- The Fair Credit Reporting Act deals with such issues as erroneous information that can undermine an individual's borrowing power.
- The Electronic Fund Transfer Act requires financial institutions to inform their customers of information disclosure policies.
- The Telephone Consumer Protection Act regulates telemarketing practices, requiring (among other things) that consumers have the opportunity to *opt out* of future solicitation by a specific company.

In the final stages of consideration of GLB, some experts pointed out that restrictions (no matter how well intended) could have unfortunate results. That had been the case in Maine, for instance, when the state attempted to protect the confidentiality of medical records. Though the Maine law that took effect early in 1999 had been discussed for years, it still had odd, unintended consequences. For example, it impeded close relatives from getting information on the condition of family members and it slowed the delivery of gifts to hospital patients. The measure was soon repealed.

Still, in passing GLB, Congress included restrictions on information use. Many members of Congress, including some of the most liberal, said that they were satisfied with the opt-out provision, the bar on transmission to third parties, and other safeguards. However, the landmark nature of Title V received insufficient notice, perhaps because the measures eventually adopted were billed as a *compromise*. The last-minute amendment allowing states to enact still more restrictions (without regard to logic or the uniformity essential for our national markets) was itself a compromise that reflected the appetite for further regulation. It demonstrated lack of understanding by some policymakers, much of the media, and consumers themselves, of how far GLB went; it also showed how unreasonable regulation could have potential adverse impact on consumers.

The Solid Case for a Moratorium

Because the chairmen of key congressional committees and some other leaders seem reluctant to propose new federal legislation so soon after GLB's enactment, Congress will probably not rush to impose additional restrictions. However, rhetorical rumblings will probably still occur in Washington, and these will likely reinforce public apprehension and keep consumer advocacy groups energized. At least some of the states, absent of legal restrictions imposed by Washington, may well enact disparate legislation that will create new difficulties.

In this atmosphere, the best argument for those opposed to new legislation is that the already strong privacy provisions of GLB, as refined in the agency regulations now being sculpted, must be given a reasonable opportunity to take hold. Indeed, Congress appeared to be heading in this direction when it ordered a 6-month study by regulators (to begin after GLB takes effect) on information sharing among affiliated providers. Therefore, Congress has good reason to place a broader moratorium on additional statutory restrictions, state as well as federal, until the new regulations are in place and tested in practice.

Trade associations and individual institutions must make this case in Washington, both to legislators and relevant executive branch officials. State capitals in which problematic legislation is pending must also get the word. The key message at the state level is that GLB contains meaningful safeguards that both protect consumers' privacy rights and allow consumers to benefit from enhanced services.

Getting the word out also means educating news organizations, which can play an important part in shaping public opinion on this issue. With editorial board meetings, background papers, op-ed articles, and other devices, the financial services industry should attempt to apply reality checks on the more expansive arguments of those who demand drastic measures now. Coverage that argues for pragmatism and patience can help calm the atmosphere and encourage legislators to think through the implications of additional reform.

In this context, the ability to resist inappropriate additional legislation is compounded by the fact that specific partisan or ideological division does not exist on this issue. Though more liberals, generally speaking, side with the privacy advocates, enough centrists and staunch conservatives are allied with them to make that faction seem broadly based. This complicates legislative strategies and also makes public relations more difficult because journalists are fond of strange bedfellows' subplots and tend to ascribe more credibility to such alliances. The industry can easily be stereotyped in the media as predictable, self-interested, and obsessed with the bottom line. The opposition is more colorful, more diverse, and (ostensibly, at least) altruistic. So service providers should meet this challenge with as many positive and precise messages as possible.

Beware of Opt In

Encourage scrutiny of what is potentially the most burdensome and impractical requirement contained in pending federal and state bills—the *opt-in* standard. The opt-in standard would force institutions to seek all customers' affirmative consent to each of those institutions' privacy practices. Administering the opt-in approach would obviously be a nightmare because of the difficulty in getting consumers to respond to paper or email requests without a clear incentive for doing so.

In one real-life test of the opt-in procedure, US West tried the system when it sought to solicit customers' permission to track patterns in telephone use for market research purposes. Though the parallel with financial services is not exact, the experience of US West underscores the problems of opt in. The company was unable to reach one-third of those whose permission was sought, despite repeated attempts. Those individuals, therefore, were not offered the services being developed by the research effort. Further, the opt-in procedure is so inherently inefficient that it costs US West nearly $40 for each consumer who was contacted.

In depicting the negative consequences of unreasonable restrictions, the distinction between harmful and benign uses of personal information should be recognized. Maintaining confidentiality about a person's medical history clearly deserves high priority, for instance, because misuse of it could affect the individual's career prospects. That is a very different situation than, say, determining that a particular person's age and financial status indicate that he or she is a plausible recipient of a letter describing annuity programs.

However, that distinction is often lost in the current political debate swirling around Title V. A bill pending in California would not only impose the opt-in requirement, but would also prescribe heavy fines for transfer of any personal financial information, public or nonpublic, even if no actual damage to the individual consumer has occurred. This bill would take privacy safeguards, as administered in the nation's largest state, to a very different and very frightening level. It would also inhibit the birth of new companies and make existing smaller enterprises leery of new ventures. Hence, competition would be discouraged and consumer choice limited.

Advocates of opt-in regulations assume that consumers do not want or have nothing to gain from one of the large opportunities available in the modern financial marketplace—carefully directed offers to those persons most likely to have a need for new products and services developed by studying data derived from consumers' behavior and resources. The ability to create such opportunities is one of the main dividends of allowing financial service providers reasonable flexibility in the use of customer information.

Finally, financial institutions have a large stake in preventing extreme restrictions. Opt in is the worst example of that threat, but not the only specter haunting the industry. The general public also has a large (if sometimes less obvious) interest in heading off unreasonable laws. The best way to avoid new statutory constraints is to raise awareness of the public's stake by focusing on specific facts:

- Increasing the efficiency of operations helps everyone because it enhances service and controls costs.
- Burdensome regulation, by contrast, will create unnecessary additional costs that inevitably trickle down to consumers.
- Unreasonable regulation imposes a special burden on companies struggling to establish themselves and on smaller existing providers. These hardships squelch competition and ultimately reduce consumer options.
- Unreasonable regulation may deprive consumers of information about products and services that could otherwise be communicated with the individual consumer's needs in mind.
- As a corollary, unreasonable regulation may consign consumers to a continued onslaught of mass-market solicitations by mail, phone, and email for *irrelevant* goods and services.
- Reasonable use of financial information is necessary to combat fraud, the price of which radiates throughout society.
- Additional legislation could well open the gates to frivolous litigation— a wasteful process that in the long run benefits no one.

The preceding list provides sound, factual principles. These principles deserve to be put forward vigorously and promptly, even as federal regulators are honing rules necessary to implement GLB. The tug of war over privacy has been going on for many years. Whatever the fate of what is now being considered, the contest will most probably continue well into the future as technology evolves. Just as financial service providers will seek to continuously improve ways of delivering their products, they would be wise to vigorously engage in the privacy debate—effectively and indefinitely.

While this chapter discussed privacy issues for corporate desktop application development technology, the next chapter discusses a mobile road warrior's laptop, which is used to maintain person-to-person reachability. Topics covered in the next chapter include, but are not limited to, laptop mobility and vulnerability; assuring privacy and security in mobile computing; and establishing secure communications for mobile users.

15

PROTECTING THE PRIVACY OF THE ROAD WARRIOR'S LAPTOP

Ubiquitous network connectivity for devices does not automatically imply continuous reachability for people. People move from place to place and switch from one network device to another. As a result, phones ring in empty offices, email cannot reach most cell phones, and spam clogs expensive, low-bandwidth links to laptops. Whereas existing mechanisms have addressed host mobility or the mobility of people within one network, few have allowed people—the ultimate and most important endpoints of communication—to roam freely, without being constrained to one location, one application, one device, or one network.

Therefore, one of the defining trends of this decade has been the explosive growth of the Internet and other communication networks. People or *road warriors* have access to a growing number of networks (Internet, cellular, pager) on a growing number of devices (laptops, personal digital assistants, cell phones, smart cards) at a growing number of locations (work, home, on the road). Unfortunately a growing problem for these road warriors is maintaining reachability; as network devices, applications, and accessible locations proliferate, other road warriors (correspondents) are less likely to be able to get in touch with a mobile road warrior at any particular time. For example, a correspondent might not have the mobile road warrior's hotel phone number, or the correspondent's email application might not interoperate with the mobile road warrior's phone. Therefore, a road warrior laptop needs to meet the following goals:

- *Maintain person-to-person reachability:* The laptop should direct the correspondent's communications to the mobile person regardless of whether the two participants have direct access to the same kind of network, device, or application.

- *Protect the mobile person's privacy:* To route communications to a mobile person, a mobile road warrior laptop must track the devices and applications through which the person is currently reachable. The laptop should not reveal this tracking information, whether current or historical, because it could be used to deduce the mobile road warrior's location and compromise his or her privacy. In addition, receiving unwanted messages is also an invasion of privacy. Many applications, such as those in many phone systems, have no way to deliver high priority communication intrusively while delivering low priority communication unintrusively. Mobile road warriors should be able to have all their incoming communications prioritized and filtered according to their preferences.
- *Extend easily to new network devices and applications:* Given the rate at which communication networks, devices, and applications proliferate, a mobile road warrior laptop must be easily extensible.
- *Be deployable without modifying existing infrastructure:* Considering the fast pace at which new networking technologies develop, a communication system that requires changes to the existing network and telecommunications infrastructure is difficult to deploy and runs the risk of becoming obsolete before it is widely available. A mobile road warrior laptop must be easily and rapidly deployable to benefit the greatest number of people.

This chapter discusses a mobile road warrior's laptop, used to maintain person-to-person reachability. The central component of the laptop tracks a mobile person's location, accepts communications on his or her behalf, converts them into different application formats according to his or her preferences, and forwards the resulting communications to him or her. In contrast to similar systems, the mobile road warrior's laptop protects the mobile user's privacy, is easily extensible to new network devices and applications, and has been deployed with no modifications to the existing network and telecommunications infrastructure. In this chapter, the design, implementation, and preliminary evaluation of the laptop is described in the form of a checklist—a service that integrates Internet and telephone communication and addresses the need for person-to-person reachability. The following topics are covered in this chapter:

- Assuring Privacy and Security in Mobile Computing
- Establishing Secure Communications for Mobile Users
- Addressing Laptop Mobility and Vulnerability: Very Technical Issues
- Responding to Industry-Specific Issues

ASSURING PRIVACY AND SECURITY IN MOBILE COMPUTING

The explosive growth of the Internet and the World Wide Web has fueled the image of personal digital assistants (PDAs), laptop computers, and mobile computing devices of all kinds as valuable *information retrieval* devices, rather than stand-alone *islands* of computation. Surveys have shown that mobile computing users want access to the Internet and their desktop, not a new *killer app* for mobile computing devices. Wireless infrastructure is rapidly being deployed to enable *untethered* mobile computing.

Even as mobile computing and network computing are gaining momentum, Internet security is sharing the spotlight. Security and authentication on open networks is already a difficult problem, even without the additional risks posed by wireless media and the additional software constraints imposed by mobile computing devices with capabilities more modest than those of full-blown laptops.

Unfortunately, security and authentication in unprotected networks such as the Internet is a difficult problem, and the wireless medium is physically easier to compromise than wired media. Much attention has been focused recently on securing this link. However, link-level encryption and authentication solve only part of the problem. Mobile users still need to authenticate themselves to services and servers higher than this level. Users of mobile computers will want access to resources in a visited mobile environment, on the strength of credentials validated by their home environment. Users of network computing devices and the service providers to which those devices connect will both want authentication for connection to the service and privacy when retrieving content, especially sensitive content such as email. Even users of pagers and similar communication devices can benefit from a mutually authenticated, secure communication channel if the mechanism is lightweight enough that it is not cumbersome to implement on such devices.

ESTABLISHING SECURE COMMUNICATIONS FOR MOBILE USERS

Wireless laptops are inherently less private than wired systems because the radio link can be intercepted without any physical tap, undetected by the transmitter and receiver. Wireless laptops are therefore especially vulnerable to eavesdropping, usage fraud, and activity monitoring—threats that will grow as wireless banking and other commercial services become available. In addition, both wired and wireless laptops need to be designed to maintain the integrity of data and systems and to assure the appropriate availability of services. Thus, security is an important issue for both commercial and military applications. For purposes of this discussion, which considers key aspects of the information security challenge but is not comprehensive, the issues can be divided into three categories: network security, radio link security, and hardware security.

Network security encompasses end-to-end encryption and measures to prevent fraudulent network access and monitoring. One mobile user-oriented framework distinguishes several levels of end-to-end encryption:

- Level 0 has no encryption, meaning that anyone with a scanner and knowledge of the communication link design can intercept a transmission. Analog cellular telephones offer this level of security, which has been a problem and has motivated security upgrades in the digital cellular standards.

- Level 1 provides low-level security such that individual conversations might take a year or more to decrypt. This level is probably secure enough for commercial telephony applications as long as an equivalent effort would be needed to decrypt subsequent conversations (*perfect forward secrecy*).

- Level 2 provides increased (perhaps by a factor of 10) security for sensitive information related to electronic commerce, mergers and acquisitions, and contract negotiations.

- Level 3 provides the most stringent level of security, meeting government and military communications requirements as defined by the appropriate agencies.

Radio link security prevents the interception of radio signals, ensuring the privacy of mobile user location information and, for military applications, active jamming (AJ) and low probability of detection and interference (LPD/I) capabilities. Link security was primarily a military concern before commercial wireless communications became prevalent. Military systems are designed to avert the detection of radio signals, jamming of communication links, and interception and decoding of messages. Many military radios are based on spread-spectrum technology, which provides both AJ and LPD/I capabilities. However, because knowledge of the spread-spectrum code would enable an adversary to intercept a spread signal, encryption is usually applied as well to prevent signal interception and message recovery. Many military techniques for reducing interception and detection are classified.

For commercial systems, the primary link-security issue is privacy, which is not typically assured. Conversations on analog cellular telephones are accessible to anyone with an FM scanner, as demonstrated by recent publication of communications involving public figures. Moreover, the location of a cellular user can be determined by triangulating the signal from two or more base stations, a feature that has been exploited successfully by law enforcement authorities. Preventing the interception of commercial radio signals is difficult, not only because communications protocols are publicized in patents and standards, but also because most communications devices have a *maintenance* mode for monitoring calls (a capability intended for testing purposes that could also be used to eavesdrop).

Commercial devices will not likely ever require a level of security equivalent to military systems, and they may not even provide the *hooks* enabling the addition of LPD/I capabilities. Similarly—although the growing use of wireless laptops and growing dependence on networked communications have heightened concerns about the possible denial of service in commercial contexts—a greater tolerance exists for private-service outages than for jamming in a military situation.

Hardware security also has different implications for commercial and military applications, although encryption keys typically need to be protected in both contexts. Commercial systems require sufficient security to prevent the fraudulent use of information in the event of theft or loss, and user databases need to be secured against unauthorized access. The military has similar requirements but at a much higher security level. The military also has additional requirements: Military devices need to be protected so that opening them will not reveal any of the specialized hardware or software technology.

Protecting the Laptop Before It Is Stolen

Suppose that someone is looking for the mobile user's laptop. It could be a business competitor, a personal enemy, or just a curious thief. How does the mobile user protect data on the laptop if the laptop is stolen? Let's take a look.

Portable computers are stolen often, according to reports from police and security experts. It recently happened to the head of technology at Qualcomm. His laptop disappeared off the podium at a national conference of business journalists recently. It's still missing, though Irvine, California, police and San Diego–based Qualcomm are both investigating.

Notebooks being stolen are very common, especially from airports, restaurants, or people's cars. That's one of the reasons the government is strict about keeping distinctions between classified and unclassified computers. Attorney General Janet Reno is currently weighing a Justice Department official's recommendation to prosecute former CIA head John Deutch, who used his home computer for classified materials from May 1995 to December 1996.

Critical Data

A quick survey of current and former employees of major Wall Street firms, law firms, banks, and consulting firms found none who protect their laptops beyond a Windows or BIOS password, which can be cracked easily by curious hackers or corporate spies. All the thief has to do is remove the hard drive from the computer and plant it in another. Even sensitive financial data are not well protected.

The analysts that are seen on CNNFn and ABCNEWS talking about stocks—if they dropped their machines, a stock report might be revealed before that report was issued to Wall Street. Fortunately, most laptop thieves don't care what's on the hard drive. The vast majority of laptop thefts are done for the purposes of stealing the hardware.

Necessary Encryption

So, how does the mobile user protect sensitive files? The answer is *encryption*. Using several inexpensive software packages, mobile users can lock away data from curious eyes. A good encryption program encodes all the documents on a hard drive when the computer shuts down. (See the sidebar, Encrypting Sensitive Data.) Privacy-sensitive mobile users should also separate their documents into groups, and leave the ones they're not working on encrypted and password protected in case the laptop is stolen while it's already on.

Encrypting Sensitive Data

Several companies produce software that lets the mobile user encrypt sensitive data. Windows 2000 and NT include an encryption feature that is good enough for most tasks. Apple's Mac OS 9 also allows mobile users to encrypt files, but not folders, from the Finder. Those systems probably won't protect against the most determined hackers or foreign operatives, but they're certainly good enough for personal files.

The mobile user should remember, though, that the encryption is only as good as the password. *Password* is a bad password. *T?7!!qisf0* is a great password. Of course, now it's a bad password because it's been shown here. Don't write down the password anywhere—people might find it—and don't lose the password. For example, the top ten most commonly used passwords are:

1. Your first, last, or kid's name
2. *Secret*
3. Stress-related words (*deadline, work*)
4. Sports teams or terms (*bulls, golfer*)
5. *Payday*
6. *Bonkers*
7. The current season ("winter," "spring")
8. Ethnic group
9. Repeated characters (*aaaaa, bbbbb*)
10. Obscenities, sexual terms

A few companies have even developed *lo-jack* tools that help the mobile user get a stolen laptop back by transmitting its location through the use of a hidden GPS tracking device embedded within the laptop. Network ICE's BlackIce Defender tries to connect back to the mobile user's corporate network and then phone home if a machine is stolen. For home users, CSS' CyberAngel and Absolute Software's CompuTrace call into their manufacturers when a computer is stolen and continually update owners as to phone numbers to which the machine's connected. CyberAngel also includes encryption; CompuTrace automatically works with law enforcement.

If a mobile user is going to visit one client, that mobile user should encrypt the files that relate to the other clients. Unfortunately, few companies seem to be getting the encryption message.

A recent industry survey found that most mobile users who have worked for consulting and startup companies (and have had many laptops) have never had encrypted hard drives for anything—for their desktop or laptop. However, even encryption can be defeated by password-cracking programs that cycle through character combinations and dictionaries to find common passwords.

The longer the password (with punctuation, upper- and lowercase and numbers), the harder it is to crack. If a mobile user chooses really simple words like *chip*, the encrypted partition can be cracked and all data grabbed.

For example, at Intel, the CEO's laptop is never left alone. Either the CEO or a staff member traveling with him always watches it. Intel applies multiple layers of password protection to laptop hard drives, encrypts files, and locks some sensitive files from being transferred to personal machines at all.

The physical asset, the laptop itself, often has a certain value. Oftentimes, the information that is contained within it could have even a higher value.

In summary, the use of remote communication devices for the mobile laptop may compromise the privacy and security of the corporate enterprise. The Chief Technology Officer (CTO) and the business manager's staff must identify those weaknesses or vulnerabilities that threaten privacy and security. Some very technical issues must be addressed by businesses as they relate to laptop mobility and vulnerability.

ADDRESSING TECHNICAL ISSUES OF LAPTOP MOBILITY AND VULNERABILITY

Laptops incorporate a broad range of technologies, including electrochemical materials, electronic devices and circuits, antennas, digital signal processing algorithms, network control protocols, and cryptography. Although all of these technologies are well advanced in other applications, laptops introduce a set of constraints and challenges beyond those addressed in the evolution of other communications networks, such as the Internet and the Public Switched Telephone Network (PSTN), which is the regular land-based phone system. These special constraints make it exceedingly difficult to design affordable laptops that meet every need. The challenges can be grouped into three categories: mobility, connectivity, and energy.

Mobility is a fundamental feature of untethered communications networks. Portable, wireless communications devices significantly enhance the mobility of users, but they also pose network design difficulties. As the communications devices move, the network has to rearrange itself. To deliver information to a mobile terminal, the network has to learn the new location(s) of the terminal and change the routing of information accordingly, sometimes at very high speeds. The rerouting must be done seamlessly without any perceived interruption of service.

A wide variety of *connectivity* problems arise when laptop communications terminals send and receive signals over the air. The signals of all the terminals are subject to mutual interference. The characteristics of the propagation medium change randomly as users move, and the mobile radio channel introduces random variation in the received signal power and other distortions, such as frequency shifts and the spreading of signals over time.

Signals that travel over the air are also more vulnerable to jamming and interception than those transmitted through wires or fibers. These limitations are often addressed with a combination of sophisticated signal processing techniques and antennas. However, these solutions add to the complexity of portable communications devices and increase power requirements.

Wireless systems pose two types of *energy* or power challenges. First, when power is radiated from an antenna, very little of it typically reaches the receiver. This phenomenon is known as *path loss*. Path loss can be partly overcome with increased transmit power, special types of antennas, and other solutions. Second, wireless terminals often carry their own power supplies in the form of batteries. Battery life is limited and is influenced by many aspects of terminal design and the network infrastructure technology. Scarce power constrains the mobile terminal's signal processing capabilities and transmit power, and therefore motivates efforts to keep these units as simple as possible. However, a low-power design cannot accommodate the most sophisticated techniques available to cope with the vagaries of the wireless channel and to support the network protocols of mobility management. In the absence of research breakthroughs that simplify these techniques, the only solution is to increase the complexity of the network, which needs to compensate for the simplicity of portable communications devices.

The challenges related to mobility, connectivity, and energy have stimulated a high level of research and development in the telecommunications industry and academia. Still, a chasm remains between the capabilities of wired and wireless communications systems. Even as commercial wireless systems evolve, additional features will be needed to meet military requirements for untethered communications. Military applications introduce additional challenges because the systems need to be rapidly deployable on mobile platforms in any one of a diverse range of operating environments; they need to interoperate with other systems; and they need protection against enemy attempts to jam, intercept, and alter information. This part of the chapter provides the technical basis for the analysis of military-commercial synergy by examining the challenges and vulnerabilities of laptop privacy, security, mobility, connectivity, and energy and the technologies devised to overcome them.

Communication Link Design

The ideal laptop would provide high data rates with high reliability and yet use minimum bandwidth and power. It would perform well in wireless propagation environments despite multiple channel impairments such as signal fading and interference. The ideal laptop would accommodate hardware constraints such as imperfect timing and nonlinear amplifiers. The laptop would have low power requirements and yet still provide adequate transmit power and signal processing. In addition, despite the system complexity required to achieve this performance level, both the transmitter and receiver would be affordable.

Such a laptop has yet to be built. In fact, many of the desired properties are mutually exclusive, meaning that trade-offs need to be made in laptop design.

Characteristics of the Wireless Laptop Channel

The characteristics of the radio channel impose fundamental limits on the range, data rate, and quality of wireless laptop communications. The performance limits are influenced by several factors, most significantly the propagation environment and user mobility pattern. For example, the indoor radio channels typically support higher data rates with better reliability than does the outdoor channel used by persons moving rapidly. The wireless laptop has the following characteristics:

- *Path loss:* Path loss is equal to the received power divided by the transmitted power, and this loss is a function of the transmitter-receiver separation.
- *Shadow fading:* A received signal is often blocked by hills or buildings outdoors and by furniture or walls indoors. The received signal power is in fact a random variable that depends on the number and dielectric properties of the obstructing objects. Signal variation due to these obstructions is called *shadow fading.*
- *Small-scale (multipath) fading:* Small-scale fading is caused by interference between multiple versions of the signal that arrive at the receiver at different times.
- *Interference:* Users of wireless laptops can experience interference from various sources. One source is frequency reuse, a popular technique for increasing the number of mobile users in a given region who can be supported by a particular set of frequencies.
- *Satellite channels:* Satellite channels (the links between a receiver or transmitter on Earth and an orbiting receiver or transmitter) have inherent advantages over terrestrial radio channels. Multipath fading is rare because a signal propagating skyward does not experience much reflection from surrounding objects (except in downtown areas with densely packed buildings).

RESPONDING TO INDUSTRY-SPECIFIC ISSUES

With the rise in popularity of business communication over the Internet and wireless laptops, issues of privacy have been the topics of increasing concern among information technology managers. The public nature of these laptops means that malicious parties can intercept communication signals and, if the signals were sent as unencrypted plain text, read whatever confidential information they desire.

In response to this problem, data encryption techniques have been developed and deployed that enable mobile users to send even the most confidential information over private networks. The use of encryption has brought the privacy level of digital wireless communication up to that of the wired telephone network, but in some cases this may not offer enough security. For stronger privacy, encryption can be deployed over an entire remote connection with the use of a Virtual Private Network (VPN), which can provide a single high-security solution for all mobile users.

Data encryption is now a necessary addition to any mobile communications technology, but the available solutions and options can be confusing. The purpose of this part of the chapter is to explain how encryption fits into the mobile data model, and what one should consider when choosing an encryption solution for mobile business communication.

How Much "Privacy" Does One Need?

Communications security is based on the premise that all confidential information has a value attached to it. This value provides an incentive for others to try to steal information. The goal of any security solution is to take away this value by making it difficult for malicious attackers to read private data. The level of security is sufficient when the attacker's required effort and expense to breach privacy are no longer worth the value of the confidential data. As an analogous example, consider that most people would comfortably leave three dollars on a table in their house—a thief wouldn't risk breaking into the house just to steal the money. On the other hand, if the amount were $3,000, then the owner may think twice about leaving it on the table—the required level of security increases as the value to a thief increases. Hence, before choosing a security solution, first consider the value of the information that is to be kept private. This value will provide a benchmark for the minimum level of security that is required.

The Baseline Requirement: Digital Wireless Encryption

In its infancy, wireless cellular communication used unencrypted analog signals. Since the signals were sent over the open air, privacy could be breached by a receiver that could intercept a specific signal. Such systems provided very little security and were obviously not fit for the needs of businesses that transmit confidential information. Modern digital wireless systems have been designed with these needs in mind and have fixed the security weaknesses of the earlier solutions.

Today, all digital cellular systems provide encryption as part of their standard service. Before a signal leaves the wireless transmitter, it is mathematically manipulated (*encrypted*) to make it unreadable to anybody but the person who is intended to receive the signal. Once the signal is encrypted, the threat of interception becomes irrelevant because a thief cannot understand the data. A thief could use computers to try to read an encrypted signal, but such an endeavor would be too expensive and would take too much time to be worth the value of the intercepted information.

When a connection is made over a cellular network, the network only provides a wireless link to the PSTN—the regular land-based phone system. All digital wireless solutions aim to provide enough encryption so that the level of privacy meets or exceeds the level of security provided by the PSTN. With modern encryption systems, the wireless link is no longer the weak point in a communication link—the level of privacy provided by a cellular communication session is at least as great as that provided by any PSTN-based session.

This use of digital wireless encryption enables one to seamlessly move between PSTN-based mobile connections using wire-based landlines to a mobile wireless solution that is just as secure. This is the baseline case for the use of mobile wireless communications—anything that a company can safely send over landlines can be sent over a cellular link with no modifications to the basic wireless service.

The Next Step: Building a Complete Data-Based Mobile Solution

Standard encryption over the wireless link may still be inadequate for a complete mobile solution. The biggest potential problem with relying on standard wireless security for all mobile needs is the fact that encryption is only provided up to the PSTN. Beyond that point, the mobile user has no control over the level of security protecting his or her communication.

This problem may limit the type of information that the mobile user is allowed to send or retrieve—many information technology managers would be wary of allowing their mobile users to transmit highly confidential information over a connection offering only PSTN-level security. The problem becomes more urgent when one considers that the mobile user may want to dial into an Internet Service Provider (ISP). In this case, unencrypted data would be sent over the Internet, which offers virtually no privacy protection.

The point to remember is that the chain of security in a mobile communication session is only as strong as its weakest link. For example, encrypting wireless data doesn't help much if the data are then sent unencrypted over the insecure Internet. In the past, most organizations have dealt with this issue by implementing different security policies for different types of connections—for example, allowing some confidential information to be sent over phone lines but only nonconfidential information over the Internet. With an increasing number of connection options available, the task of implementing and enforcing multiple security policies is becoming complex for the SA and more inconvenient for the mobile user.

To simplify and resolve problems such as these, many organizations are choosing to expand the use of encryption in their mobile communications as part of an effort to implement one strong security policy over their entire organization. This has resulted in a new class of products and services called the *Virtual Private Network* (VPN). A VPN enables an organization to send confidential data over the Internet by first encrypting the data to keep them private from snoopers. The use of encryption means that VPN security does not depend on the type of connection or the intermediate links, and it can provide the same level of security for all mobile users. This gives mobile users the freedom to connect to the network, however they choose, without having to worry about what kind of information they can send. The result is a flexible, all-encompassing solution suitable for all mobile users.

VPN Advantages

VPN products and services are poised to become the remote access solution of choice for both large and small business for three primary reasons:

1. They are relatively inexpensive compared to traditional dial-in services.
2. They can offer a large amount of security policy control.
3. Perhaps most important to the mobile user, they are very flexible.

VPN solutions can save a lot of money over traditional dial-in services. Since VPNs can send all of their data over the Internet, the mobile user does not need to dial directly into the corporation. Instead, the mobile user needs only to connect to the Internet, no matter where in the world he or she is. In most cases, this will mean connecting through an ISP. With ISP roaming services widely available today, connecting to the Internet through an ISP often requires no more than a local call within any major city in the world. This translates to direct savings in phone charges. Rather than paying long-distance charges for every minute that a remote employee is connected, the corporation pays a small monthly fee to the ISP; and the only phone charges are for local calls. Additionally, since a VPN offloads to the ISP the responsibility of providing a reliable dial-up Internet connection, more money is saved when the corporation no longer needs to administer and maintain pools of modems for dial-in users. VPNs can also be relatively inexpensive to deploy. The VPN service can be incrementally phased into a corporation and can coexist with current mobile access solutions.

A second advantage of VPNs is that they can offer a great amount of policy control to the security administrator (SA). Most VPN solutions give the SA some degree of control over the strength of encryption used by the VPN, and some products allow detailed control over a variety of security preferences from mobile user authentication requirements to access rights, often on a user-by-user basis. Combined with sophisticated mobile user tracking software, these products allow full monitoring and policy enforcement to be accomplished easily for all mobile users. If the SA needs to implement slightly different policies for different mobile users or different types of information, then this centralized control can be very useful.

For mobile users, the biggest advantage of VPNs is their flexibility. Since the level of encryption provided by the VPN is unaffected by the communication technology used, a remote employee can use any type of connection desired. Whether the mobile user connects to the Internet directly, through an ISP over a landlline, or through an ISP over a wireless line, the level of privacy achieved is consistent. This provides the freedom to use the most convenient connection without having to worry about a security policy for that type of connection. From the SA's standpoint, a wide spectrum of VPN products and services are available for finding a solution that matches the organization's needs for policy control, deployment, and maintenance. At first glance, the great number of different VPN solutions can seem confusing, but this variety ensures that a company will be able to find the right combination of features to match its needs.

Choosing the Right VPN

When looking at possible VPN solutions for an organization, the SA must weigh the three major factors discussed previously: cost, security policy control, and flexibility. The costs of various VPN solutions can vary widely. While in the long run most VPNs will save money over traditional remote access solutions, deployment and maintenance costs may be a concern. Many VPN products grow more complex as features are added to increase security and policy control, and this complexity will affect the deployment and especially maintenance costs accordingly. The SA should consider the type of information that mobile users will want to send over the VPN; the level of control that needs to be exercised over security policy; and how much knowledge exists in the organization for maintenance of the VPN system. These considerations may help narrow the choices of VPNs that match an organization's cost needs. Many companies choose to save money by incrementally deploying a new VPN. The existing remote access solution may be maintained or slowly phased out as the new VPN is deployed or initially outsourced to an ISP.

Security policy control can include everything from the level of encryption and what authentication mechanism is to be used, to the level of granularity that can be applied to mobile user profiles, to the amount of monitoring and logging that can be done on mobile user sessions. Greater policy control often results in a more flexible solution but also adds cost due to the increased complexity of the VPN. Many organizations prefer to have a greater amount of control over their solution. They may be unwilling to trust their security to an outside company (if the VPN is outsourced to an ISP, for instance), or they may want greater freedom to let their VPN policies evolve in the future. However, this additional control comes at a cost; if a company just needs a basic VPN to provide standard service, this solution is available at a relatively inexpensive price.

Flexibility of the VPN solution is of particular concern to mobile users who want to log in to the corporate network from various locations using various connection technologies. One of the most important VPN features for mobile users is the ability to *roam*, or use the VPN from any major location in the world. Some VPN products do not provide this ability—for example, some services may require that the mobile user be directly connected to a specific server to use the VPN. Mobile users should also have the ability to use various connection technologies with the VPN. For example, whether the mobile user wants to connect through a direct Internet connection, a land-based phone call, or a wireless connection makes no difference. Most VPNs that provide roaming will be connection agnostic in this manner. For the SA, flexibility may mean that the VPN should be able to evolve along with the needs of the organization and with changing ISP and Internet technologies. For example, the SA may want a scalable VPN that can grow as the company grows, or a highly modular solution that can work in conjunction with a variety of ISP services.

VPN Models

The VPN market is still evolving, and vendors are continuing to look for the right combination of features that will broadly appeal to a large number of organizations. An organization looking to implement a new VPN solution can choose from a great variety of options that offer different combinations of features and different usage models. The many options, though, can also quickly become confusing. Each VPN solution brings its own benefits with respect to cost, policy control, and flexibility. Tradeoffs between each of these factors should be considered as different VPN solutions are compared.

For the mobile user, a spectrum of VPN solutions usually represent some combination of two broad models. At one end of the spectrum are VPN solutions that are self-deployed and maintained exclusively by the organization using the VPN. In this model, the ISP is used only for the purpose of connecting to the Internet. If an organization is not prepared to exclusively manage its own VPN, it may wish to outsource some of its VPN services to the ISP. As the amount of outsourcing increases, a second model emerges where all of the VPN services are handled by the ISP. In this model, the organization using the VPN may have little or no VPN maintenance responsibilities.

Self-Deployed VPN Solutions

A self-deployed VPN solution requires an organization to purchase, deploy, and maintain its own VPN. In this model, the organization purchases and installs VPN hardware or software products at its home office and on each remote user's computer. Self-deployed solutions can offer all-encompassing security that is under the full control of the corporation.

The biggest advantage of a self-deployed VPN is *flexibility*. Since the VPN is only installed at the endpoints of the remote connection, any type of intermediate connection can be used. Whether the remote user connects via wireless, Internet, telephone, or any other technology makes no difference—the VPN provides the same level of end-to-end privacy.

Another advantage of self-deployed VPN flexibility is that the company keeps complete control over the maintenance of the VPN and can modify the VPN as needed to adjust to changing mobile user demands or security policies. A self-deployed VPN also frees the organization to outsource whatever maintenance duties it sees fit, and to keep control of duties it wants to perform in house.

A self-deployed VPN can also offer very good policy control features. An organization running its own VPN is free to choose whatever security policies it sees fit. The organization can keep its security policies as simple or complex as it chooses and is free to change the policies as often as needed. If precise policy control or session logging is desired, many products offer such features. The drawback to being responsible for all VPN policy control is that it can often become one of the most complex aspects of maintaining a VPN. In response to this concern, many VPN providers offer additional tools to aid in policy control duties.

Usually, the biggest worry about implementing an in-house VPN is the cost. A large and complex VPN solution can grow to be fairly expensive and, depending on the expertise available in an organization, additional startup costs may be associated with training personnel for VPN deployment and maintenance. For very small organizations, this expense may not justify a self-deployed VPN. However, most companies will find that over the long-term this cost is worth having a flexible end-to-end security solution and keeping control of important security duties, in addition to the savings that VPNs offer over traditional dial-in services.

ISP VPN Solutions

Many ISPs are beginning to offer VPNs as a premium service. In this model, some of the difficult or expensive aspects of a VPN are outsourced to the ISP. ISPs offer varying levels of VPN service. Some services will handle most aspects of VPN maintenance, while others may only handle certain parts and leave other aspects—for example, user authentication—up to the client. Using the right service, the one that matches an organization's needs, can result in a low-cost solution that is easier to implement.

The primary advantages of ISP VPN services are *cost savings* and *simplicity*. By outsourcing the VPN to an ISP, an organization can avoid having to train or hire employees to deploy and maintain the VPN system. This cost saving comes in addition to the savings in long distance calls and dial-in maintenance that comes with all VPN solutions. Depending on how much of the VPN is outsourced, leveraging the ISP can also make deployment and maintenance of the VPN much easier. Many ISP services don't require any software to be loaded onto the remote client, and they often will handle administrative duties such as security policy control. This added simplicity could be especially beneficial to small businesses that don't want to go through a lot of expense and trouble to deploy a VPN for a small number of employees. Outsourcing can also simplify incremental deployment of a VPN solution. For example, an organization can continue using its existing modem pools or current mobile access solution while slowly transitioning employees to the ISP VPN service, or it can even use the ISP's VPN concurrently with an in-house VPN deployment.

While a company can simplify security policy maintenance by outsourcing it to the ISP, this loss of policy control can be a disadvantage. The ISP may not offer enough options to match the needs of the company, or the company may simply decide that security policy is too important to trust to external vendors. Outsourcing encryption duties to the ISP can also be risky. Although data will be safely encrypted by the ISP when sent over the Internet, before reaching the ISP the data are transmitted as clear text. In most cases, the connection between the remote user and the ISP will be over a landline or wireless phone connection. If strong encryption is used by the ISP, this connection may then become the weak link of the remote session. This situation may be unacceptable to some organizations if the VPN is to be used for the transmission of highly confidential information. Recognizing this problem, many ISPs offer customers the ability to extend encryption all the way to the client. However, this solution usually involves giving up some of the advantages in simplicity and ease of deployment that make outsourcing attractive.

One factor in which some ISP VPNs may be lacking is flexibility. If critical VPN services are housed by the ISP, then a direct connection to that specific ISP may be required to ensure security. If the *base* ISP provides pieces of the VPN that cannot be substituted for by other ISPs, then mobile users may not be able to use the VPN when roaming. ISPs have different ways of trying to solve this problem, from putting additional software on the remote clients to partnering with other ISPs to provide VPN roaming. In most cases, this problem will involve bringing some VPN duties in house.

The Right VPN for the Organization

Given the many choices, choosing the best VPN for an organization can be a confusing process. The two models previously discussed are broad categories of VPN offerings that contain many different products. These products may overlap in functionality and features. The best solution for an organization's needs may lie in between these models, with some combination of ISP outsourcing and in-house deployment. A self-deployed VPN can provide maximum flexibility and control but may not be fully worth the additional start-up cost and complexity for some small organizations. For larger organizations, an ISP-based VPN can be used as a pilot, or as a temporary solution to aid in the migration to an in-house system. The in-house solution will save more money in the long run and will likely provide a more flexible solution that can cover all data privacy needs of the corporation.

Once the decision is made that a VPN can offer privacy and convenience to an organization with cost savings over traditional dial-up, all that is left is to decide which factors best match the situation and the needs of the mobile users. Likely the right VPN solution will lie somewhere between a completely self-deployed product and a completely outsourced service.

Using Encryption to Solve Mobile Privacy Issues

Encryption has given organizations many new options for protecting the confidential data of their mobile users. The use of encryption in wireless communications has made wireless just as secure as landline PSTN sessions. Organizations that want further security, or that want the freedom to send confidential data over the Internet or any other connection medium, can implement encryption across all mobile communication links by deploying a VPN. A VPN lets users securely send data over any type of connection, can greatly simplify security policy control, and can save the corporation money in mobile access costs. Self-deployed VPNs offer a high level of flexibility and control, and they can protect all confidential information as soon as it leaves the internal corporate network. However, self-deployed VPNs may be too expensive for very small organizations. ISP VPNs are well suited for small implementations or as temporary solutions, but special attention must be paid that the needs of mobile users are satisfied. The right solution for a company will be one that best balances its needs for cost, policy control, and flexibility in a VPN.

While this chapter discussed the privacy and security issues surrounding a remote user's laptop, the next chapter provides a successful remote access solution.

16

PROTECTING THE PRIVACY OF REMOTE ACCESS AND TELECOMMUTERS

Remote access is a dynamic market segment of the networking industry exploding with opportunity. More and more companies, realizing that this technology is essential to remain competitive in the global marketplace, have either adopted or plan to adopt a remote access solution. Because of the impact it can have on the bottom line, remote access has moved from a departmental-level decision to a strategic enterprise-level decision.

As the key decision maker, the network manager is faced with choosing an enterprise-level remote access solution that satisfies the needs and requirements of a very diverse employee population. According to a recent industry study by Gartner Group,[i] 78 percent of employees or telecommuters conduct work from home after regular business hours, 53 percent are business travelers, 47 percent are from the mobile workforce such as sales and technical support personnel, 40 percent are telecommuters, and 31 percent are employees in small branch offices. All major job functions are represented—including IT, sales and marketing, engineering, customer service, and research and development. Combine telecommuters' usage needs with individual application requirements and wide-area transmission options and the decision becomes extremely complicated. But all these needs can be addressed easily with a solution known as *remote access*.

Remote access is a network manager's ideal solution. The concept is simple: Connect anyone, anywhere, to any network resource, at any time. Most importantly, make it a *total solution* that is simple to use and easy to manage. Remote access will also receive a financial officer's endorsement because the cost of ownership easily justifies the capital expenditure. It is cheaper than all the other traditional remote access options currently available. To provide a successful remote access solution, a network vendor must address four key areas:

1. The solution's client connectivity interface for both the telecommuter and the network manager
2. The types and requirements of applications that need to be accessed
3. Current or future wide-area transmission options available
4. The total product solution

UNDERSTANDING CLIENT CONNECTIVITY MODELS AND INTERFACES

The solution's client connectivity interface is critical to both telecommuters and network managers. All industry studies show that both groups, regardless of their level of technical expertise, require an interface that is easy to use and has point-and-click access. A *point-and-click* interface for telecommuter and network managers is no longer viewed as a benefit or convenience: It is an expectation and a solution requirement.

ACCESSING APPLICATIONS REMOTELY

In the corporate environment, applications are based on two different architectures: a client-server architecture and the traditional multiuser host (or mainframe-terminal emulation) architecture. According to Forrester Research, 60 percent of corporate applications have been ported or developed for a client-server architecture. The remaining 40 percent are still considered multiuser host applications. Moreover, even in organizations where the client-server model is deployed, access to legacy mainframe or minicomputer-based applications is frequently required.

A multiuser host architecture connects multiple *dumb* terminals to a mainframe or minicomputer. Based on time-sharing applications, multiple users can access the same computer simultaneously via a terminal or a PC that emulates a terminal. The architecture is based on an operating environment such as UNIX or VMS.

In a client-server architecture, the work between the client (such as a remote PC) and the server (a powerful computer or host at the corporate office) is shared so that each device performs the tasks it can do most efficiently. The client computer runs its own applications programs, but uses the file, print, and communications services of a large and powerful central file server. The file server uses a network operating system (NOS) such as UNIX, Windows NT, NetWare, or AppleTalk to support the transfer of data from a variety of computers. Client-server applications are either developed specifically for this architecture or have migrated from a mainframe application. Many workgroup applications use the client-server architecture for a shared pool of information.

Each classification of application has been developed to optimize the operating environment (for multiuser host applications) or the network operating system (for client-server applications). A remote access solution must support both of these.

Remote access offers the telecommuter an unlimited number of resources regardless of the technology on which the application is based. Access to email, database files, printers, and applications such as MSWord and spreadsheet programs are now the minimum requirements for the majority of remote users. Telecommuters also require the capability to transfer files to and from the network quickly and easily. Additionally, there is a growing need for telecommuters to access workgroup applications such as sales force automation, materials resource planning, order/entry, accounting, and project tracking systems. These applications require that information be updated and exchanged among multiple individuals who input, receive, or analyze the specialized data.

In addition to using the traditional client-server and multiuser host applications, remote users can easily dial-out and take advantage of the resources available through community networks such as the Internet, America Online, and CompuServe. These networks offer a huge range of resources for home or business use, including email, at-home shopping, corporate *home page* information, bulletin boards, and entertainment. Subscribers can access information services such as specialized electronic libraries or databases of business news and statistics. Updated versions of software products are available as well. Video games and other sources of entertainment are readily available. And, subscribers can exchange information with other members worldwide.

A number of other *vertical* applications are also just a remote access session away. Telemedicine is one example that is receiving increased visibility. It is a technology that marries telecommunications, videoconferencing, and medical technologies to deliver health care from a distance. Most projects connect doctors at urban hospitals with patients in rural areas, but telemedicine also has international network possibilities. Telemedicine advocates contend that the technology will save lives and money and that it is the next revolution in health care.

UNDERSTANDING WIDE-AREA TRANSMISSION OPTIONS

In addition to the operating environment and the network operating system, many of the newer and revolutionary applications depend on the wide-area transmission environment referred to as the *cloud*. The cloud supports the simultaneous transmission of voice, data, and video information and also offers telecommuters a seat on the information highway and its endless array of resources.

A remote access solution must be compatible with all of the public transmission facilities available as well as the multiple protocols associated with each. Because up to 60 percent of the total remote access solution cost is in the cost of dialing in, many vendors believe enterprisewide remote access will be outsourced to the telephone carriers. They are turning their focus and resources to this segment of the market.

FINDING THE TOTAL PRODUCT SOLUTION FOR REMOTE ACCESS

A total product solution will connect anybody, anywhere, to any application at any time, regardless of the wide-area transmission option utilized or the protocols being run on the network. The concept must be transferable to all vertical markets, including those networks outsourced to the public carrier system, private networks, and Internet providers.

In recent industry studies, network managers cited the key pieces for solving the remote access puzzle as ease of access for telecommuters, connection-transfer speed, reliability, ease of management, cost of ownership, privacy, and security. A product must also support mixed traffic environments and must offer access to any application without having to use multiple connections.

Network managers are inundated daily with calls by telecommuters requesting assistance in connecting to the network and its resources. Easy access for the telecommuter is essential because it directly affects the network manager's workload and his or her capacity to address other critical issues associated with managing a complex service. The typical network manager also receives a significant number of calls demanding increased connection-transfer speeds and problems with reliability. Hence, these issues are all key aspects to the decision-making process.

Configuration and network management often becomes a challenging process as the number of telecommuters on a network increases and as net-

across the country to the other side of the world. The remote workers can be a company's branch office employees, full- or part-time telecommuters, traveling professionals, customers, suppliers, or business partners. (See the sidebar, "Telecommuting Facts.")

Telecommuting Facts

Telecommuting, or teleworking, is one of the fastest growing segments of the remote networking phenomenon. Telecommuters include executives, managers, customer support representatives, sales professionals, editors, programmers, and other information workers who access their enterprise's network from home. Here are just a few of the facts about telecommuting:

• Telecommuting results in an average work time increase of three hours per day per worker (Gartner Group).
• Telecommuters at Pacific Bell exhibited 36 percent less absenteeism than other employees.
• Companies save from $4,000 to $6,000 per year per telecommuter on facilities costs (Gartner Group).
• The number of telecommuters will continue to increase at the rate of more than 11 percent per year (Link Resources).

Remote networking cuts across industry lines and international borders. It affects a growing number of workers that include executives and engineers, secretaries and salesmen, doctors, and delivery truck drivers. This diverse group has two things in common: the need to communicate with colleagues and business associates in other locations and the need to access critical information housed on the corporate network. Today's sophisticated digital technologies and advanced communications services meet these needs—faster, easier, and less expensive than ever before. According to companies with remote networks already in place, remote networking includes a long list of benefits:

• Increased sales
• More effective customer support
• Faster response to customer needs
• Quicker project completion
• Increased job satisfaction
• Expanded presence in regional areas
• Improved corporate communications

- Better employee retention
- Faster product development cycles[ii]

With these advantages, the main issue with remote networking today is not *if*, but *how*. The traditional analog modem bank is become obsolete with advances in technology and deregulation in the telecommunications industry. Organizations now have three far more capable and affordable options to the modem bank: private networks with digital access concentrators, outsourced wholesale access arrangements with network service providers (see Table 16–1), and the Internet-based virtual private networks (VPNs).

Selecting the right network service provider is critical to the success of the remote networking solution. Whether an organization wants to use a national provider or multiple local ones, consider each to be a strategic partner. Table 16–1 shows a checklist of considerations for selecting the best possible network service provider(s). Depending upon the particular organization's situation, some listed factors may be irrelevant or relatively unimportant, but be sure to thoroughly evaluate all factors and all network service providers.

In general, distance determines which of the preceding alternatives is the most cost effective. Long-distance remote networking needs, especially for a company's cross-country and international users, are best served by a VPN. Private networks and wholesale arrangements make more sense for local remote networking needs, such as telecommuting programs.

ADDRESSING INTERNAL AND EXTERNAL SECURITY THREATS OF REMOTE USAGE

Remote usage management involves two systems: one for managing the equipment and the other for administering network usage. Every vendor has its own system for managing its own equipment.

Managing equipment is ideally a centralized function in a remote network. Remote users normally lack the technical skills to troubleshoot problems and prefer not to be bothered by routine system maintenance and upgrades. Normally, the management system is provided by the vendor of the remote access systems and should have most of the following features:

- Auto discovery and dynamic mapping of the end-to-end network topology with both physical and logical groupings of all equipment and links

CHECKLIST FORM: CONSIDERATIONS FOR SELECTING THE BEST POSSIBLE NETWORK SERVICE PROVIDER(S)

Date: _____

The IT management staff responsible for such information held by the enterprise should ensure that the following tasks have been completed (check all tasks completed):

___ 1. Support for the full spectrum of WAN options (analog modems, cellular, ISDN, Frame Relay, Switched 56, T1/E1/PRI, X.25 and DSL).

___ 2. Digital modem technology for improved link reliability and support of an open architecture for the latest in 56 Kbps analog modem technology.

___ 3. Multilink Protocol Plus (MP+) advanced dynamic bandwidth management to accommodate telecommuter integrated access devices.

___ 4. Standards-based compression (bandwidth on demand and compression work together to deliver optimal throughput as needed, and only as needed, to minimize service fees).

___ 5. Comprehensive security and privacy provisions, especially IPSec, and a reputation for administering security.

___ 6. Support for L2TP, PPTP, ATMP, and IPSec tunneling to accommodate existing protocols and applications.

___ 7. High-speed backhaul links to the Internet backbone for good performance.

___ 8. Redundancy to assure adequate uptime for mission-critical needs.

___ 9. Service Level Agreement (SLA) uptime guarantees and confirmation reporting.

___ 10. Tiered Quality of Service (QoS) options ranging from "best effort" to an "absolute" guarantee of throughput and latency.

___ 11. End-to-end monitoring, operating, and troubleshooting capabilities.

___ 12. Value-added features, such as Voice over IP (VoIP), IO multicast, and IP faxing.

___ 13. Value-added services, including consulting, network design, systems integration, ongoing support, remote user help desk, extranet management, data backup, Web hosting, electronic commerce, etc.

___ 14. POP locations near all remote users and sites, or national/international "roaming" agreements with other service providers, to minimize or entirely eliminate long-distance fees.

___ 15. Call Detail Reporting (CDR) to track usage by all remote users.

___ 16. Central site or distributed pricing and billing arrangements, including bundled and managed service offerings.

___ 17. Long-term financial stability and viability.

Table 16–1. Considerations for Selecting the Best Possible Network Service Provider(s) Checklist

- Real-time network monitoring of physical and logical WAN links and traffic conditions, with fault alert or alarm generation based on remote user-defined thresholds
- Networking monitoring that assesses actual throughput on WAN lines and helps control delivery of contracted SLA and QoS guarantees
- Capacity planning and performance trending through collection and analysis of traffic statistics that show both the remote usage levels and patterns of all users or sites
- Baselining of normal operating conditions to help determine overall network health and capacity needs
- Integrated, statistical accounting to track network traffic by remote user, department, or site for bill- back or other purposes
- Remote configuration management for bringing new locations online, as well as coordinating networkwide updates and changes
- A means of comparing actual versus intended equipment configurations
- Device-oriented fault detection and diagnostics for pinpointing and troubleshooting specific equipment problems
- A trace function that tracks traffic through the network, end to end, to help isolate bottlenecks and other problems
- A way to examine the WAN's physical and data link layers, as well as assess actual throughput of dial-up and dedicated WAN links
- Compatibility with industry standards, like the Simple Network Management Protocol (SNMP)

Remote Usage Security Policy

A good remote usage security policy has the following characteristics:

1. *An Information Technology System and Network Maintenance Policy* that describes how both *internal* and *external* maintenance people are allowed to handle and access technology. One important topic to be addressed here is whether remote maintenance is allowed and how such access is controlled. Another area for consideration is outsourcing and how it is managed.
2. A *Violations Reporting Policy* that indicates which types of violations (privacy and security, internal and external) must be reported and to whom the reports are made. A nonthreatening atmosphere and the possibility of anonymous reporting will result in a greater probability that a violation will be reported if it is detected.

Completely Defined Security Plans for Remote Usage

All sites should define a comprehensive remote usage security plan. This plan should be crafted as a framework of broad guidelines into which specific policies will fit.

This framework should be in place so that individual policies can be consistent with the overall site security and privacy architecture. For example, having a strong policy with regard to Internet access and having weak restrictions on modem usage is inconsistent with an overall philosophy of strong security and privacy restrictions on external access.

A remote usage security plan should define the list of network services that will be provided, which areas of the organization will provide the services, who will have access to those services, how access will be provided, who will administer those services, etc.

The plan should also address how incidents will be handled. Each site should define classes of incidents and corresponding responses. What about a systematic scan of systems?

For sites connected to the Internet, the rampant media magnification of Internet-related security and privacy incidents could overshadow a (potentially) more serious internal security problem. Likewise, companies who have never been connected to the Internet may have strong, well defined, internal policies that fail to adequately address an external connection policy.

Separation of Services

A site may wish to provide its remote users with many services, some of which may be external. These services should be isolated onto dedicated host computers for a variety of security and privacy reasons.

The services that a site may provide will usually have different levels of access needs and models of trust. Services that are essential to the security, privacy, or smooth operation of a site would be better off being placed on a dedicated machine with very limited access. Essential services should not be placed on a machine that provides other services that have traditionally been less secure or that require greater accessibility by remote users who may accidentally suborn security.

A site should also distinguish between hosts that operate within different models of trust (all the hosts inside of a firewall and any host on an exposed network). Remote usage security is only as strong as the weakest link in the chain. Several of the most publicized penetrations in recent years have been through the exploitation of vulnerabilities in electronic mail systems. The intruders were not trying to steal electronic mail, but they used the vulnerability in that service to gain access to other systems.

If possible, each service should be running on a different machine whose only duty is to provide a specific service. This helps to isolate intruders and limit potential harm.

Deny-All or Allow-All Models

Two diametrically opposed underlying philosophies can be adopted when defining a remote usage security plan: *deny-all* or *allow-all*. Both alternatives are legitimate models to adopt, and the choice between them will depend on the site and its needs for remote usage security.

The first option is to turn off all services and then selectively enable services on a case-by-case basis as needed. This can be done at the host or network level as appropriate. This model, the *deny-all* model, is generally more secure than the allow-all model. Successful implementation of a *deny-all* configuration requires more work and a better understanding of services. Allowing only known services provides for a better analysis of a particular service or protocol. It also provides for the design of a remote usage security mechanism suited to the site's security and privacy levels.

The other model, the *allow-all* model, is much easier to implement, but is generally less secure than the *deny-all* model. Simply turn on all services (usually the default at the host level) and allow all protocols to travel across network boundaries (usually the default at the router level). As remote-usage security holes become apparent, they are restricted or patched at either the host or network level.

Each of these models can be applied to different portions of the site, depending on functionality requirements, administrative control, site policy, etc. For example, the policy may be to use the *allow-all* model when setting up workstations for general use, but to adopt the *deny-all* model when setting up information servers such as an email hub. Likewise, an *allow-all* policy may be adopted for traffic between LANs internal to the site, but a *deny-all* policy may be adopted between the site and the Internet.

The SA should be careful when mixing the allow-all and deny-all philosophies. Many sites adopt the theory of a hard *crunchy* shell and a soft *squishy* middle. They are willing to pay the cost of security and privacy for their external traffic and require strong security measures, but they are unwilling or unable to provide similar protections internally. This combination works fine as long as the outer defenses are never breached and the internal users can be trusted. Once the outer shell (firewall) is breached, subverting the internal network is trivial.

Identify Real Needs for Services

A large variety of services may be provided both internally and on the Internet at large. Managing remote usage security is, in many ways, managing access to services internal to the site and managing how internal users access information at remote sites.

Services tend to rush like waves over the Internet. Over the years many sites have established anonymous (anon) FTP servers, gopher servers, WAIS servers, WWW servers, etc., as they became popular—whether or not they were particularly needed. The SA should evaluate all new services with a skeptical attitude to determine if they are actually needed or just the current fad sweeping the Internet.

Bear in mind that security and privacy complexity can grow exponentially with the number of services provided. Filtering routers need to be modified to support the new protocols. Some protocols are inherently difficult to filter safely (RPC and UDP services), thus providing more openings to the internal network. Services provided on the same machine can interact in catastrophic ways. For example, allowing anonymous FTP on the same machine as the WWW server may allow an intruder to place a file in the anonymous FTP area and cause the HTTP server to execute it.

Protecting the Services

The many types of services each have their own remote usage security requirements. These requirements vary based on the intended use of the service. For example, a service that should only be usable within a site (NFS) may require different protection mechanisms than a service provided for external use. Sufficient security may be to protect the internal server from external access. However, a WWW server, which provides a home page intended for viewing by remote users anywhere on the Internet, requires built-in protection. That is, the service, protocol, or server must provide the remote usage security required to prevent unauthorized access and modification of the Web database.

Protection requirements will usually differ for internal services, those meant to be used only by users within a site, and external services, those deliberately made available to users outside a site. Therefore, internal services should be isolated to one set of server host computers and the external services to another set of server host computers. That is, internal and external servers should not be located on the same host computer. In fact, many sites go so far as to have one set of subnets (or even different networks) that are accessible from the outside and another set that may be accessed only within the site.

Organizations are becoming increasingly interested in using Intranets to connect different parts of the organization (or divisions of a company). While this document generally differentiates between external (public) and internal (private), sites using Intranets should be aware that they need to consider three separations and take appropriate actions when designing and offering services. An Intranet service is not public, yet it is not as completely private as a service to a single organizational subunit. Therefore, an Intranet service needs its own supporting system, separated from both external and internal services and networks.

One form of external service deserves some special consideration: anonymous or guest access. This access may be either an anonymous FTP or a guest (unauthenticated) login. Anonymous FTP servers and guest login user IDs must be *carefully isolated* from any hosts and file systems from which outside users should be kept. Another area of special consideration concerns anonymous, writable access. A site may be legally responsible for the content of publicly available information, so the information deposited by anonymous remote users should be carefully monitored.

A site should carefully examine the services that it will provide in order to determine how to protect them. The most popular and frequently used services—name service, password-key service, authentication-proxy service, electronic mail, WWW, file transfer, and NFS—are the most obvious points of attack. Also, a successful attack on one of these services can produce disaster all out of proportion to the innocence of the basic service.

Authentication

For many years, the prescribed method for authenticating remote users has been through the use of standard, reusable passwords. Originally, these passwords were used by remote users at terminals to authenticate themselves to a central computer. At the time, no networks (internally or externally) existed, so the risk of disclosure of the clear text password was minimal. Today, systems are connected together through local networks, and these local networks are further connected together and to the Internet. Remote users are logging in from all over the globe; their reusable passwords are often transmitted across those same networks in clear text, ripe for anyone in between to capture. And indeed, the Computer Emergency Response

Team (CERT)/Coordination Center and other response teams are seeing a tremendous number of incidents involving packet sniffers that are capturing the clear text passwords.

With the advent of newer technologies like one-time passwords (S/Key), one-time transaction credit cards, PGP, and token-based authentication devices, people are using passwordlike strings as secret tokens and pins. If these secret tokens and pins are not properly selected and protected, the authentication will be easily subverted.

ESTABLISHING SECURE COMMUNICATIONS FOR REMOTE USERS

According to Request For Comments 2196 (RFC 2196),[iii] because of the Web's ease of use and the powerful ability to concentrate information services, it is growing in popularity exponentially. The majority WWW servers who are accessed by persons requesting their services, accept some type of direction and action from those said persons. Taking a request from a remote user and passing the provided information to a program running on the server to process the request, is the most common remote access example. Security holes can therefore be created by programs that are not written with security and privacy in mind. With that in mind, confidential information should not be located on the same host as that server, especially if a Web server is available to the Internet community. Also, the Web server should have a dedicated host that is not *trusted* by other internal hosts.

Today, many sites are colocating WWW service with their FTP service. This usually occurs for anon-FTP servers that only provide information (ftp-get). *Anon-ftp puts*, in combination with WWW, might be dangerous. In other words, they could result in modifications to the information that a site is publishing to the Web; and, the security and privacy considerations for each service could end up being made different.

TRAINING REMOTE USERS ON ISSUES AND PROCEDURES RELATED TO PRIVACY AND SECURITY

When selecting secret tokens, take care to choose them carefully. Like the selection of passwords, they should be robust against brute force efforts to guess them. That is, they should not be single words in any language, any common, industry, or cultural acronyms, etc. Ideally, they will consist of long pass phrases that combine upper and lower case characters, digits, and symbols.

Once chosen, these secret tokens must be protected. Some are used as pins to hardware devices (like token cards), and these should not be written down or placed in the same location as the device with which they are associated. Others, such as a secret Pretty Good Privacy (PGP) key, should be protected from unauthorized access.

When using cryptography products, like PGP, take care to determine the proper key length and ensure that remote users are *trained* to do likewise. As technology advances, the minimum safe key length continues to grow. Make sure the site keeps up with the latest knowledge on the technology so that the Security Administrator (SA) can ensure that any cryptography in use is providing the protection the SA believes it is.

Handling Security and Privacy Incidents

This part of the chapter provides guidance to be used before, during, and after a computer security and privacy incident occurs on a host, network, site, or multisite environment. The operative philosophy in the event of a breach of computer security is to react according to a plan. A plan should be followed for all breaches, whether the breach is the result of an external intruder attack, unintentional damage, a student testing some new program to exploit a software vulnerability, or a disgruntled employee. Each of the possible types of breaches should be addressed in advance by adequate contingency plans.

Traditional computer security, while quite important in the site's overall security and privacy plan, usually pays little attention to how to actually handle an attack once one occurs. As a result, when an attack is in progress, many decisions are made in haste and can damage efforts to track down the source of the incident, to collect evidence to be used in prosecution efforts, to prepare for system recovery, and to protect the valuable data contained on the system.

One of the most important, but often overlooked, benefits for efficient incident handling is an economic one. Having both technical and managerial personnel respond to an incident requires considerable resources. If staff members are *trained* to handle incidents efficiently, less staff time is required when an incident occurs.

Due to the worldwide network, most incidents are not restricted to a single site. Operating system vulnerabilities apply (in some cases) to several millions of systems, and many vulnerabilities are exploited within the network itself. Therefore, all sites with involved parties should be informed of the incident as soon as possible.

Another benefit is related to public relations. News about computer security incidents tends to be damaging to an organization's stature among current or potential clients. Efficient incident handling minimizes the potential for negative exposure.

A final benefit of efficient incident handling is related to legal issues. In the near future, organizations may be held responsible if one of their nodes is used to launch a network attack. In a similar vein, people who develop patches or workarounds may be sued if the patches or workarounds are ineffective, resulting in compromise of the systems, or if the patches or workarounds themselves damage systems. To circumvent possible legal problems, the organization should know about operating system vulnerabilities and patterns of attacks, and then take appropriate measures to counter these potential threats.

Preparing and Planning for Incident Handling

Proper incident handling depends on being prepared to respond to an incident before the incident occurs in the first place. This preparation includes establishing a suitable level of protections to help a site prevent incidents and to limit potential damage resulting from them when they do occur. Protection also includes preparing incident handling guidelines as part of a contingency plan for the organization or site. Written plans eliminate much of the ambiguity that occurs during an incident and also lead to a more appropriate and thorough set of responses. The proposed plan should be tested through *dry runs* before an incident occurs. An organization might even consider conducting two parallel dry runs, one of which is performed by a tiger team (a team of specialists who try to penetrate the system's security).

Learning to respond efficiently to an incident is important for a number of reasons:

1. Protecting the assets that could be compromised
2. Protecting resources that could be utilized more profitably if an incident did not require their services
3. Complying with government or other regulations
4. Preventing the use of the compromised systems in attacks against other systems (which could incur legal liability)
5. Minimizing the potential for negative exposure

As in any set of preplanned procedures, goals must be set for handling an incident. These goals will be prioritized differently depending on the site. A specific set of objectives can be identified for dealing with incidents:

1. Figure out how it happened.
2. Find out how to avoid further exploitation of the same vulnerability.
3. Avoid escalation and further incidents.
4. Assess the impact and damage of the incident.
5. Recover from the incident.
6. Update policies and procedures as needed.
7. Find out who did it (if appropriate and possible).

Depending on the nature of the incident, a conflict may occur between analyzing the original source of a problem and restoring systems and services. Overall goals (such as assuring the integrity of critical systems) might be the reason for not analyzing an incident. However, all involved parties must be aware that without analysis the same incident may happen again.

The written plan for handling incidents should prioritize the actions to be taken during an incident. Sometimes an incident may be so complex that responding properly to everything at once is impossible—priorities are essential. Although priorities will vary from institution to institution, the following suggested priorities may serve as a starting point for defining an organization's response:

- *Priority one:* Protect human life, privacy, and people's safety; human life always has precedence over all other considerations.
- *Priority two:* Protect classified and sensitive data. Prevent exploitation of classified and sensitive systems, networks, or sites. Inform affected classified and sensitive systems, networks, or sites about penetrations that have already occurred. Be aware of regulations by the site or by government.
- *Priority three:* Protect other data (including proprietary, scientific, and managerial data) because loss of data is costly in terms of resources. Prevent exploitations of other systems, networks, or sites. Inform affected systems, networks, or sites about actual penetrations.
- *Priority four:* Prevent system damage (loss or alteration of system files, damage to disk drives, etc.). Damage to systems can result in costly downtime and recovery.
- *Priority five:* Minimize disruption of computing resources (including processes). Shutting a system down or disconnecting from a network may be better than risking damage to data or systems. Sites will have to evaluate the trade-offs between shutting down and disconnecting, and staying up. Service agreements may require keeping systems up even in light of further damage occurring. However, the damage and

scope of an incident may be so extensive that service agreements may have to be overridden.

When defining priorities, once human life, privacy, and national security considerations have been addressed, saving data is generally more important than saving system software and hardware. Although any damage or loss during an incident is undesirable, systems can be replaced. However, the loss or compromise of data (especially classified or proprietary data) is usually not an acceptable outcome under any circumstances.

Another important concern is the effect on others, beyond the systems and networks where the incident occurs. Within the limits imposed by government regulations, affected parties should be informed as soon as possible. Due to this topic's legal implications, the process of informing others should be included in the planned procedures to avoid further delays and uncertainties for the administrators.

Any plan for responding to security and privacy incidents should be guided by local policies and regulations. Government and private sites that deal with classified material have specific rules that they must follow.

The policies chosen by a site on how it reacts to incidents will shape the response. For example, creating mechanisms to monitor and trace intruders makes little sense if the site does not plan to take action against the intruders if they are caught. Other organizations may have policies that affect plans. For example, telephone companies often release information about telephone traces only to law enforcement agencies.

Handling incidents can be tedious and can require any number of routine tasks that could be handled by support personnel. To free the technical staff, the response plan might identify support staff that will help with tasks like photocopying, faxing, etc.

Actually Handling an Incident

Certain steps are necessary when handling an incident. In all activities related to security and privacy, the most important point is that all sites should have policies in place. Without defined policies and goals, activities undertaken will remain without focus. Management and legal counsel should define the goals in advance.

One of the most fundamental objectives is to restore control of the affected systems and to limit the impact and damage. In the worst case scenario, the only practical solution may be shutting down the system or disconnecting the system from the network.

As the activities involved are complex, try to get as much help as necessary. While trying to solve the problem alone, real damage might occur due to delays or missing information. Most SAs take the discovery of an intruder as a personal challenge. By proceeding this way, other objectives as outlined in the local policies may not always be considered. Trying to catch intruders may be a very low priority, compared to system integrity, for example. Monitoring a hacker's activity is useful, but allowing the hacker continued access might not be worth the risk.

MONITORING REMOTE USERS FOR PRIVACY VIOLATIONS

Walk-up connections are network connection points that provide a convenient way for remote users to connect a portable host to a network. Consider whether the company needs to provide this service, which allows any remote user to attach an unauthorized host to the network. A walk-up connection increases the risk of attacks via techniques such as IP address spoofing and packet sniffing. Remote users and site management must appreciate the risks involved. If the SA decides to provide walk-up connections, plan the service carefully and define precisely where it will be provided so that the SA can ensure the necessary physical access security.

A walk-up host should be authenticated before its remote user is permitted to access resources on the network. As an alternative, it may be possible to control physical access. For example, if the service is to be used by students, the SA might only provide walk-up connection sockets in student laboratories. If the SA is providing walk-up access for visitors to connect back to their home networks (to read email, etc.) in the facility, consider using a separate subnet that has no connectivity to the internal network.

Keep an eye on any area that contains unmonitored access to the network, such as vacant offices. It may be sensible to disconnect such areas at the wiring closet, and consider using secure hubs and monitoring attempts to connect unauthorized hosts.

Authenticating Dial-in Users

A username and password check should be completed before a remote user can access anything on a network. Normal password security and privacy considerations are particularly important.

Remember that telephone lines can be tapped, and intercepting messages to cellular phones is quite easy. Modern high-speed modems use more sophisticated modulation techniques, which makes them somewhat more difficult to monitor, but hackers may know how to eavesdrop on one's lines. For this reason, the SA should use one-time passwords if at all possible.

A single dial-in point (a single large modem pool) is helpful so that all remote users are authenticated in the same way. Remote users will occasionally mistype a password. Set a short delay (say two seconds) after the first and second failed logins, and force a disconnect after the third. This will slow down automated password attacks. Do *not* tell the remote user what was incorrect—the username, the password, or both.

Choosing the Opening Banner Carefully

Many sites use a system default contained in a message-of-the day file for their opening banner. Unfortunately, this default message often includes the type of host hardware or operating system present on the host. This banner can provide valuable information to a potential intruder. Instead, each site should create its own specific login banner, which should only include necessary information.

Display a short banner, but don't offer an inviting name. For example, don't use *University of XYZ, Student Records System*. Instead, give the site name, a short warning that sessions may be monitored, and a username-password prompt. Verify possible legal issues related to the text that is put into the banner.

For high-security applications, consider using a blind password (that is, give no response to an incoming call until the remote user has typed in a password). This effectively simulates a dead modem.

Coordinating Local Managers and Personnel

Remote users must know how to report suspected incidents. Sites should establish reporting procedures that will work both during and outside normal working hours. Help desks are often used to receive these reports during normal working hours, while beepers and telephones can be used for out-of-hours reporting.

When an incident is under way, a major issue is deciding who is in charge of coordinating the activity of the multitude of players. A major mistake is having a number of people who are each working independently, but are not working together. This situation will only add to the confusion of the event and will probably lead to wasted or ineffective effort.

The single Point of Contact (POC) may or may not be the person responsible for handling the incident. The person in charge of the incident will make decisions as to the interpretation of policy applied to the event. In contrast, the POC must coordinate the effort of all the parties involved with handling the event.

NOTE: For each type of communication contact, a specific *Point of Contact* (POC) should be defined. The POC may be technical or administrative in nature and may include legal or investigative agencies as well as service providers and vendors. When establishing these contacts, decide how much information will be shared with each class of contact. Define, ahead of time, what information will be shared with the remote users at a site, with the public (including the press), and with other sites.

The POC must be a person with the in-depth technical expertise to successfully coordinate the efforts of the system managers and remote users involved in monitoring and reacting to the attack. Care should be taken when identifying the POC. The POC should not necessarily be the same person who has administrative responsibility for the compromised systems since often such administrators have knowledge only sufficient for the day-to-day use of the computers.

Another important POC function is maintaining contact with law enforcement and other external agencies to assure that multiagency involvement occurs. Legal constraints and management decisions will determine the appropriate level of involvement.

A single POC should also be the single person in charge of collecting evidence. As a rule of thumb, the more people that touch a potential piece of evidence, the greater the possibility that it will be inadmissible in court. To ensure that evidence will be acceptable to the legal community, evidence should be done while following predefined procedures in accordance with local laws and legal regulations.

One of the most critical tasks for the POC is the coordination of all relevant processes. Responsibilities may be distributed over the whole site, involving multiple independent departments or groups. Responding to an incident will require a well-coordinated effort in order to achieve overall success. The situation becomes even more complex if multiple sites are involved. With multiple sites, a single POC at one site may not be able to adequately coordinate handling the entire incident. Instead, appropriate incident response teams should be involved.

The incident handling process should provide some escalation mechanisms. In order to define such a mechanism, sites will need to create an internal classification scheme for incidents. An appropriate POC and procedures will be associated with each level of incident. As an incident is escalated, the POC may change, and this change will need to be communicated to all others handling the incident. When a change in the POC occurs, the old POC should brief the new POC in all background information.

Dealing with Law Enforcement and Investigative Agencies

If an incident has legal consequences, the organization must establish contact with investigative agencies (the FBI and Secret Service in the United States) as soon as possible. Local law enforcement, local security offices, and campus police departments should also be informed as appropriate. This part of the chapter describes many of the issues that will be confronted, but each organization will have its own local and governmental laws and regulations that will influence how it interacts with law enforcement and investigative agencies. The most important point to make is that each site needs to work through these issues.

A primary reason for determining the POC well in advance of an incident is that once a major attack is in progress, there is little time to call these agencies to determine exactly who the correct point of contact is. Another reason is that the organization must cooperate with these agencies in a manner that will foster a good working relationship and that will follow the working procedures of these agencies. Knowing the working procedures in advance and the expectations of the agencies' points of contact will help. For example, since evidence gathered needs to be admissible in any subsequent legal proceedings, prior knowledge of how to gather such evidence is required. A final reason for establishing contacts as soon as possible is that it is impossible to know the particular agency that will assume jurisdiction in any given incident. Making contacts and finding the proper channels early on will make responding to an incident go considerably more smoothly.

If an organization or site has a legal counsel, the POC needs to notify this office soon after learning that an incident is in progress. At a minimum, the organization's legal counsel needs to be involved to protect the legal and financial interests of the site. A few of the legal and practical issues are as follows:

1. Whether a site or organization is willing to risk negative publicity or exposure to cooperate with legal prosecution efforts.

2. *Downstream liability:*   If the POC leaves a compromised system as is so it can be monitored and then another computer is damaged because the attack originated from the organization's system, the site or organization may be liable for damages incurred.

3. *Distribution of information:*   If a site or organization distributes information about an attack in which another site or organization may be involved or information about vulnerability in a product that may affect the ability to market that product, then that site or organization may again be liable for any damages (including damage of reputation).

4. *Liabilities due to monitoring:*   The site or organization may be sued if users at the site or elsewhere discover that the site is monitoring account activity without informing users.

5. Unfortunately, no clear precedents have been established on the liabilities or responsibilities of organizations involved in a security and privacy incident or who might be involved in supporting an investigative effort. Investigators will often encourage organizations to help trace and monitor intruders. Indeed, most investigators cannot pursue computer intrusions without extensive support from the organizations involved. However, investigators cannot provide protection from liability claims, and these kinds of efforts may drag out for months and may take a lot of effort.

On the other hand, an organization's legal council may advise extreme caution and suggest that tracing activities be halted and an intruder shut out of the system. This in itself may not provide protection from liability and may prevent investigators from identifying the perpetrator.

The balance between supporting investigative activity and limiting liability is tricky. When making a decision about what to do during any particular incident, the organization will need to consider the advice of legal counsel and the damage the intruder is causing (if any).

Legal counsel should also be involved in any decision to contact investigative agencies when an incident occurs at the site. The decision to coordinate efforts with investigative agencies is most properly that of the site or organization. Involving legal counsel will also foster the multilevel coordination between the site and the particular investigative agency involved, which in turn results in an efficient division of labor. Another result is that the organization is likely to obtain guidance that will help avoid future legal mistakes.

Finally, the legal counsel should evaluate the site's written procedures for responding to incidents. These procedures should be given a *clean bill of health* from a legal perspective before they are actually carried out.

When dealing with investigative agencies, the POC must verify that the person who calls asking for information is a legitimate representative from the agency in question. Unfortunately, many well-intentioned people have unknowingly leaked sensitive details about incidents, allowed unauthorized people into their systems, etc., because a caller has masqueraded as a representative of a government agency.

A similar consideration is using a secure means of communication. Because many network attackers can easily reroute electronic mail, avoid using electronic mail to communicate with other agencies (as well as others dealing with the incident at hand). Nonsecured phone lines (the phones normally used in the business world) are also frequent targets for tapping by network intruders, so be careful!

No set of rules has been established for responding to an incident when the local government becomes involved. Normally in the United States, except by legal order, no agency can force an organization to monitor, to disconnect from the network, to avoid telephone contact with the suspected attackers, etc. Each organization will have a set of local and national laws and regulations that must be adhered to when handling incidents. Each site should be familiar with those laws and regulations and should identify in advance and get to know the contacts for agencies with jurisdiction.

Containing the Incident Damage

The purpose of *containment* is to limit the extent of an attack. An essential part of containment is decision making (determining whether to shut a system down, disconnect from a network, monitor system or network activity, set traps, disable functions such as remote file transfer, etc.).

Sometimes this decision is trivial; shut the system down if the information is classified, sensitive, or proprietary. Bear in mind that removing all access while an incident is in progress obviously notifies all users, including the alleged problem users, that the SA is aware of a problem; this may have a deleterious effect on an investigation. In some cases, the SA should remove all access or functionality as soon as possible, then restore normal operation in limited stages. In other cases, risking some damage to the system is worthwhile if keeping the system up might enable the SA to identify an intruder.

This stage should involve carrying out predetermined procedures. The organization or site should, for example, define acceptable risks in dealing with an incident, and should prescribe specific actions and strategies accordingly. Having predefined procedures is especially important when a quick decision is necessary and contacting all involved parties to discuss the decision is not possible. In the absence of predefined procedures, the person in charge of the incident will often not have the power to make difficult management decisions (like to lose the results of a costly experiment by shutting down a system). A final activity that should occur during this stage of incident handling is the notification of appropriate authorities.

Following Up

Once the SA believes that a system has been restored to a safe state, holes and even traps could still be lurking in the system. One of the most important stages of responding to incidents is also the most often omitted—the follow-up stage. In the follow-up stage, the system should be monitored for items that may have been missed during the cleanup stage.

The most important element of the follow-up stage is performing a postmortem analysis. Exactly what happened, and at what times? How well did the staff involved with the incident perform? What kind of information did the staff need quickly, and how could they have gotten that information as soon as possible? What would the staff do differently next time?

After an incident, those involved should write a report describing the exact sequence of events: the method of discovery, correction procedure, monitoring procedure, and a summary of lessons learned. This report will aid in the clear understanding of the problem. Creating a formal chronology of events (including time stamps) is also important for legal reasons.

A follow-up report is valuable for many reasons. It provides a reference to be used in case of other similar incidents. It is also important to quickly obtain a monetary estimate of the amount of damage the incident caused. This estimate should include costs associated with any loss of software and files (especially the value of proprietary data that may have been disclosed), hardware damage, and manpower costs to restore altered files, reconfigure affected systems, and so forth. This estimate may become the basis for subsequent prosecution activity. The report can also help justify an organization's computer security and privacy effort to management.

RESPONDING TO
INDUSTRY-SPECIFIC ISSUES

Finally, let's take a closer look at some industry, specific issues with regard to net security and privacy for telecommuters. To start with, how safe are online resume banks in general? Can someone *steal* information from another?

Resume banks like *Monster.com, Headhunter.com,* and *HotJobs.com* can be considered relatively safe from hackers. The safety is dependent upon the safety measures each resume bank has in place. Most resume banks require membership with a unique user name and password. Some also give the individual the option to have his or her resume searchable or not. If a resume is searchable, then employers can do a database query; if the resume fits their criteria, it will be made available to them to see. If the resume is not searchable, then it is in the database for the individual's use only and cannot be seen by others. Another option that some resume banks offer is employer filters. With this option an individual can specify which employers are blocked from being able to see the resume. This option is helpful if the individual doesn't want the current employer to know of his or her job search.

If an individual has concerns about a particular resume bank, then he or she should read the resume bank's privacy policy. Most resume banks will make a reasonable effort to keep information private and will not distribute personal information to outside parties without permission. If the individual finds the privacy policy unacceptable, then the resume should not be posted at that resume bank.

Hacker Access

The risk of hacker access depends upon how secure the connection is. If the connection is from a properly configured UNIX or NT remote access server, then the risk is low. Then the real issue is how stringent the company's password policy is. Any remote access connection uses standard authentication techniques. In the case of NT, the remote user logs in using the same user name and password as used for logging in locally. A weak password policy makes hacking in easier. A strong password policy requires that all passwords be at least eight characters long and contain a combination of letters, numbers, and special characters. A weak password is *toast*. It is less than eight characters, is only letters, and is a common word. A strong password is *u1b$u4s$*. It is eight characters long and contains letters, numbers, and special characters, yet it is easy to remember.

Another alternative is to set up a Virtual Private Network (VPN) between the telecommuter and the corporate network. A VPN gives a secure encrypted link from home to the office. A VPN negates the worry about sensitive information being intercepted as it travels over the airways.

Using the Internet to Access the Intranet

A properly configured Intranet involves very little risk. For example, when the URL was typed in for one company's Internet site, a few creative modifications to the URL brought up that company's private Intranet site. That company forgot one very important step when they set up their Intranet. They forgot to restrict access to internal IP addresses only. Once that security and privacy hole was fixed, the Intranet was secure again.

Some other simple measures can also add a little more security and privacy to an Intranet to keep prying eyes out. One is to name the virtual Web something that is less than the obvious. In other words, for a company named *abc*, don't make the virtual Web for the Intranet */abc/*. Another good rule to follow is to make the Web page names a little cryptic. If a page in the accounting section of the Intranet lists monthly expenditures, don't name it *expenditures.html*. Name it something like *exp1311.html*. Also, password-protect all pages that contain sensitive data. This will prevent unauthorized people, whether from outside or inside the organization, from seeing stuff that they shouldn't.

While this chapter provided a successful remote access solution, the final chapter discusses the future of privacy management. It discusses how the challenges of long-term privacy management fall into two major categories: the evolution of privacy laws and policies, and adapting information technology to meet privacy management requirements.

END NOTES

[i] Gartner Group Headquarters, 56 Top Gallant Road, P.O. Box 10212, Stamford, CT 06904, USA, 2001.

[ii] Infonetics Research, 255 West Julian Street, Suite 402, San Jose, CA 95110, United States, 2001.

[iii] Barbara Y. Fraser, "RFC 2196: Site Security Handbook," Software Engineering Institute, Carnegie Mellon University, 5000 Forbes Avenue, Pittsburgh, PA 15213, 2001.

17

THE FUTURE OF PRIVACY MANAGEMENT

The long-term privacy management challenges that organizations face fall into two major categories: (1) the evolution of privacy laws and policies and (2) the adaptation of information technology to meet privacy management requirements. Currently little consistency or alignment exists between privacy needs and actual privacy management. As laws change in the future, better information technology (IT) solutions will be available to help manage privacy. But this evolution will require time and considerable effort.

Legal requirements for managing information privacy will become more complex as laws evolve and social pressures increase. The legislative and political process is just beginning to churn and will take time to mature. There will be many attempts to make sense of privacy needs, and balancing privacy needs with social, political, economic, and business conditions will take time. Socially oriented legislation in areas such as civil rights and environmental protection has taken several decades to evolve and to come into balance with overall social conditions. In the area of privacy, just as in civil rights and environmental protection, the dialogue and political process will continue to be riddled with political conflict among interest groups. These evolutionary processes will continue to make the job of privacy managers challenging and perhaps sometimes even extremely difficult. Privacy managers will likely have very few dull moments as privacy policies and laws evolve.

THE CONTINUING EVOLUTION OF INFORMATION TECHNOLOGY

Many of the problems that organizations face in managing the privacy of information are tied to the technology used to collect, process, store, and maintain information. The basic nature of information technology, in a historical perspective, is that information technology only does what humans design it to do. From 1920 through the early 1990s, the producers of information technology developed and marketed the product equivalent of a blank slate. Computer systems, in their blank-slate condition, were acquired by organizations that then developed their own version of information management systems by writing software internally or by purchasing off-the-shelf software products and adapting them to meet the organization's needs. As more organizations started performing the same or similar information processing tasks, IT manufacturers recognized a market for integrated software solutions that are designed to support specific business processes or to meet the needs of specific business environments.

There are two excellent examples of the movement from the blank-slate computer system to the business-oriented IT solutions. In the late 1980s, IBM introduced the AS/400 family of computer systems as the first highly integrated system that provided a platform for software developers to create easy-to-use business solutions for all types of business environments. Thus law firms, construction companies, medical offices, and many other businesses were able to acquire computers that did not need extensive programming in order to meet their business needs. This was possible because information-processing expertise had evolved over a 70-year period and software developers had learned by doing. A critical mass of business environments had been computerized, and a sufficient number of programmers had learned what was required to support different types of businesses. This culmination of experience, knowledge, and skill was packaged into vertical-business IT solutions that could support a specific type of business from top to bottom and provide necessary support in accounting, inventory control, and human resource management.

A second example, which we are now seeing evolve, is Internet and World Wide Web software. In 1994, organizations that wanted to have a Web presence or enter ecommerce had to take blank-slate computer systems and then hire programmers and developers to create a custom solution for their business. By 1999, several off-the-shelf software solutions were on the market that could provide Web-site management or ecommerce support for almost any type of organization, thus eliminating the need for each organization to invent its own wheel. During 1999 and 2000, the off-the-shelf Web software products rapidly evolved and can now provide more functionality and are more stable products overall. However, even though these types of products are rapidly evolving, they are still relatively immature. Over the next five years, the off-the-shelf Web software product will mature and reach a higher level of stability and help meet more information management needs.

THE EMERGENCE OF
THE TRUSTED ENVIRONMENT

The database software that drives most business applications is extremely flexible and can be used to manage data for almost any business process. Although this flexibility is an asset, a high level of flexibility can become an obstacle in two ways. First, getting the most out of database software requires a cadre of highly skilled programmers and administrators who must be capable of interpreting business rules and translating those rules into functions that control how data can be used. Second, even when an organization has a sufficiently skilled workforce to use database technology, the emergence of supply chain systems and interconnections across organizations still can put data at risk. These risks arise from the potential of abuse by some member of the supply chain and from increased exposure to weaknesses somewhere in the supply chain.

Software organizations will seek alternative methods of deploying IT solutions in order to overcome the exposure to risk in a supply chain environment, to reduce the cost of having to hire and train highly skilled software personnel, and to maximize the benefits of new off-the-shelf applications. Several methods to achieving these goals have been tried in the past, including outsourcing entire IT operations and implementing enterprise resource planning and management systems from major software producers. These methods still have a high potential of solving the problems of information control, risk avoidance, and cost reduction. However, no one approach completely addresses all of the needs that an organization faces in managing technology and maintaining privacy.

The evolutionary direction of IT products and services is toward the creation and maintenance of a trusted environment, which requires the following elements:

- Management of supply chain systems (by third-party organizations) that meet the highest levels of system availability, data security, and privacy management standards
- Utilization of information technology (from producers that develop and market hardware and software products) that meets stringent security standards and has high levels of interoperability
- Restricted membership in supply chains only to companies that adhere

to safe harbor principles and that deploy IT products that comply with stringent security standards and have high levels of interoperability
- Financial liability and legal consequences for third-party supply chain managers, technology suppliers, and supply chain participants for failure to meet standards or for the violation of safe harbor principles

The emergence of trusted environments will take about five years. Currently no clear leader among third-party companies has enough experience and the capability of supporting a trusted environment model. In addition, no universal standard on security exists, and technology producers are, for the most part, still creating proprietary technology. Existing Web-based trading communities and marketplaces do not meet all of the criteria for trusted environments, and none have been in existence long enough to gain a solid reputation in the traditional business community. Also, potential antitrust and fair trade issues need to be addressed before the trusted environment is politically acceptable.

Although these obstacles are indeed formidable, the need for privacy management and the continued growth of ecommerce are trends that will help to foster the emergence of the trusted environment. Another more practical issue, the taxation of ecommerce, may also contribute to the emergence of the trusted environment because the underlying transaction technology could also facilitate the payment of sales taxes to hundreds of taxing entities. Safe harbor principles, which are gaining universal acceptance, will also increase the pressure for trusted environments.

THE INFLUENCE OF POLITICAL AND ECONOMIC FORCES

Privacy is a political issue that is never going to go away. As legislative bodies attempt to deal with privacy laws and as regulatory agencies attempt to police compliance with privacy laws, trusted environments may be the best safe havens for businesses to turn to in order to reduce regulatory scrutiny of their operations. If companies were to cooperate in the development of trusted environments, they could more readily keep regulators at a more comfortable distance and also satisfy legislators who are pushing for greater privacy protection on the Internet. Thus the trusted environment could help to simultaneously satisfy many constituencies.

Economics will also help drive the emergence of trusted environments because privacy regulations will increase the cost of doing business. Privacy laws in the future will be complex and more plentiful. Staying in compliance with the myriad of privacy laws, especially in cross-border ecommerce transactions, will become more expensive over time. In addition, stiff penalties will be likely for privacy violations. This complexity, combined with the potential for financial liability, will force many companies to move toward trusted environments in order to avoid the risk of economic instability and perhaps to merely stay in business. Regardless of how trusted environments evolve or which IT companies become leaders in providing trusted environment technology or services, one thing is for sure—the basic cost of doing business is going to increase.

GLOSSARY

PRIVACY TERMS

Access: The third principle of fair information guidelines, along (1) Notice, (2) Choice, and (4) Security. This refers to the users' ability to view and contest the accuracy and completeness of data collected about users.

Affirmative customization: Refers to a site's or a service provider's use of personal data to tailor or modify the site's content or design to specifications affirmatively selected by a particular individual. For example, a user may permit a shopping site to use the record of the user's book purchases to make recommendations of other publications that may interest the user. The site will thus display a list of its recommendations every time the user visits.

Aggregate: Refers to data that are combined together without releasing personally identifiable information. The statistic *70 percent of users of this Web site live in New York City* is an example of aggregated information.

Anonymity: A condition in which an individual's true identity is not known. A customer's online service provider may allow the customer, as a subscriber, to participate in online activities anonymously (not known at all) or pseudonymously (taking on a different identity). (See also "Pseudonymity" and "Pseudonymous profiling.")

BBBOnline: The Better Business Bureau's Online (http://www.bbbonline.org/) privacy-seal program that certifies eligible Web sites if they conform to baseline privacy standards. The program requires its licensees to implement certain fair information practices and to submit to various types of compliance monitoring in order to display a privacy seal on their Web sites.

Blocking software: A computer program that allows parents, teachers, or guardians to *block* access to certain Web sites and to other information available over the Internet. All blocking software has filtered the information before blocking access to it. (See also "Filtering software.")

Choice: The second principle of fair information guidelines, along with (1) Notice, (3) Access, and (4) Security. This refers to companies' providing consumers with options regarding whether and how personal information collected from them may be used for purposes beyond those for which it was provided.

Client-based filter: A software program that an individual installs on a computer to block access to inappropriate material, to prevent kids from accessing the Internet at certain times, or to prevent kids from revealing personal information. (See also "Filtering software" and "Blocking software.")

Collection: Online collection of personal information (such as shopping preferences, interests, and physical contact information) occurs in two ways. First, data may be collected through a user's input of information, such as during a financial transaction or acquisition of a membership. Second, detailed personal information may be collected while the user engages in *passive* online activity—for example, when the user peeks into chat rooms, glances at bulletin boards, or browses through online libraries. When a user ftps a file, the user's actions may generate a personally identifiable record. The user's personal information may thus be collected and stored while the user believes that he or she remains anonymous.

Commercial online service: An online service that maintains a closed proprietary network, providing a variety of information and other services to its subscribers. A commercial online service generally provides its own content, forums, and information available only to its subscribers.

Commercial service: General term for large online services. These services are like special clubs that require membership dues. Besides providing access to the Internet, commercial services have lots of content, games, and chat rooms that are available only to members.

Completion and support of current activity: Refers to a site's, or a service provider's, use of an individual's personal information to complete the activity for which it was provided, such as the provision of information, communications, or interactive services, for example, to return the results from a Web search, forward email, or place an order.

Consent: Explicit permission given to a Web site by a visitor to handle that visitor's personal information in specified ways. Web sites that ask users to provide personally identifiable information should be required to obtain *informed consent*, which implies that the company fully discloses its information practices prior to obtaining personal data or permission to use that data.

Content: The actual text of a communication or information sent. Includes text of emails, bulletin board postings, chat room communications, files, and graphics. Content does not include routing information, the date, time, or subject of the message, or other transactional data.

Cookie: A piece of information unique to a user that the user's browser saves and sends back to a Web server when the user revisits a Web site (the Web server is the computer that *hosts* a Web site that the user's browser downloads or sees). The server *tells* the user's browser where to put the cookie on the server. Cookies contain information such as log-in or registration information, online *shopping cart* information (the user's online buying patterns in a certain retail site), user preferences, what site the user came from last, etc. CookieCentral (http://www.cookiecentral.com/) provides detailed information on Internet cookies and how to stop them.

Correction: User ability to alter incomplete or inaccurate personal information that a company has collected. Collectors of private data should always give the user the ability to make additions and corrections.

CPNI: Consumer Proprietary Network Information, which applies to telephone usage data, including the location, duration, and frequency of phone calls.

Data category: A significant attribute of a data element or data set that may be used by a trusted engine to determine what type of element is under discussion, such as physical contact information.

Data element: An individual data entity, such as last name or telephone number.

Data mining: The practice of compiling information about Internet users by tracking their motions through Web sites, recording the time they spend there, what links they clink on, and other details that the company desires, usually for marketing purposes. (See also "Online profiling.")

Demographic and socioeconomic data: Data about an individual's characteristics, such as gender, age, and income.

Digital Storm: A new generation of analytic tools, currently being developed by the FBI, to sift and link data from disparate sources. Currently, law enforcement agencies have access to a growing volume of digital information, which is often minimally protected.

Disclosure: Refers to companies' practice of making an individual's personal information available to third parties (marketing lists, other organizations that provide similar services, etc.).

Downstream data use: Refers to companies' practice of disclosing personal information collected from users to other parties *downstream* to facilitate a transaction. For example, a content provider may disclose a user's personal information to a shipping company that will deliver the order to the user's house. The content provider may also disclose the user's personal information to a billing or credit card company in order to charge the user for the transaction.

Encryption: Technology that scrambles digital content, with the use of a private code for secure transmission.

Enforcement: A principle of fair information guidelines, along with (1) Notice, (2) Choice, (3) Access, and (4) Security. This refers to the use of a reliable mechanism to impose sanctions for noncompliance with the preceding information practices. The 1998 FTC Report entitled *Records, Computers, and the Rights of Citizens* identified enforcement as one of the core fair information principles and as a critical ingredient in any government or self-regulatory program that seeks to ensure privacy online.

Equable practice: An information practice that is very similar to another in that the purpose, recipients, and identifiable use are the same or more constrained than the original, and the other disclosures are not substantially different. For example, two sites with otherwise similar practices that follow different—but similar—sets of industry guidelines.

Fair Information Practices: Privacy guidelines, predating the online medium, that were enumerated in the 1973 report released by the U.S. Department of Health, Education, and Welfare, which addressed privacy protections in the age of digital data collection. The principles—(1) Notice, (2) Choice, (3) Access, and (4) Security—have been developed and recognized by agencies in the United States, Canada, and Europe. The 1998 FTC Report entitled *Records, Computers, and the Rights of Citizens* also identified *enforcement* as one of the core fair information principles.

Fairness: A goal of Fair Information Practices, which requires a company to use personal information only for the purpose for which it was initially collected.

Filtered ISP: An Internet Service Provider (ISP) that automatically blocks access to content that is inappropriate for children. Each filtered ISP uses its own criteria to decide which Web sites are inappropriate. When choosing a filtered ISP, parents and other caretakers should make sure the company's criteria are consistent with their own values and judgments.

Filtering software: Software that sorts information on the Internet and classifies it according to content. Some filtering software allows the user to block certain kinds of information on the Internet. (See also "Blocking software," "Client-based filter," and "Server-based.")

Financial information: Information about an individual's finances, including account status and activity data such as account balance, payment or overdraft history, and information about an individual's purchase or use of financial instruments, including credit or debit card information. Purchase information alone does not constitute financial information. (See also "Purchase information.")

Firewall: A security device that places a protective *wall* around a computer or network of computers, keeping it from being accessible to the public.

Flaming: Sending a nasty piece of email or posting a nasty comment in a newsgroup or discussion group—usually in response to a posting that offended someone.

Gateway: Generally any device that provides access to another system. For example, an ISP might be called a gateway to the Internet; also a hardware device that connects a local network to the Internet.

Health information: Personal data that may be collected by a site or a service provider about an individual's physical or mental health, sexual orientation, use or inquiry into health care services or products, and purchase of health care services or products.

ICANN: The Internet Corporation for Assigned Names and Numbers. The nonprofit international organization responsible for domain names management.

ICRA: Internet Content Rating Alliance rating system. A rating system for Web content. (See also "RSACi.")

Individual profiling: Refers to a site's or a service provider's use of personal data to create or build a record on the particular individual or computer for the purpose of compiling habits or personally identifiable information of that individual or computer. For example, online stores may recommend products based on the visitor's purchasing history on the specific Web site or online in general.

Informed notice: Notice of information practices cannot be truly effective unless that notice is clearly written and noncoercive. Users are *informed* when they know and understand who collects their personal information and the purposes for which it is collected. Notice of information practices is particularly important when an Internet user participates in a *passive* activity under the illusion of anonymity. Providing advance notice is crucial when personal information is used for purposes unrelated to those for which a user has initially disclosed it.

IP: Internet Protocol. The computer language that allows computer programs to communicate over the Internet.

ISP: Internet Service Provider. A company that sells access to the Internet, most often through a local phone number. ISPs are usually distinguished from commercial services that link to the Internet, but also offer additional services, such as content and chat, that are only available to their subscribers.

Kids' Web site: A Web site for children under 13 years old (or those sites that know that their visitors are under 13 years old).

Limitation on collection: Refers to the established principle that collection of personal data should be limited to information that is necessary to complete a transaction. For instance, an online service provider that requires an individual to provide a copy of that individual's tax returns as a condition of becoming a subscriber obviously collects more information than it requires to process a membership. When personally identifiable information is not necessary to support the initial activity, users should have the opportunity to restrict or deny its collection.

Location data: Information that can be used to identify an individual's current physical location and track that individual as the location changes.

Mailing list: An email-based discussion forum dedicated to a topic of interest. An interested Internet user can subscribe to a mailing list by sending an email message that contains appropriate instructions to a specific email address. The computer that houses the mailing list program maintains a list of subscribers and routes all posted messages to subscribers' electronic mailboxes. Mailing lists are either publicly or privately maintained, and can be either moderated or unmoderated.

Monitoring software: A type of software product that allows a parent or caretaker to monitor the Web sites or email messages that a child visits or reads without necessarily blocking access.

Navigation and click-stream data: Refers to user data passively generated by browsing the Internet. Includes information regarding the links on which a user clicks, pages a user visits, and the amount of time spent on each page.

Netiquette: The rules of cyberspace civility. These are usually applied to the Internet where manners are enforced exclusively by fellow users.

Notice: The first principle of fair information guidelines, along with (2) Choice, (3) Access, and (4) Security. Refers to data collectors' disclosure of their information practices prior to collecting personal information from consumers. In the online context, *notice* means that Internet users learn from the online service provider or Web site whether and to what extent the service or site collects and uses their personal information.

OECD guidelines: Privacy guidelines issued in late 1980 by the Organization for Economic Cooperation and Development. Although broad, the OECD guidelines set up important standards for future governmental privacy rules; the guidelines underpin most current international agreements, national laws, and self-regulatory policies.

One-time tailoring: Refers to a site's or a service provider's use of personal data, only for a single visit to the site and not used for any kind of future customization, in order to tailor or modify the site's content or design even though not affirmatively selected by the particular individual. For example, an online store may suggest items a visitor may wish to purchase based on the products that the visitor has already placed in the shopping basket.

Online contact information: Information that allows an individual to be contacted or located on the Internet, such as the email address. Often, this information is independent of the specific computer used to access the network. (See also "Physical contact information.")

Online Privacy Alliance (OPA): The OPA (http://www.privacyalliance.org), a group of more than 80 global corporations and associations, was created to lead and support industry self-regulatory initiatives. The OPA identifies and advances online privacy policies across the private sector; supports the development and use of self-regulatory enforcement mechanisms and activities; supports the development and use of user empowerment technology tools designed to protect an individual's privacy; and supports compliance with strong enforcement of applicable laws and regulations. See OPA's privacy policy guidelines (http://www.privacyalliance.org/resources/ppguidelines.shtml).

Online profiling: The practice of aggregating information about consumers' preferences and interests, gathered primarily by tracking their online movements and actions with the purpose of creating targeted advertisement using the resulting profiles. (See also "Individual profiling" and "Data mining.")

Operator: The person who is responsible for maintaining and running a Web site.

Opt in: An option that requires an individual's explicit consent for the use, and disclosure of, the individual's personal information beyond the original, primary purpose for which it was collected.

Opt out: An option that allows an individual to prevent the use, and disclosure of, the individual's personal information beyond the original, primary purpose for which it was collected.

P3P: (See "Platform for Privacy Preferences Project.")

Personally identifiable transactional data: Information that describes an individual's online activities such as the Web sites that an individual has visited, addresses to which an individual has sent email, files that an individual has downloaded, and other information revealed in the normal course of using the Internet. *Transactional data* differ from the content of a communication since they are not the actual substance of an individual's communication, but rather the information *about* an individual's communication. Traditionally, the content of an individual's communications received greater statutory protection than transactional data. Recent legislative developments, however, have strengthened privacy protections for transactional data since it became widely acknowledged that transactional data might reveal as much sensitive information as the actual content of a communication. Also, personal user preferences tracked by a Web site via online cookies are also considered personally identifiable when linked to other personally identifiable information provided by online users.

Physical contact information: Information that allows an individual to be contacted or located in the physical world, such as a telephone number or an address.

PICS: Platform for Internet Content Selection. PICS is a technology that allows Web browsers to read content ratings of Web sites, but it is not a rating system itself.

Platform for Privacy Preferences Project (P3P): A set of software-writing guidelines developed by the World Wide Web Consortium (W3C), the standard-setting body for the Web. P3P is designed to provide Internet users with a clear understanding of how personal information will be used by a particular Web site. It empowers users to avoid sites that do not meet their privacy preferences.

Policy: A collection of one or more privacy statements together with information that provides the identity, URI, assurances, and dispute resolution procedures of the service covered by the policy.

Political information: User information which may be collected by a site or a service provider regarding membership in or affiliation with groups such as religious organizations, trade unions, professional associations, and political parties.

Preference data: Data, which may be collected by a site or a service provider, about an individual's likes and dislikes—such as favorite color or musical tastes.

Privacy policy: A page or pages on a Web site that describe privacy policies (what personal information the site collects, how it uses it, with whom the site shares it, and whether users can exercise control over the use of their personal data).

Pseudonymity: A condition in which an individual has taken on an assumed identity. (See also "Anonymity.")

Pseudonymous profiling: Refers to a site's or a service provider's use of personal data to create or build a record of a particular individual, or computer that is tied to a pseudonymous identifier without tying personally identifiable information (such as name, address, phone number, email address, or IP address) to the record. This profile is usually used to determine the habits, interests, or other characteristics of individuals but not to attempt to identify specific individuals.

Public forums: Refers to digital entities such as bulletin boards, public directories, or commercial CD-ROM directories, where personal user data may be distributed by a site or a service provider.

Purchase information: Information actively generated by the purchase of a product or service, including information about the method of payment.

Recipient: Refers to the legal entity, or domain, beyond the service provider and its agents where personal user data may be distributed. May include delivery services, unrelated third parties, and public forums.

Repository: A mechanism for storing user information under the control of the user agent.

RSACi: Recreation Software Advisory Council's Internet rating system. A rating system for Web content that uses PICS technology. RSACi was recently renamed the Internet Content Rating Alliance (ICRA).

Secondary use: Refers to using personal information collected for one purpose for a second, unrelated purpose. A fundamental fair information principle is the provision of the opportunity for a user to choose if that user wants personal information used for a secondary purpose. The principle allows a user to provide personal information for a specific purpose without the fear that it may later be used for an unrelated purpose without that user's knowledge or consent.

Security: The fourth principle of fair information guidelines, along with (1) Notice, (2) Choice, and (3) Access. It refers to data collectors' responsibility to take reasonable steps to ensure that information collected from consumers is accurate and secure from unauthorized use. Online services can safeguard data in a number of ways, including passwords, audit trails, and encryption.

Server-based filter: Unlike client-based software, which is installed on an individual's own computer, a server-based filter works on a host server (for example, a Web server) generally located at an ISP or a company's LAN. A user's computer is connected to this server so that the user can receive only the Web pages that are not filtered on the server.

Spam: Hundreds of unsolicited *junk* email containing advertising or promotional messages sent to a large number of people or one person at the same time. Sometimes people or companies send sexually explicit unsolicited email, known as *porn spam*.

State management mechanisms: Mechanisms for maintaining a stateful (active-state) session with a user or for automatically identifying users who have visited a particular site or accessed particular content previously. Cookies are a state management mechanism.

Subscription data: Information that an individual provides to an online service when that individual signs up to become a member. Subscription data usually include the individual's name, physical address, email address, billing information, and telephone numbers.

Time limiting software: Software that allows time limits to be set for access to the Internet or software programs such as games.

Transparency: A goal of Fair Information Practices that requires a company to inform users of what personal information the company collects and how the information is used.

TRUSTe: An online privacy-seal program (http://www.truste.com/) that certifies eligible Web sites and holds sites to baseline privacy standards. It requires its licensees to implement certain fair information practices and to submit to various types of compliance monitoring in order to display a privacy seal on their Web sites.

Trustmark: An online seal awarded by TRUSTe to Web sites that agree to post their privacy practices openly via privacy statements, as well as to adhere to enforcement procedures that ensure that those privacy promises are met. When a user clicks on the TRUSTe trustmark, that user is taken directly to the privacy statement of the licensed Web site.

Unique identifiers: Nonfinancial identifiers issued for purposes of consistently identifying the individual. These include government-issued identifiers such as social security number, as well as identifiers issued by a Web site or service.

User agent: A privacy program designed to mediate interactions with services on behalf of the user under the user's preferences. A user may have more than one user agent, and agents need not reside on the user's desktop. Any user agent must be controlled by and act on behalf of only the user.

INDEX

ABOUT THE AUTHORS

Michael Erbschloe is a world-renowned information technology consultant, author, and educator. The Vice President of Computer Economics, an influential technology think tank, Erbschloe has authored more than 2200 articles for leading publications and his research work has appeared in *Fortune*, *The Wall Street Journal*, *U.S. News & World Report*, *The Washington Post*, and many others.

John Vacca is an information technology consultant and author of over 30 books and 370 articles on topics including Internet security, programming, and systems development. Vacca previously served as the computer security specialist for NASA's space station program and the International Space Station Program. His books include *Internet Security Secrets*, *The Cabling Handbook*, *Satellite Encryption*, and *Virtual Reality*. Vacca was also one of the security consultants for the MGM movie *AntiTrust*.